News with a View

News with a View

*Essays on the Eclipse
of Objectivity
in Modern Journalism*

Edited by BURTON ST. JOHN III *and*
KIRSTEN A. JOHNSON

McFarland & Company, Inc., Publishers
Jefferson, North Carolina, and London

LIBRARY OF CONGRESS CATALOGUING-IN-PUBLICATION DATA

News with a view : essays on the eclipse of objectivity in modern
journalism / edited by Burton St. John III and Kirsten A.
Johnson.
    p.   cm.
Includes bibliographical references and index.

ISBN 978-0-7864-6589-7
softcover : acid free paper ∞

1. Journalism — Objectivity.   I. St. John, Burton, 1957–
II. Johnson, Kirsten A., 1974–
PN4784.O24N48 2012
070.4'42 — dc23   2012005697

BRITISH LIBRARY CATALOGUING DATA ARE AVAILABLE

Front cover design by David K. Landis (Shake It Loose Graphics)

Manufactured in the United States of America

McFarland & Company, Inc., Publishers
  Box 611, Jefferson, North Carolina 28640
    www.mcfarlandpub.com

To my wife, Dana, who has been a consistent source of support and encouragement. And to my children, Melissa and Aaron, who keep teaching me the value of listening.— Burton St. John III

To my husband and best friend, Scott, who has always supported me. I know I wouldn't be where I am today without his constant encouragement.
And to my daughter Sarah, who has gracefully tolerated being dragged along to classes, meetings, and presentations over the past 10 years. You're truly the best girl in the world!— Kirsten A. Johnson

Table of Contents

Introduction: Challenges for Journalism in a Post-Objective Age
    BURTON ST. JOHN III *and* KIRSTEN A. JOHNSON   1

Part I. Historical Perspectives   9

1. "Gagged, Mincing Neutrality": Horace Greeley on Advocacy
    Journalism in the Early Years of the Penny Press
    DAXTON R. "CHIP" STEWART   11

2. The Pride and Reward of Falisfication: Post-Objectivity as
    Post-Responsibility
    AARON BARLOW   26

3. A New Model of Objectivity: Investigative Reporting in the
    Twentieth Century
    GERRY LANOSGA   42

Part II. Contemporary Examinations   59

4. Conversational Journalism and Journalist-Audience Relations:
    New Rules, New Voices
    DOREEN MARCHIONNI   61

5. The Sociality of News Sociology: Examining User Participation
    and News Selection Practices in Social Media News Sites
    SHARON MERAZ   78

6. Why Contribute? Motivations and Role Conceptions among
    Citizen Journalists
    DEBORAH S. CHUNG *and* SEUNGAHN NAH   97

7. Morality, the News Media, and the Public: An Examination
    of Comment Forums on U.S. Daily Newspaper Websites
    SERENA CARPENTER *and* ROBIN BLOM   116

Part III. Global Considerations 133

8. Post-Objectivity and Regional Russian Journalism
   WILSON LOWREY *and* ELINA ERZIKOVA 135

9. Journalism from the Perspective of "We": How Group
   Membership Shapes the Role of the Community Journalist
   JOHN A. HATCHER 153

10. Engagement as an Emerging Norm in International News
    Agency Work
    JOHN JIRIK 170

Part IV. Objectivity and Theory 187

11. Why Objectivity Is Impossible in Networked Journalism
    and What This Means for the Future of News
    DAVID MICHAEL RYFE 189

12. Disrespecting the Doxa: The *Daily Show* Critique of CNN's
    Struggle to Balance Detachment and Connectedness
    BURTON ST. JOHN III 205

13. Gatekeeping in the Digital Age: A New Model for a
    Post-Objective World
    KIRSTEN A. JOHNSON 222

14. Contemporary News Production and Consumption:
    Implications for Selective Exposure, Group Polarization,
    and Credibility
    ETHAN HARTSELL, MIRIAM J. METZGER *and* ANDREW J.
    FLANAGIN 238

About the Contributors 259

Index 263

Introduction:
Challenges for Journalism
in a Post-Objective Age

Many people will say that journalistic objectivity is impossible. Every decision a reporter makes, about which quote to use, etc. — is a subjective one.... But at its core, journalism is about finding out the truth, whenever that is humanly possible. So that is the profession's most important mandate.

— Mark Jurkowitz, Pew Research Center,
Washington Post online, October 23, 2008

The concept of objectivity provides ... journalists with distinct professional norms to guide their daily practices, while it also serves the public good. Indeed, by revealing the truth to an audience, objective journalists can pride themselves on unveiling ... what some would like to leave in the dark, to hide from the public.

— Sandrine Boudana, New York University, 2011

For decades, the field of journalism has maintained that it uniquely offers news consumers daily accounts that are accurate representations of truth. Modern journalism, most notably since the end of World War I, has justified that claim by pointing to its adherence to objectivity — a stance that asserts that journalists, as dispassionate chroniclers, provide the facts, data, experts, and context that news consumers need to understand the day's events.

But there are signs that the primacy of the objectivity orientation is not enough to meet the needs of today's citizens. News consumers increasingly maintain that they do not have a press that provides them with the credible information they need to make decisions in a democracy. In late 2009, the Pew Research Center for the People and the Press revealed that 63 percent of Americans say news stories are often incorrect (*Public evaluations*, 2009). Not surprisingly, many Americans indicate an aversion to traditional news accounts; an early 2010 Pew survey found that only a little more than half of all Americans (56 percent) say they regularly follow the news (*How Internet*, 2010).

A series of events are contributing to this credibility problem for journalism — a wave of occurrences that the objectivity stance appears ill-equipped to address. First, the official "gatekeepers" of news — traditional journalists — are dwindling. For example, print newsrooms now employ 25 percent fewer reporters since 1990 (*The State*, 2008). Not surprisingly, newsrooms face the problem of having enough reporters to cover local happenings, verify breaking news, or fact-check the assertions, data and context offered by their sources. And as journalistic resources constrict, many in the public — from individuals up to large corporate interests — see that they can leverage a combination of online platforms and increasingly more affordable digital equipment (flipcams, smart phones, etc.) to assert that they too can construct news accounts (Bowman & Willis, 2003; Gillmor, 2006; Shirky, 2008; St. John, 2008). Finally, as has been well known about traditional news media for decades, individuals, exhibiting selective exposure, turn to news accounts that reflect their viewpoints. A Pew Research report in the fall of 2010 revealed that an individual's ideology continues to influence what news sources he or she will attend to. For example, approximately 80 percent of the audience for FOX News's Sean Hannity classify themselves as conservatives; conversely, the *New York Times* and MSNBC's Rachel Maddow program have audiences that are dominated by self-described liberals (*Americans Spending*, 2010).

All of these factors place traditional journalism in the uncomfortable position of addressing what it means to be a truly credible purveyor of news in an age when people can self-select both their consumption and production of news. This is a vitally important question to address now because, as journalism historians have long pointed out, the press has understood truth to be reified through what Boudana (2011, p. 395) has called the "performance of objectivity." We maintain, however, that within the daily routines of the news room such performances are actually an approximation of objectivity. That is, journalistic objectivity has revealed itself to be less a journalistic performance of scientific practice and more a guiding light and a "glorious goal" (Smith, 1978, p. 153) that orients the reporter toward the items that will be encountered each day (McNair, 1998; Mindich, 1998). While some have maintained its nascent form emerged in the 19th century (Kaplan, 2002; Schiller, 1981), objectivity has been particularly notable as a benchmark of an increasingly professionalizing journalism since the end of World War I (Janowitz, 1975; Schudson, 1978; St. John, 2010). Since then, it has been seen as an enduring ethic that has spread from the west into other advanced and developing nations (Hachten & Scotton 2006; Ward, 2010). Nonetheless, over the latter half of the 20th century, objectivity came under attack as a "strategic ritual" (Tuchman, 1972) that prevented journalism from offering the fuller range of information and viewpoints needed in a society. Other journalistic approaches arose — new journalism, the alternative press (and advocacy journalism), investigative journalism, and the public journalism movement of the late 20th century — but they have not dethroned traditional journalism's emphasis on objectivity. In fact, objectivity remains a foundational premise for the organization of reports in a way that appears "common sense" so that the various needs of news owners, news workers, and the news-consuming public appear to be readily met every day. It is so endemic in mainstream journalism that scholar David Mindich noted that, if journalism was a religion, objectivity would be its "supreme deity" (1998, p. 6).

Within just a few years after Mindich's assertion, the early part of the 21st century has represented a time of transition for objectivity. There are two major forces being exerted on objectivity during this time of transition — the proliferation of channels by which audiences can receive their news, and the ever-increasing availability of easy-to-use and low-cost online publishing tools. Audiences now have more opportunities to get news than they ever have and this has led to increased competition among journalists, which in turn impacts the way journalists do their jobs (Cunningham, 2003; Deuze, 2011). For example, audiences can now get the news immediately online from any number of traditional and/or non-traditional information sources, which forces journalists to react and filter the news quickly for the audience. Social networking platforms, like Facebook and Twitter, have made it very easy for audiences to share information with others without traditional news workers serving as intermediaries. This has forced journalists to go beyond just putting information in the newspaper, on newscasts, or on their websites. Now journalists must co-mingle with the audience in a space that is not solely reserved for news, which can lead journalists to step past the bounds of objectivity in order to connect with audiences in this new environment. Additionally, because of this increased competition media outlets are constantly monitoring each other, which can lead to more interpretation of facts, as opposed to original reporting, because journalists assume that their audience already knows the elementary story facts (Schudson, 2003).

The other major force exerted on objectivity during this time of transition is the advent of easy-to-use online tools, which has signaled an age when anyone with a computer, Internet connection, and an interest in storytelling, can be a journalist. Gillmor (2006) recognized the rise of citizens as journalists and encouraged professional journalists to not abandon their traditional journalistic roles to users. Instead, he encouraged news workers to acknowledge that many users are now part of the journalistic process. Professional journalists, he said, should continue to maintain high standards, especially accuracy and fairness. He also noted that providing context is a new and important role for journalists. Furthermore, the advent of users posting stories on blogs and other sites that support user-generated content has also forced journalists to reconsider objectivity in reporting practices. When citizens place stories on sites there is no promise of objectivity. In fact, just the opposite is often true. Stories on these sites usually contain opinions, and are often unfinished when posted online, with the expectation that readers will correct inaccuracies (Phillips, 2011). The journalistic waters have also become muddied as many traditional media reporters now have blogs or Twitter accounts where they can feel, at least online, more free to express their opinions on the news of the day.

Not surprisingly, since the early 2000s, scholars have not only reexamined objectivity, but gatekeeping practices as well. They noted that journalists began to struggle with how to incorporate user-generated content into their work (Harrison, 2010; Robinson, 2011; Singer & Ashman, 2009; Usher, 2010). Initially, professional journalists resisted releasing control of the news gate because of credibility and trust issues, but now many journalists are realizing they have no choice but to acknowledge user-generated content. In a study of the 2004 presidential campaign, Singer (2006) found that major U.S. newspaper Web site editors posted content online intending that coverage to be a starting point for the audience and acknowledging that the story may grow and change depending upon user input. This signaled a major shift in how traditional media viewed the storytelling process. By in large, prior to 2000, a story was thought to be complete when it was printed or posted online. Post-2000, we see a willingness on the part of traditional media to acknowledge that the audience can be a vital part of the storytelling process.

In 2005 Bruns introduced the idea of "gatewatching" as opposed to gate-keeping. Gatewatching is the idea that those who have an interest in a story will collect and aggregate news and then present it to the audience via the Web. The content is considered unfinished because the audience always has a chance to interact with it. According to Bruns, this collaborative news gathering and storytelling can lead to the demise of journalistic objectivity. He argued that news coverage has begun changing from an industrial model of journalism where one journalist covers a news beat and then reports, to a model where multiple people cover a story and present their individual perspectives. Singer (2011) argued that all of these individual perspectives can lead to ever-increasing tides of information that may actually change the role of the journalist from one who simply reports, to one who filters this deluge of information for different audiences. Since journalists no longer have such influential control over what information is available to audiences, various sectors of the public no longer simply hold different opinions from one another, but can also hold entirely different sets of facts (Manjoo, 2008).

The widespread use of the Internet and the increasing affordability and bandwidth power of smart phone technology has broadened audiences and turned those who were once only consumers of information into producers of information. Additionally, social networking technologies like Twitter and Facebook have made it very easy for people to share information among themselves, without the help of traditional media. Audience proclivities for subjectivity within the news are also apparent through the popularity of online-only news sites. A proliferation of Web-based outlets like the Huffington Post, the Drudge Report and Salon.com take the news and craft it to appeal to the political, social, and economic interests of niche audiences. What we see now, with the rise of subjectivity as news, are accounts of reality that jut away from journalistic norms and, too often, contain a litany of information that may or may not be true.

This new landscape of news no longer features a sense of sharp corners and clear-cut edges bounded by the established field of journalism. Instead, the ability of a news consumer to actually contribute to the construction of news accounts provides the potential for some counterbalances to problems inherent within journalism's objectivity routines. The local knowledge of citizens interjected into news stories can, for example, allow for richer and deeper coverage of ongoing concerns like education, health care, affordable housing, development, and environmental concerns. Indeed, without such local knowledge, objectivity orientations have led to journalists relying too much on privileged experts/authority figures who shape the news frame through agenda-driven talking points and de-contextualized facts and data.

However, a too-credulous course correction toward "everyone is a journalist" can saddle the news (and journalism) with a subjectivity that imperils accuracy. As Manjoo (2008) pointed out, it can be confusing, and perhaps even dangerous, when audiences are left to construct stories on their own based upon different sets of facts. Citizens may end up taking action against a person or organization due to assumptions made after reading misguided reporting or stories that contain conflicting information, he said.

However, today's journalism has no choice — it must grapple with the fact that citizens have more ability than ever to subjectively offer renderings of what they consider news. We maintain that the potential benefits, and the looming dangers, of extensive subjectivity in the news must be acknowledged and tackled by the professional press. As subjectivity is increasingly valued by consumers and news producers, traditional journalists need to incorporate "post-objective" stances into their thinking. Included in such an approach are (1) acknowledging wider spectrums of viewpoints, (2) embracing transparency, and (3) engaging the public by actively educating/updating the citizenry as to the issues, policies, and facts that are germane to their lives. Many traditional media outlets are gradually incorporating some of these three ideals. Practically all traditional media websites now have areas where citizens can comment on news content and offer differing viewpoints that can stimulate conversations among audience members. A next step in making this a richer experience for news consumers is for professional journalists to moderate these discussions to correct any misconceptions and to keep the discussions focused and productive. Secondly, the idea of transparency in reporting is being embraced by journalists to a greater degree now than in the past. In many ways, reporting online has made this easier, as there is now space for reporters to offer information on their background and training, which could offer clues to the audience as to any biases journalists may harbor. If there is to be true transparency between journalists and audience members more information regarding reporters must be made available. Audiences need to know who is reporting information, what affiliations they may have to the stories they are reporting, and under what conditions these stories are being reported. Thirdly, traditional journalists must find new ways to make sure the information they are communicating to audiences is relevant and meaningful. For example, Real Simple Syndication (RSS) feeds are a step in that direction, as audiences can set up information filters with the hope that only the most relevant information will be passed along to them. As a growing amount of information is collected about each individual's online patterns and preferences it should become easier for news organizations to figure out which information will be most useful to each individual audience member. Some news outlets take further steps to make information relevant to the community. Many news organizations now allow citizen journalists to contribute stories; the aim is that these non-professionals write stories that are interesting and relevant to fellow members of their communities. For example, HartsvilleToday is a citizen journalism website created as a partnership between the *Hartsville Messenger* and the University of South Carolina. The site allows citizens to post stories about topics of interest to them.

This book offers new examinations of how the traditional notion of objectivity is changing as professional journalists grapple with a rapidly evolving news terrain — one that has become increasingly crowded by those with no journalistic credentials. As such, these developments call upon the 21st-century journalist to question the value of traditional notions of objectivity. Instead of a sense of objectivity as a "supreme deity" (Mindich, 1998, p. 6), the journalistic field would be better served by identifying how news with a view can lend itself to more thorough, credible, and pertinent accounts of reality. Embracing user-generated content in a newsroom does not necessarily mean that objectivity must be abandoned, but the pseudo-scientific journalistic objectivity markers of distance, balance and factuality are no longer enough. Citizens are already displaying a preference for relating to, and constructing, post-objective news accounts that stress connections, context, values, and transparency. While the soundness (e.g., credibility, accuracy) of some of the resulting stories may be questionable, the efforts also point to the promise of new frameworks through which mainstream journalism can revitalize its authenticity and relevance. As such, the contributors to this volume offer their perspectives on post-objectivity in the news; their observations stimulate thought and conversation about news with a view in both theory and practice.

References

Americans spending more time following the news. (2010, September 12). Washington, DC: Pew Research Center for the People and the Press.

Boudana, S. (2011). A definition of journalistic objectivity as performance. *Media, Culture & Society, 33*(3), 385–398.

Bowman, S., & Willis, C. (2003). *We media.* Retrieved Oct. 14, 2011, from http://www.hypergene.net/wemedia/weblog.php

Bruns, A. (2005). *Gatewatching: Collaborative online news production.* New York: Peter Lang.

Cunningham, B. (2003). Re-thinking objectivity. *Columbia Journalism Review, 42*(2), 24–32.

Deuze, M. (2011). What is journalism? Professional ideology of journalists reconsidered. In D. Burkowitz (Ed.), *Cultural meanings of news* (pp. 17–32). Thousand Oaks, CA: Sage.

Gillmor, D. (2006). *We the media: Grassroots journalism by the people, for the people.* Sebastopol, CA: O'Reilly.

Hachten, W., & Scotton, J. (2006). *The world news prism: Global information in a satellite age.* Malden, MA: Blackwell.

Harrison, J. (2010). User-generated content and gatekeeping at the BBC hub. *Journalism Studies, 11*(2), 243–256.

How Internet and cell phone users have turned news into a social experience. (2010, March 1). Washington, DC: Pew Research Center for the People and the Press.

Janowitz, M. (1975). Professional models in journalism: The gatekeeper and the advocate. *Journalism Quarterly, 52*(4), 618–626, 662.

Kaplan, R. (2002). *Politics and the American press: The rise of objectivity, 1865–1920.* Cambridge, England: Cambridge University Press.

Manjoo, F. (2008). *True enough: Learning to live in a post-fact society.* Hoboken, NJ: John Wiley and Sons.

McNair, B. (1998). *The sociology of journalism.* New York: Oxford University Press.

Mindich, D. T. Z. (1998). *Just the facts: How "objectivity" came to define journalism.* New York: New York University Press.

Phillips, A. (2011). Transparency and the new ethics of journalism. *Journalism Practice, 4*(3), 373–382.

Public evaluations of the news media: 1985–2009. (2009, September 12). Washington, DC: Pew Research Center for the People and the Press.

Robinson, S. (2011). *Someone's gotta be in control here.* In D. Burkowitz (Ed.), *Cultural meanings of news* (pp. 151–164). Thousand Oaks, CA: Sage.

St. John, B. (2008). Not biting the hand that feeds them: Hegemonic expediency in the newsroom and the Karen Ryan/Health and Human Services Department video news release. *Journal of Mass Media Ethics, 23*(2), 110–125.

_____. (2010). *Press professionalization and propaganda: The rise of journalistic double-mindedness, 1917–1941.* Amherst, NY: Cambria Press.

Schiller, D. (1981). *Objectivity and the news: The public and the rise of commercial journalism.* Philadelphia: University of Pennsylvania Press.

Schudson, M. (1978). *Discovering the news.* New York: Basic Books.

_____. (2003). *The sociology of news.* New York: W. W. Norton.

Shirky, C. (2008). *Here comes everybody: The power of organizing without organizations.* New York: Penguin.

Singer, J. (2006). Stepping back from the gate: Online newspaper editors and the co-production of content in campaign 2004. *Journalism & Mass Communication Quarterly, 83*(2), 265–280.

_____. (2011). The socially responsible existentialist: A normative emphasis for journalists in a new media environment. In D. Burkowitz (Ed.), *Cultural meanings of news* (pp. 53–66). Thousand Oaks, CA: Sage.

Singer, J., & Ashman, I. (2009). Comment is free, but facts are sacred: User generated content and ethical constructs at the Guardian. *Journal of Mass Media Ethics, 24*(3), 3–21.

Smith, A. (1978). The long road to objectivity and back again. In G. Boyce, J. Curran, & P. Wingate (Eds.), *Newspaper history from the 17th century to the present day* (pp. 153–171). London: Sage.

The state of the news media 2008. (2008, March 17). Washington, DC: Pew Research Center for the People and the Press.

Tuchman, G. (1972). Objectivity as strategic ritual: An examination of newsmen's notions of objectivity. *American Journal of Sociology, 77*(4), 660–679.

Usher, N. (2010). Goodbye to news: how out-of-work journalists assess enduring news values and the new media landscape. *New Media & Society, 12*(6), 911–928.

Ward, S. (2010). *Global journalism ethics.* Montreal: McGill–Queen's University Press.

PART I

Historical Perspectives

1

"Gagged, Mincing Neutrality"

Horace Greeley on Advocacy Journalism in the Early Years of the Penny Press

Daxton R. "Chip" Stewart

The three decades preceding the start of the Civil War were times of drastic change in the newspaper industry. The roots of our modern understanding of journalism were evident in the creation of the first daily newspapers and the first penny newspapers in this era. It was a period that historian Michael Schudson called "a revolution in American journalism" when coverage shifted from editorial opinions to news and facts more readily available to working-class readers (Schudson, 1978, p. 14). It was during this era that Horace Greeley emerged as one of the most popular and outspoken journalists. His opinions and ideas on the role of the press in society and the debates they inspired helped to shape modern understandings of how journalism ethics and professionalism developed during the American daily newspaper's infancy.

The newspaper world was changing, and Greeley had no shortage of ideas about how this world should be run. It was during these early years of the Penny Press, when Greeley founded and ran *The New-Yorker* and *The New York Tribune*, that he publicly mulled over the role of a free press in the United States. He engaged in regular debates within his pages about the ethical duties of journalists, particularly focusing on the press's self-imposed obligations to serve society and contribute to democracy.

Previous historical research about Greeley's approach to journalism has focused on incidents during and shortly after the Civil War, when Greeley used the press to bolster his favored political candidates, to curry favor with President Lincoln, and ultimately to support his own run for the presidency (Borchard, 2007, 2010; Williams, 2006). But these experiences contrast somewhat with the journalism philosophy Greeley developed during the previous quarter century, an era of Greeley's daily experience in journalism that has received less attention from scholars. It was in the 1830s and 1840s that the notion of impartiality in reporting started to attract the interest of American newspaper publishers, with the Penny Press marking "a significant milestone in an evolutionary process" leading to objectivity becoming the industry standard (Huntzicker, 1999, p. 183). However, Greeley was a vocal dissenter to such thoughts of neutrality and impartiality, preferring instead to blend his roles as "the journalist, the practical politician, and the moralist" in a way that allowed him to speak freely about important matters of the day (Hale, 1950, p. 79).

This chapter focuses on the development of Greeley's philosophy of journalism in the pre–Civil War era, when he bucked his colleagues and rivals who were moving toward a model of an objective, neutral press. Through examination of Greeley's writings in *The New-Yorker* and *The New York Tribune* and his 1868 autobiography, *Recollections of a Busy Life*, this study focuses on Greeley's beliefs about the importance of a non-neutral, independent press and the moral duties journalists have to society through their power to advocate and spread policy messages to the people.

Method

Historical research was applied to examine Greeley's thoughts about journalism ethics before the Civil War. Initially, a review of secondary sources, including numerous biographies of Greeley, was conducted to inform a brief section regarding the historical context and background of the early days of the Penny Press, during which Greeley emerged as one of the most important figures in American journalism and politics in the nineteenth century.

The bulk of this chapter relies on a review of Greeley's writings during his early days as a journalist in the Penny Press era. The two newspapers Greeley founded, *The New-Yorker* and *The New York Tribune*, were examined using the archives available in the library of the University of Texas at Austin. The weekly *New-Yorker* was examined from its first edition in 1834 to its final issue in 1841. The daily *New York Tribune* was examined from its first issue in April 1841 to December 1842.[1] Hard copies of these publications, either in printed or microform format, were reviewed for articles dealing with ethical matters involving the practice of journalism. Greeley's subsequent accounts of this era, detailed in his autobiography and some of his letters, are also included as primary sources. A contemporary biography of Greeley, written in 1855 by James Parton, and including excerpts of articles from the 1830s and 1840s, was also used to examine Greeley's thoughts about journalism in this era.

Journalist, Politician, and Reformer in the Penny Press Era

Greeley was born near Amherst, Massachusetts, in 1811, the son of a Scotch-Irish farmer. He grew up cherishing the rural life of farmers and supporting the causes of the poor and the working class. It is questionable whether journalism or politics was Greeley's first true love, but he would get a full share of both. After decades as an editor and publisher, Greeley was "among the most famous, and most easily recognized, Americans of his day" (Williams, 2006, p. 293) helping him become the candidate of both the Democrats and the Liberal Republicans for president in 1872, an election he would lose to Ulysses S. Grant. Weeks later, Greeley died at age 61.

Greeley spent his entire professional life at least partially in the newspaper business. He also spent a great amount of time in the world of politics, starting out as a staunch Whig supporter, then helping to found the Republican Party (Borchard, 2006), later serving one term in the U.S. House of Representatives before his failed presidential run. But whether as a journalist or a politician, Greeley fancied himself as a reformer who wished to make the American system of democracy work for every citizen.

He dabbled in nearly every possible reform movement and political campaign, and spoke out on many crises of American society during this period. His life as an editor, writer, and publisher guided his philosophy about the proper role of the press in American society. Biographer Lurton D. Ingersoll wrote that Greeley considered the freedoms guaranteed by the First Amendment and the implied duty of the press to enlighten society about public issues as central to serving the "welfare of the People," which he saw as "the true object of government" (1873, p. 111). At different times, Greeley took part in movements such as abolitionism, socialism, feminism, temperance, and protectionism, all of which he saw as ways for Americans to achieve the highest ideals of democracy (Stoddard, 1946). He saw the newspaper as the perfect instrument for effecting change through these reform movements. A free, unfettered press would be able to bring small, even unpopular reform movements into the public eye for consideration and possible approval. As the head of a daily newspaper in New York in the mid-nineteenth century, Greeley had a broad platform from which he could spread his messages of reform.

It was in this era that the newspaper industry was undergoing radical changes that would shape the future of journalism. Before the 1830s, newspapers were almost exclusively of two types: political propaganda papers and commercial journals. The political papers were created and almost fully funded by political parties, with additional backing coming through advertising purchased by supportive businesses. The other type of newspaper, the commercial journal, was aimed purely at businessmen trying to keep up with the financial world. While these papers routinely reported on some broader developments in the news, Schudson said they were, in actuality, "little more than bulletin boards for the business community" (1978, p. 15).

Both the commercial and political papers of the early nineteenth century were expensive and not very timely. They were published weekly or monthly, were sold only by subscription, and usually cost at least six cents per issue, or six to ten dollars a year for a subscription (Parton, 1855). This price was only affordable to the affluent, and with the arrival of the economic depression of the 1830s, these journals were even further out of the reach of the middle and lower classes (Emery & Emery, 1984). But revolutions in the technology of the printing press, and the determination of printers such as Greeley to reach a more middle-class market, led to the creation of a number of cheap daily papers (Tucher, 1994). These papers covered more general interest news, and because of significant advertising revenues, they were priced for daily sale on the streets (Emery & Emery, 1984). By 1830, the first successful daily newspapers had begun to flourish in New York, after the creation of *The Morning Courier and New-York Enquirer*, the *Journal of Commerce*, and *The New York Evening Post* (Parton, 1855). When Benjamin Day founded *The New York Sun* and sold it for a penny an issue, it was another step in the newspaper revolution. The "penny paper" became an institution in journalism — the inexpensive daily that has lasted to the present. The focus of the *Sun* was not politics or commerce, but instead news of interest to the common person, often sensational in nature. Day called this "human-interest" news, covering "local happenings and news of violence" (Emery & Emery, 1984, pp. 140–141).

The move from politically-sponsored newspapers and commercial publications to inexpensive dailies raised new issues about freedom of the press and the duties of the press to society. Greeley found himself at the heart of these debates.

Independence, Not Neutrality

Greeley was a young man in the journalism industry as this transition took place, starting in 1826 as a 15-year-old apprentice for a writer for *The Northern Spectator*, a Whig party publication in Vermont. After a brief stint at *The Erie Gazette* in Pennsylvania in 1831, he moved to New York, where he worked a number of printing jobs, including commercial publications. In 1833, he published the nation's first penny newspaper, *The New York Morning Post*, aimed at the large immigrant population moving into the city. However, the *Post* failed after only a few weeks of publication (Huntzicker, 1999). He founded his first successful newspaper in New York, a six-cent weekly called *The New-Yorker*, on March 22, 1834. It was a publication independent of political parties that included literature, foreign letters, poetry, book reviews, and an "Editorial-Political" section where Greeley commented on social and political events of the day. In 1838, Greeley began printing *The Jeffersonian*, a weekly publication financed by Whig politicians and supporters. After a year, he stopped printing that paper and started *The Log-Cabin*, another weekly that supported the Whigs and its presidential candidate William Henry Harrison. This paper, however, was not funded by the party, allowing Greeley more freedom to comment without concerns about party censorship.

After Harrison won the 1840 presidential election, Greeley returned his full attention to *The New-Yorker*, but with new plans. The rapid growth of daily penny papers, specifically James Gordon Bennett's scandalous *New York Herald*, intrigued Greeley. In particular, Greeley wanted to target as readers an "active and substantial middle class" (Tucher, 1994, p. 170). After being "incited ... by several Whig friends" (Greeley, 1868, p. 166) including party boss Thurlow Weed, Greeley secured a loan and began *The New York Tribune*, the publication with which he would be identified for the rest of his career in journalism. The first issue was published on April 10, 1841, just four days after Harrison died from an illness he contracted during his inauguration. Announcing the launch of the paper in *The Log-Cabin*, Greeley said the *Tribune* would be financially independent of the Whigs, but would also nevertheless be a Whig-supporting publication, as opposed to the *Herald* and *Sun*, which declared themselves politically neutral (Greeley, 1841b). The daily issue cost a penny in the *Tribune*'s first year, and two cents per issue the next year (Parton, 1855).

Publication of the *Tribune* took up most of Greeley's time, and after four months, he ceased publishing *The New-Yorker* and focused his energies on the *Tribune*. It was in these two publications that Greeley expressed his opinions about the important political and social matters of the day, including his thoughts about the practice and philosophy of journalism.

Greeley saw a need to break out of the political party patronage system that was common during the early years of the penny press. He advocated financial freedom from political parties to further the notion of a free and independent press. However, while he advocated independence from political parties, he did not agree with emerging notions of objectivity that were becoming common in his competitors' publications. Instead, he repeatedly challenged the ideal of unbiased or neutral newspapers as best equipped to foster meaningful political dialogue.

Before founding the *New-Yorker* and the *Tribune*, Greeley published papers for the Whig party. *The Log-Cabin* and *The Jeffersonian* were openly funded and supported by Whigs as propaganda for the party's presidential campaign in 1840. While *The New-Yorker* was not politically subsidized, it had frustrated Greeley by following the mainstream course of keeping political commentary neutral, "avoiding as far as possible any allusion to or interference with party politics, local or National" (Greeley, 1837a, p. 383). But, upon creation of the *Tribune*, Greeley moved to a style that allowed him more leeway to express his opinions without limitations imposed by either political patronage or notions of objectivity. While he continued supporting Whigs in his politics and his newspaper, he did not want his publication to be beholden to the Whig party through financial support, as was the case with *The Log Cabin* and *The Jeffersonian*. Greeley did not overly denigrate "avowed party" papers, writing that "an openly party paper will, nine times out of ten, speak out its honest thought" (Greeley, 1841e, p. 2). Meanwhile, he noted, "a neutral paper seldom or ever can" speak what it believes to be the honest truth (Greeley, 1841e, p. 2). Further, he thought these so-called neutral papers were disingenuous, a "counterfeit of Independence" that were, in reality, "venomous slaves of party" (Greeley, 1841e, p. 2). Instead, he preferred the route of "manly independence" in which he had the option to criticize the party he supported (Greeley, 1841e, p. 2). Comparing the American press to that of Europe, he noted that in America, "the press is generally more servile in its devotion to or fear of party, more timorous in the expression of new, singular, or unpopular opinions, more slavish in its submission to the imperious will of patronage, than in any other part of the world," in spite of the freedoms guaranteed by the First Amendment (Greeley, 1841a, p. 635).

But because Greeley was an intensely political man, he could not fathom the press avoiding involvement in the coverage of campaigns and elections, which he viewed as central duties of the press to American society. To be able to comment on politics, express his honest opinions, and still be able to stay involved in Whig politics, Greeley created the *Tribune* as a non-neutral but independent publication, reflecting upon its founding:

> My leading idea was the establishment of a journal removed alike from servile partisanship on the one hand and from gagged, mincing neutrality on the other. I believed there was a happy medium between these extremes — a position from which a journalist might openly and heartily advocate the principles and commend the measures of that party to which his convictions allied him, yet frankly dissent from its course on a particular question, and even denounce its candidates if they were shown to be deficient in capacity or (far worse) in integrity [Greeley, 1868, p. 137].

It was this course that the *Tribune* followed, supporting the Whig party in general but chastising the party when it took a course Greeley did not support.

He was proud of the independence of the paper, and in a famous statement made in a letter to Whig political boss Thurlow Weed, Greeley wrote, "I owe what little chance of usefulness I may have to the impression that I do no man's bidding but speak my own thoughts" (Stoddard, 1946, p. 321).

At the *Tribune*, the notion of objectivity was not an option. The Whig sympathies of Greeley were at the heart of nearly every editorial decision at the *Tribune*, both for news and opinion articles. He refused to be bound by the "imbecile epithet" of "neutrality," which he said was a major hindrance for other New York newspapers (Greeley, 1837a, p. 383).

Greeley saw true neutrality as impossible and believed it impeded the ability of the press to provide insight to its readers. This was a major topic of debate among the editors of the early penny newspapers, and Greeley regularly denounced James Gordon Bennett of the *Herald* and Benjamin Day of the *Sun* for claiming to be neutral when, in fact, they actively supported the candidates and policies of the Democratic Party (also known at the time as the Loco-Focoists, the term often used by Greeley to describe and deride them). In the first edition of the *Tribune*, under the headline, "A Plain Talk to Whigs," Greeley discussed the topic of objectivity, deriding the *Sun*:

> But that Editor as bitterly, we do not doubt sincerely, Loco-Foco in all his associations and sympathies, and his writings are thoroughly imbued with the spirit of his party.... Every great question of National and State Policy is ably, dexterously discussed in its columns, with much caution and plausibility of manner, but in a spirit of deadliest hostility to the Whigs [Greeley, 1841d, p. 2].

He went on to say that Bennett's *Herald* was "a little less bitter in its hostility, but hardly less thorough" than the *Sun* and commented that *The Journal of Commerce* "views every public opinion through Van Buren spectacles" (Greeley, 1841c, p. 2).

Bennett, Day, and later Henry J. Raymond of *The New York Times* differed from Greeley in their views about the meaning of objectivity, as Bennett explained in 1835:

> We shall support no party — be the organ of no faction or coterie, and care nothing for any election or candidate from president down to constable. We shall endeavor to record facts on every public and proper subject, stripped of verbiage and coloring, with comments when suitable, just, independent, fearless, and good-tempered [Bennett, 2003, p. 169].

These editors, critical of Greeley, still provided heated opinions on matters of the day in their editorial pages, but they tried to separate commentary from the news stories. Raymond, who worked for Greeley at the *Tribune* before taking over as editor of the *Times*, wrote that Greeley's great fault was moving away from the neutrality espoused in the *New-Yorker* (Maverick, 1870, p. 361).

In his prospectus for the *Times*, Raymond announced that his paper was "not established for the advancement of any party, sect, or person," and that while Raymond may adhere more to the Whig party than any other, the *Times* would be "free from bigoted devotion to narrow interests" (Raymond, 1870, p. 94).

Greeley obviously disagreed, understanding that the opinions of editors would necessarily make their way into the publication as the paper also provided the public "facts rather than arguments ... which may assist them in forming opinions, rather than opinions ready formed for their adaptation" (Greeley, 1837a, p. 409). Whether writing for the politically-supported *New-Yorker* or the more independent *Tribune*, he charged the other papers with treachery in their claims of neutrality. He asserted that his own open and honest support of a party was more effective and honest, "filling the expectations" of the paper's Whig supporters; his competitors, he said, attempted to confuse the public by pretending to be neutral (Greeley, 1837a, p. 409).

Greeley's criticisms of his peers and their so-called neutrality earned him several enemies. Greeley accused the *Sun* of a "conspiracy to crush the *New York Tribune*" by encouraging "the boys in [the *Sun's*] office ... to whip the boys engaged in selling the *Tribune*." Such physical attacks, he maintained, were revenge for his criticisms of his competitors' political and editorial policies. Greeley, in turn, sent young men to take "retributory measures" against the boys from the *Sun* office who were flogging his newsboys (Greeley, 1841e, p. 3). Greeley relished the dispute, covering it in great detail and requesting that the *Sun* provide his company with a free printing press as a token of goodwill, "until the *Sun* shall cease to be the slimy and venomous instrument of loco-focoism it is, jesuitical and deadly in politics and grovelling in morals" (Parton, 1855, p. 195). The incident ultimately worked to the benefit of the *Tribune*, earning sympathy from the public and attracting a wider readership.

Greeley openly discussed what he saw as the hypocrisy of his contemporaries, who claimed to be impartial and neutral and yet could not break free of the political patronage and partisanship that was inherent in the early American press. Press historian John Nerone (1987) found that the emergence of an impartial, neutral press in this era is more myth than reality, noting the actual lack of political neutrality by Bennett and Raymond, who also had political ambitions. Greeley recognized this, and called out other New York publishers for their hypocrisy. In doing so, he invited debate about the proper role of the press in a democracy that went beyond questions of partisanship and neutrality. Greeley's vision of journalism at the *New-Yorker* and the *Tribune* demonstrated his belief that the press had a responsibility to the public. The Constitutional guarantee of a free press called for a journalism of advocacy, education, and reform.

Moral Duty to the Public

Greeley saw potential dangers in Penny Press practices during their earliest days. One development of this era was a move by the *Sun* and the *Herald*, followed by other publications nationwide, toward "emphasizing local news, human interest stories, and entertainment underwritten by increased circulation accompanied by higher advertising rates" (Huntzicker, 1999, p. 32). Greeley recognized the importance of reporting human interest stories, but he took a different approach than Bennett, who was criticized by rival editors in New York for his tendency to publish the sensational and scandalous in the *Herald*. Greeley was troubled by what he saw as Bennett's lack of principles or sense of duty to the public, as biographer William Harlan Hale said:

> An editor, as Greeley saw it, should be by trade both an entertainer and an inspirer. In order to succeed, he must be adventurous and resourceful; but the more he did succeed, the more he fell under moral obligation to the community as a whole, for his duty was to serve it on weekdays almost as much as a pastor did on Sundays [Hale, 1950, p. 78].

A press that overemphasized murders and scandals and perpetrated hoaxes on the public, Greeley noted, was "a tremendous engine for good or evil — possibly evil in its savage infancy; certainly for good in its chastened maturity" (Greeley, 1841a, p. 635).

As a reformer and politician, Greeley saw the "good" of the press as the ability to educate and reform. He would use the press to support many of his "isms" — socialism, abolitionism, and feminism among them — which he saw as furthering the cause of liberty and democracy in America (Stoddard, 1946). In *The New-Yorker*, Greeley criticized other papers that avoided commentary and discussion of such reform movements and any other important political issues, saying that other journals were

> unanimously and profoundly silent with regard to those great questions of political economy, constitutional principle, or more simply, party antagonism, which are and should be the theme of discussion not merely in the halls of legislation, but at the Exchange, in the market place, the village gathering, and on the deck of the steamboat [Greeley, 1837a, p. 383].

Greeley maintained that the *Sun* and the *Herald* ignored this realization and, instead, strove to sell as many papers as possible by featuring sensational stories of crime, scandal and human interest. By comparison, Greeley reported that he sought more intellectual discussion in the *New-Yorker* and the *Tribune*. He treasured education of the working class in particular, writing in an essay in 1870 that he aimed his publications "for the great mass of intelligent, observant, reflecting farmers and mechanics," which he saw as the intended beneficiaries of his reform movements (Ingersoll, 1873, pp. 497–498). He worked, he said, to "lift the Laboring Class ... out of ignorance, inefficiency, dependence, and want, and place them in a partnership" with the wealthy and politicians (Greeley, 1868, p. 508). This stance was based on the tenets of Fourierism, a pre–Marxian form of socialism, a position that Greeley debated with Raymond of the *Times* within a series of letters published in the *Tribune*.[2]

Besides supporting the causes of the working class, Greeley also allowed the voices of women to be heard in the columns of the *Tribune*, a rarity at the time. He provided coverage of the controversial Women's Rights movement at the Seneca Falls Convention in 1848 and he supported feminist thinkers of the day (Jones, 1947). Most prominent among these was Margaret Fuller, a feminist writer whom Greeley hired as a literary reviewer and editor, supporting her notion that it was "the right of Woman to be regarded and treated as an independent, intelligent, rational being, entitled to an equal voice in framing and modifying the laws she is required to obey" (Greeley, 1868, p. 175).

By making the *Tribune* a public forum for debate on controversial issues, Greeley put into practice his view of the role of a non-neutral, independent free press in democratic society. As was the case with the discussion with Raymond about Fourierism, Greeley opened his columns for other debates, including a dispute over the propriety of divorce (which Greeley opposed) in 1853. Although Greeley typically allowed dissenting views, he was charged by debate opponent Stephen Pearl Andrews as a hypocrite who "used the power of the press" to "apply 'the gag' and 'suppress' me" after refusing to publish one of Andrews' rebuttals in the *Tribune* (James, Greeley, & Andrews, 1889, p. 7–8). But this appears to be a rare exception to Greeley's policy of allowing opposing views to be published in his paper, regardless of where he stood on an issue. In fact, Greeley is credited with creating the interview story, where he allowed important people to present their arguments (Jones, 1947). In 1859, Greeley published an important "first" for an interview story — he was the first reporter to interview Mormon leader Brigham Young (Stoddard, 1946). While Greeley called the Mormons a cult and said he did not believe Young's ideas, he recognized Mormonism as an important public movement and allowed Young to be heard, letting the public be the judge of the truth (Ingersoll, 1873).

However, Greeley's broad views on freedom of the press and the role of the press as a forum were not unlimited. With these freedoms came a duty for the press to be responsible in covering the events of the day. Greeley noted that the press had the ability to do great evil to society, but nowhere did he see this as more true than in coverage of murders and other violent crimes.

He called such reporting "deplorable," saying that reporting of such events would "tend only to demoralize or dissipate the minds of their readers" (Greeley, 1841a, p. 635). He feared fostering "familiarity with crime" through constant reporting of it and accused his competitors of "making murderers" (Greeley, 1841d, p. 2). Further, he called for the *Herald* and the *Sun* to cease such coverage "for the sake of ... social security" and criticized both publications for using sensationalist reporting styles to sell more newspapers while disregarding the public welfare. By constant reporting of violent crimes, Greeley argued, "a formidable barrier against sin is thus broken down and destroyed forever" (Greeley, 1841a, p. 635).

Advertisements also troubled Greeley. As he noted upon the launch of the *Tribune*, Greeley intended that the paper would avoid not only the "immoral and degrading Police Reports," but also distasteful "advertisements and other matter which have been allowed to disgrace the columns of our leading Penny Papers" (Greeley, 1841b, p. 2). Greeley charged rival publications with accepting all advertisements. The *Herald* had a policy of publishing nearly any advertisement, including those by quack doctors, snake-oil salesmen, abortionists, and "women of notorious reputation" (Jones, 1947, p. 279). This policy led to what has come to be known as the "Moral War" against the *Herald* by church leaders and rival publishers (Tucher, 1994, pp. 170–171). Greeley attacked such advertising policies, preferring instead to publish advertisements only for items such as books, educational classes, public lectures, and property for sale or lease (Greeley, 1837b, p. 265). He praised papers such as the *Journal of Commerce* for rejecting advertisements from "theaters and lotteries" calling them morally unacceptable. He viewed the modern popular theater as depraved and saw lotteries as a form of gambling contradictory to Christian principles (Greeley, 1837a, p. 383).

Greeley saw that these publications took almost any kind of advertising to financially support a form of objective reporting that focused too often on murderers and rapists. Too much emphasis on neutrality and independence allowed for such abuses; Greeley believed that such markers of autonomy should be secondary to publishers' moral responsibilities. He found hypocrisy in other publishers' claims that "the wretched plea of the duty of the Press to Society" required them to report objectively on bloody crimes (Greeley, 1841d, p. 2). Publication of the "pestiferous, death-breathing history" of a murderer's guilt, he said, may have "put some hundred dollars in their purse" (Greeley, 1841d, p. 2), but at the cost of publishers' duty to a decent and just society.

Greeley clearly thought that the press's high-minded claim "that it is bound to keep the public informed of such acts" was actually cynical, profit-driven, and not motivated by a desire to serve "the good of their fellow-men" (Greeley, 1841d, p. 2). But he had hope that, by ridding itself of "bloody murders" and depraved advertising, the press would be raised to its proper level in American discourse, saying, "[W]e have faith that a revolution has commenced which we must go on till the character of the press generally is purified and elevated, its independence asserted, and its influence extended" (Greeley, 1841a, p. 635).

Conclusion

Horace Greeley was a critically important figure in the Penny Press revolution, when daily newspapers affordable to the masses became commonplace, and the concept of news coverage shifted from political and commercial issues to sensational and human interest news. In his early years as the founder and editor of *The New-Yorker* and *The New York Tribune*, Greeley reflected on this historic shift and its implications for the press, which he saw as central to the promise of democracy.

Greeley's emphasis on the independence of publishers from political parties, the dysfunctional reporting practices, and the presence of unscrupulous advertisers — rather than the too often self-serving claims of neutrality or objectivity — makes him a journalist who was ahead of his time. Bill Kovach and Tom Rosenstiel, in their manifesto *The Elements of Journalism* (2001), noted, like Greeley, that it is the "independence of spirit and mind, rather than neutrality, that journalists must keep in focus" (p. 97). Greeley believed it was dishonest for journalists to hold themselves out as independent or neutral, particularly aiming his venom at the *Sun*, which he said was "eternally prating of its independence" and had no "decent pretext for its claim of neutrality" (Greeley, 1841e, p. 2). To Greeley, the *Sun* and others that emulated its supposed neutrality were "counterfeit," showing only "the independence of the spy in priest's supplice [sic] — of the pirate with the white flag flying" (Greeley, 1841e, p. 2).

Greeley also thought it was a key function of the press to take stands and embrace reforms it thought could benefit society. However, he also deemed it critical that the press no longer be financially beholden to political parties, and some distasteful advertisers, so that journalists could freely criticize the society they were supposed to be scrutinizing. While Greeley's stand was often ridiculed by contemporary publishers in New York, it foreshadowed a more modern view of responsible journalism than that of his contemporaries and competitors.

Contemporary scholars have challenged the extent to which neutrality and objectivity truly existed during the early Penny Press era. While Nerone (1987) noted that the early Penny Press papers, particularly in New York, "invoked political neutrality" as a reaction against "the novel partisanism of the 1820s" he suggested that the development of objectivity as a standard in this era is more myth than fact (p. 390). Further, he saw this "ancestor myth" as a tool for legitimizing the modern practice of objective journalism, noting the power of the argument that "[t]o locate your roots in a glorious past is to clothe yourself in glory" (p. 400). However, if the modern news media can recognize that the emergence of an objective, neutral press was more of a myth than reality, as Nerone maintained, then there is another glorious past to contend with: One in which an independent but non-neutral press, vocally supported and acted out by Greeley in his Penny Press publications, were important contributors to democratic thought and action in the pre–Civil War era.[3] By realizing how Greeley long ago challenged neutrality as merely a cloak that partisan journalists wore to hide their own important ideas about reform and policy — or their own baser economic survival motivations — modern journalists can see both the honesty and the power of authenticity. Such genuineness is the best road, Greeley proclaimed in 1841, to journalistic integrity:

> The true, honest course for an individual would seem to be not to attempt Editorship until he has studied the great public questions of the day, and formed his opinions upon them; then, in coming before the public, he should frankly, candidly avow what those opinions are. Having done this, he is prepared to act with freedom and independence, and to give his arguments the weight of his known convictions [Greeley, 1841e, p. 2].

The first decade of the penny press era ushered in several changes to the way journalism was practiced, and Greeley's public arguments for an independent, advocacy-minded press provide valuable insight to the development of journalism ethics. While most biographers and scholars pay attention to Greeley's ethical compromises during the Civil War, a more consistent philosophy can be found in Greeley's earlier writings in the *New-Yorker* and the *Tribune*. This philosophy of independence and moral duty, nearer to the reality than the mythology of the Penny Press era, provides guidance to the modern role of journalism as an essential tool for encouraging debate, advocating reform, and engaging the public in the daily practice of democracy.

Greeley's experience as an independent, non-objective publisher calling for a journalism of reform and advocacy made him a controversial, but enduring, figure in the field. Journalists today can draw some parallels from Greeley's experience as well. Greeley worked in a time of technological innovations that made news media cheaper and more accessible to a broader audience, providing ample opportunity for the journalism field to try new ways of doing business. His competitors sought to increase circulation and serve the public interest through their purported neutrality, which Greeley saw as harmful to open discussion of policy matters central to American democracy at best, and cynically disingenuous at worst. Instead, Greeley preferred to emphasize his independence from political party funding — "We glory in independence" he wrote in the early years of the *Tribune* (Greeley, 1841e, p. 265) — which allowed him to participate as a voice for reform, whether as a Whig, a socialist, an abolitionist, or a Republican. This honest advocacy, driven by a sense of moral duty to the public, helped Greeley succeed as a publisher and politician. Independence liberated him, allowing him to present an authentic voice of reform to the audience and develop a business model that emphasized an authenticity that distinguished him from his supposedly neutral competitors. In eschewing blind objectivity, he found an audience and served his conscience and moral duty more effectively. Today's journalists, facing the demands that come from new technologies and new competitors, would do well to heed Greeley's call to avoid neutrality and advocate for a journalism that operates from an enhanced sense of duty to the public.

Chapter Notes

1. These were the only pre–Civil War issues available in the archives accessible to the author.

2. In his contemporary biography, Parton (1855) noted that this discussion "finished Fourierism in the United States" (p. 171) after Greeley advanced radical ideas such as outlawing land ownership.

3. During the Civil War, as the *Tribune* became financially troubled and as Greeley sided with President Lincoln in efforts to keep the union together, Greeley surrendered some of this independence, famously making a deal with Lincoln to provide favorable coverage in exchange for better access to information about the war from the Lincoln administration. However, in spite of this secret deal, biographer Robert C. Williams (2006) noted that Greeley "remained typically independent" and sometimes criticized the president (p. 226).

References

Bennett, J. G. (2003). The Herald and the great role of the newspaper. In D.A. Copeland (Ed.), *The antebellum era: Primary documents on events from 1820 to 1860* (pp. 168–169). Westport, CT: Greenwood (Reprinted from the *New York Herald*, 1835, May 6).

Borchard, G. A. (2006). From pink lemonade to salt river: Horace Greeley's utopia and the death of the whig party. *American Journalism, 32*(1), 22–33.

_____. (2007). The New York Tribune and the 1844 election: Horace Greeley, gangs and the wise men of Gotham. *American Journalism, 33*(1), 51–59.

_____. (2010). Revolutions incomplete: Horace Greeley and the forty-eighters at home and abroad. *American Journalism, 27*(2), 7–36.

Emery, E., & Emery, M. (1984). *The Press and America* (Vol. 5). Englewood Cliffs, NJ: Prentice-Hall.

Greeley, H. (1837a, March 4). To our patrons. *The New-Yorker*, p. 383.

_____. (1837b, August 26). Scary statistics. *The New-Yorker*, p. 265.

_____. (1841a, March 13). To our friends. *The New-Yorker*, p. 635.

_____. (1841b, April 8). New York Tribune. *The Log Cabin*, p. 2.

_____. (1841c, April 10). A plain talk to whigs. *The New York Tribune*, p. 2.

_____. (1841d, April 19). Peter Robinson and the newspaper press. *The New York Tribune*, p. 2.

_____, (1841e, April 26). An independent press and a party press. *The New York Tribune*, p. 2.

_____. (1841f, May 4). Conspiracy. *The New York Tribune*, p. 3.

_____. (1868). *Recollections of a busy life*. New York: J.B. Ford & Co.

Hale, W. H. (1950). *Horace Greeley: Voice of the people*. New York: Harper & Brothers.

Huntzicker, W. E. (1999). *The popular press, 1833–1865*. Westport, CT: Greenwood.

Ingersoll, L. D. (1873). *The life of Horace Greeley*. New York: Beekman.

James, H., Greeley, H., & Andrews, S. P. (1889). *Love, marriage, and divorce and the sovereignty of the individual*. Boston: Benj. R. Tucker.

Jones, R. W. (1947). *Journalism in the United States*. New York: E.P. Dutton & Co.

Kovach, B., & Rosenstiel, T. (2001). *The elements of journalism*. New York: Crown.

Maverick, A. (1870). *Henry J. Raymond and the New York press for thirty years*. Hartford, CT: A.S. Hale & Co.

Nerone, J. C. (1987). The mythology of the penny press. *Critical Studies in Mass Communication, 4*(4), 376–404.

Parton, J. L. (1855). *The life of Horace Greeley: Editor of "The New-York Tribune," from his birth to the present time*. New York: Mason Brothers.

Raymond, H. J. (1870). New York Daily Times; A new morning and evening daily newspaper. In A. Maverick (Ed.), *Henry J. Raymond and the New York press for thirty years* (pp. 93–95). Hartford, CT: A.S. Hale & Co. (Reprinted from the *New York Daily Times*, 1851).

Schudson, M. (1978). *Discovering the news*. New York: Basic Books.

Stoddard, H. L. (1946). *Horace Greeley*. New York: G.P. Putnam's Sons.

Tucher, A. (1994). *Froth & scum: Truth, beauty, goodness, and the ax murderer in America's first mass medium*. Chapel Hill: University of North Carolina Press.

Williams, R. C. (2006). *Horace Greeley: Champion of American freedom*. New York: New York University Press.

The Pride and Reward
of Falsification

Post-Objectivity as Post-Responsibility

AARON BARLOW

One of the unexpected consequences of the digital revolution has been the rise of a particular type of pseudo-journalism, a type with a surprising impact, sometimes even approaching that of traditional journalism. In an earlier age, its practitioners would have been run out of the profession. Today, even when exposed as fraudulent, this kind of work can lead to great success. This pseudo-journalism isn't the work mainly of bloggers, as some might expect. Nor is it the work of those journalists who have abandoned traditional news venues, striking out as independent news producers who use digital tools. Instead, it is the work of ambitious political activists who see American journalism's failures as an opportunity to advance themselves and their causes. This pseudo-journalism has no allegiance to traditional journalistic objectivity or responsibility. Instead, it clothes itself in the regalia of the profession, yet exists outside of well-established journalistic norms. This pseudo-journalism has no regard for the ethics or standards that journalists have attempted to establish and uphold for well over a century and half.

Pseudo-journalism has arisen partly from the fact that, with digital tools, it is extremely easy and cheap to produce something that looks like journalism without having to do the real work of investigating and reporting. But its heritage is a great deal more complex, harkening back to slightly before the 1830s and stretching forward to the 1980s collapse of American journalism and the lack of respect for the profession that ensued.

Writing just before the end of the 20th century, and on the eve of the explosion of Internet journalism, Davis "Buzz" Merritt, former editor of the *Wichita Eagle*, highlighted journalism's fixation on "objectivity." He saw it as a weakness that had already helped in the downfall of the traditional American news media:

> The notion of objectivity carries with it a requirement for something called *balance*. The idea is that journalists, being conduits, should carefully offer both sides of virtually any matter under discussion. Every assertion more arguable than that the Earth is round must be matched by a contending assertion. Invoking this axiom supposedly removes any obligation ... and risk ... on the part of the reporter that people with different views will be offended or left out of the discussion [1998, p. 26].

Striving for balance sometimes makes journalists look weak — and dishonest. Giving equal weight to two sides with a straight face makes the journalist risible and easily dismissed. It calls into question the entire structure of the industry. It makes assertions of rigor and honesty in the profession seem self-serving, at best. Take, for example, this claim from Leonard Downie, former editor of *The Washington Post*, and Associate *Post* Editor Robert Kaiser:

> Quality is hard. No market researcher or consultant can teach a news organization how to be good. That requires years of tradition, persistent high standards, intelligence and determined professionalism. Unfortunately, frivolous news values were easy to embrace, easy to pursue and easy to defend as the best way to cope with a competitive marketplace [2003, p. 251].

When a false balance is invoked, the line between "quality" and "frivolous" is blurred. The professional press's quest for quality — influenced by the objectivity orientation's emphasis on balance — sometimes translates into the journalist, and the organization behind him or her, avoiding any overt evaluative position. Viewers and readers were never fooled by this and, as a result, never believed in the "objectivity" or "quality" the journalists professed. In actuality, the press long ago embraced "frivolous news values" not only through ease or competition, but because the public had stopped seeing the news media as anything but frivolous, anyway.

Merritt wanted this alarming development countered by a new emphasis on deliberation, on creation of discussion with broad consequences in mind, not simply immediate gain. But deliberation is a difficult process, and one requiring all of us, journalists included, to put aside their biases. In her book *Outfoxed*, on Rupert Murdoch and the Fox News Channel, Alexandra Kitty (2005) wrote:

> News is supposed to present an accurate and truthful picture of reality. Watching a newscast is supposed to give the viewer the lowdown on what really transpired, who were the good guys and who were the bad. The trouble is that our wishes and beliefs continually cloud our assessment of what's really out there. The same biases that distort our vision also distort the vision of journalists. No one is truly safe from subjective biases, but an honest reporter takes extra effort to address his or her own personal prejudices before filing a story [p. 65].

This is what viewers once expected from journalists — not lack of opinion, but recognition of the bias in all of us along with a willingness to keep personalities out of the story. Viewers are not stupid, but they know their own limits as well as the limits of those informing them. The public once believed that the press would, above all, be mindful of its fallibility and counter its weaknesses with a relentless search for the truth. Said Fenton (2005), the "news media's job is supposed to be unscrambling that spin, separating truth from lies." But, he pointed out, "it's just not working anymore" (p. 82). He noted that "the public simply doesn't know what's going on much of the time. They don't know who to trust and what to believe" (p. 82). After all, as David Halberstam (2007) said, "when it comes to big stories, more often than not the networks do it in a preening way — look, not only are we here, but we've sent our *anchorman* just to prove how important the story is" (p. 16). The story becomes less important than the teller.

In reaction to what many saw as the corrupt preening of the American news media, new voices arose, ones not associated with traditional media outlets. Influenced by the "new journalists" of the generation before them, by people like Hunter Thompson, Terry Southern, and Tom Wolfe, more recent self-described journalists ignored the constraints that had grown up around the profession, striking out to entertain as much as to inform. These latter-day new journalists, frequently identified simply as bloggers, often did try to move towards more overtly serious commentary (like the new journalists, they generally left traditional reporting to the professional venues). However, like Thompson, Southern and others, they rarely subscribed to the constraints that had grown around journalism, seeing those as signs of a hide-bound, nearly moribund mainstream media. In their wake have come others, people who also have taken on some of the trappings of journalism but without the substance. Having seen the news media as increasingly shallow and having observed the inchoate honesty of the bloggers, these pseudo-journalists have taken the *image* of honesty and combined it with the *image* of objectivity, and now offer something that can only be called post-objective journalism if it is to be considered journalism at all.

Accelerating the growth of post-objective journalism has been the increased celebrity of the profession. Not only were journalists themselves becoming media stars in the wake of the Vietnam War and Watergate, but celebrities were taking on the role of journalist. Downie and Kaiser (2003) noted that, in 2000, Leonardo DiCaprio "interviewed" President Bill Clinton for Earth Day, for ABC News:

> By traditional journalistic standards, this was a howler. Use a boyish actor to conduct an interview with the president of the United States? Make that a boyish actor who had openly, fervently taken sides on the issues that would be the subject of the interview? [pp. 222–223].

There was no great outcry about this development because viewers already saw politicians and journalists as entertainers. They no longer took any of them seriously. People could present themselves as journalists (or as politicians); it did not matter. They no longer needed the substance of experience, training, or organization behind them. They needed nothing but belief in themselves and in their vision of the world.

Belying its name, post-objective journalism draws heavily on the past of American journalism. It harkens back to the early 19th century, when newspapers were explicit political organs tied to political parties and government patronage for economic success. Behind post-objective journalism also lies a foundational view of the world where belief, not exploration, is the start of understanding. On the first page of his book *Righteous Indignation*, Andrew Breitbart, one of the exemplars of post-objective journalism, used "I knew" twice and "I had read" (with no sources) three times, assuming that what he "knew" about the Association of Community Organizations for Reform Now (ACORN) was true on its face (he became instrumental in the sting that brought the organization down). In his worldview, it seems, the things he knew or read are truths needing no examination, much like truths depicted in the Bible — or like the concepts offered by Ayn Rand's objectivism.[1] The same appears to be true for all post-objective journalists. For them, belief trumps true balance every time.

What is examined in the world, and discovered in it, for those like pseudo-journalist Breitbart, works only where it confirms what one already knows. This is not unusual. In a study published in *Political Behavior* in 2010 called "When Corrections Fail: The Persistence of Political Misperceptions," Brendan Nyhan and Jason Reifler discussed what they call the

> backfire effects that ... seem to provide further support for the growing literature showing that citizens engage in "motivated reasoning." ... The results show that direct factual contradictions can actually strengthen ideologically grounded factual beliefs — an empirical finding with important theoretical implications [p. 323].

They began their study based on past work in the field of psychology showing that people are "goal-directed information processors" (p. 307) but biased ones who evaluate the information they receive mainly on the basis of whether or not it conforms to their own established ideas. To the post-objective journalist, this attitude releases them from any need to strive for balance. There is another side of this as well: The pseudo-journalists recognize that people who create even "legitimate" news stories might believe they are objective even while at the same time altering evidence and crafting stories that promote specific viewpoints. For people like Breitbart, reporting beliefs as news creates a semblance of reality around their beliefs and is no different from what they imagine mainstream journalists are doing.

Before the explosion of do-it-yourself journalism that resulted from the growth of the Internet and its new publication venues, structures of objectivity had governed just how far a journalist could go in creating a story. In great part, the modern impetus for objectivity began with CBS radio's first attempts to establish its news branch as a legitimate source of information on the eve of World War II. As mainstream journalism began to fall into disrepute half a century later, so did respect for its self-promoted objectivity. The journalists set themselves up for what is, essentially, parody by the likes of Breitbart — a parody that takes itself every bit as seriously as the journalists do themselves.

Many of the new post-objective journalists are quickly uncovered as partisans, yet they continue to churn out stories that reach large audiences. They convince themselves and many others that they are operating honestly. Like Nyhan and Reifler's consumers of news, exposure of error and deceit seems only to further confirm pseudo-journalists' prior beliefs and their faith in truths that were decided upon long before their stories were composed.

It is in this sense that such journalists become post-objective: They use the trappings of objectivity while manipulating information to produce proof of the point or belief that had brought them to the story in the first place. Objectivity, no longer a standard, becomes a tool, its semblance a means to an end. It had earlier become, in too many cases, nothing more than appearance and a means for creating spin, itself another of the developments that have led to the downfall of mainstream journalism. By 2000, the Fox News Channel had become a dominant media presence. Run by Roger Ailes, a long-time media adviser for conservative candidates, it advertises itself as "fair and balanced," but its entire purpose is to provide a counterbalance for what many on the right see as a liberal slant to the rest of the news media. In an interview with comedian Jon Stewart on June 19, 2011, host Chris Wallace of *Fox News Sunday* stated, "I think we're the counterweight. I think that [NBC news has] a liberal agenda and I think that we tell the other side of the story" (Sheppard, 2011, para. 6–10). As Fenton (2005) wrote, "the public now believes the media to be utterly politicized and partisan — caught up in its own spin" (p. 85). He continued:

> The triumph of spin is largely the news media's own fault. Certainly the industry got caught in a pincer from both flanks, politicians on the one hand and owners on the other. But we took sides with them, and allowed them to influence our judgment; indeed they became part of our business and we theirs. On the political front, too many journalists became political mouthpieces while remaining journalists — and others simply took the King's shilling, as it were, and went to work officially for politicians [pp. 86–87].

Seeing this, partisan activists have had no compunction about styling themselves as journalists, and the public has had little reason not to accept them as such.

Breitbart, and his sometimes associate James O'Keefe, have become two of the most successful post-objective journalists of the new digital age. Their work has been influential and effective, even destructive, especially as it relates to current sensibilities regarding credible journalism. Acting as political activists as well as journalists, their attributes reflect those found in the newspapers of the early years of the American republic, and they look back to the muckrakers a century later for inspiration. However, they take advantage of the contemporary cultural stage, where mistrust of media motives and the prevalence of spin have created an atmosphere where none of the more traditional news venues are much trusted at all.[2] People now look simply for those espousing views they already agree with and try to sidestep what they see as spin (which is generally what they disagree with). The public is vulnerable to those who present "objectivity" with a wink to the audience, who are supposed to be in on the deception. The work of pseudo-journalists like Breitbart and O'Keefe deliberately looks similar to the journalism of vetted and edited objective products of the mainstream media, even though it falls apart on close examination by anyone who has an eye for credible journalism. However, their work continues to garner notice — especially by traditional news operations — even when defects are exposed.

Though Breitbart and O'Keefe probably would resent the term post-objective as applied to them here, they do operate within a milieu of belief masquerading as truth, and are manipulating data to create realities that resonate with key audiences. Writing about successful viral marketing, Henry Jenkins (2006) said that creators "sought to create images that are vivid, memorable, and evocative. And most important, the content had to be consistent with what people more or less already believed about the world" (p. 207). This is a truth that the post-objective journalists understand all too well and turn to for furthering their political agendas. They want to create vivid and believable stories to effect certain political ends. That the stories might later fall apart is irrelevant. It is only important that they be believable at first sight.

The contemporary post-objective journalist, though tapping into older movements in journalism, arose as the Internet age made it easier for almost anyone to pose as a journalist, sometimes creating the image of a legitimate, citizen-directed news organization. The tools of the World Wide Web made it possible to create a site online with every appearance of legitimacy. The most notable early successful example is the Talon News website and its "reporter" Jeff Gannon. An erstwhile male escort, Gannon managed to become a regular part of the White House press corps through use of day passes; he even managed to ask President George W. Bush a question during a news conference on January 26, 2005. How did this happen? Fenton (2005) quoted an anonymous media insider:

> Any idiot with a White House Press pass ... can come to the press secretary's daily briefing and ask whatever off-the-wall question he or she wishes ... all the person on the podium needs to do is ... call on a reporter whose questions or area of interest was guaranteed to change the topic [p. 105].

Those "idiots" can be useful to have around to deflect serious questions, but they can also turn into something disturbing for both the news media and the broader political discourse, as happened in the Gannon case. All this is possible because "politicians and the media have conspired to infantilize, to dumb down, the American public. At heart, politicians don't believe that Americans can handle complex truths, and the news media, especially television news, basically agrees," said Fenton (2005, p. 83). The Gannon scandal, however, revealed that politicians and the traditional media were both as dumb as they thought the American people were, and could be misled just as easily.

Gannon's exposure didn't come from the press corps, but from bloggers. Gannon, whose real name is James Guckert, was called by name by President Bush on national television. Gannon responded with a short statement and a question:

> Senate Democratic leaders have painted a very bleak picture of the U.S. economy. Harry Reid was talking about soup lines. Hillary Clinton was talking about the economy being on the verge of collapse. Yet in the same breath they say that Social Security is rock solid and there's no crisis there. How are you going to work — you've said you are going to reach out to these people — how are you going to work with people who seem to have divorced themselves from reality? [Savage & Wirzbicki, 2005, para. 10].

The spin and obvious political bias of this statement and question galvanized a number of bloggers, including Susan Gardner (who then blogged as SusanG at the liberal Daily Kos), to start looking into whom this "reporter" was. What they found was that Talon News, the creation of Robert Eberle, seems to have been little but a means for allowing Guckert to receive day press passes to the White House, something he had managed to do for well over a year. Though it looked like almost any news website of the time, Talon News was an empty shell, simply a means for inserting a ringer into the White House press corps. It was nothing more than an attempt to use the trappings of objective journalism for the purposes of a political movement. Offering only the thinnest of a journalistic veneer, Talon News was one of the first high-profile examples of post-objective journalism. Within weeks of the exposure of Gannon as Guckert, Talon News disappeared.

James Fallows wrote that the real purpose of journalism "is to satisfy the general desire for information to have meaning. [But] people want to ... see what the details add up to. Journalism exists to answer questions like, 'What is really going on?' and 'Why is this happening?'" (pp. 129–130). The problem, as Nyhan and Reifler discovered, is that many people want that answer to conform to preexisting conceptions of the world; they want news that validates their worldviews. Post-objective journalism exists to provide just this sort of affirmation. Look at Guckert's question to Bush: the answer is assumed in the question. It is here where the heart of this new journalism is found. Its questions are never meant for shedding light on new answers but for confirming old assumptions.

Post-objective journalists share the characteristic of self-promotion, again something that is rooted in American journalism but also taps into (and exploits) journalism's links to our cultural myths:

> Every culture has its official folklore. In ancient times medicine men transformed tribal legends to enhance their own status. The twentieth century is no different, but the high priests who communicate mythic dogmas now do so through great centralized machines of communication — newspaper chains, broadcast networks, magazine groups, conglomerate book publishers, and movie studios. Operators of these systems disseminate their own version of the world. And of all the legends they generate none are so heroic as the myths they propagate about themselves [Bagdikian, pp. 177–178].

Benjamin Franklin, William Randolph Hearst, Edward R. Murrow, Walter Cronkite: these were celebrities in their own days (and partly by their own creation), but the sheer number of celebrities from the field of journalism today far outstrips the past. Anyone can now aspire to that celebrity, as Gannon and Talon News demonstrated, no matter their background either in experience or education. Add in the possibilities inherent in digital technologies and the line between journalists and their audiences has blurred:

> [People] are no longer mere readers, listeners, or passive viewers. Instead, affordable Internet technology and highly interactive, easy-to-use applications have enabled individuals to become active users and participants in public conversations. As a consequence, it's no longer a few professional journalists or powerful media conglomerates with strong commercial interests who define what we as a society talk and care about. Rather, the public agenda in the digital age is increasingly influenced by the observations, experiences, and concerns of all of us in our roles as citizens [Palfrey & Gasser, p. 264].

That's the optimistic view. The reality, as we have seen, can be far more nefarious, with the public agenda increasingly shaped by those seeing opportunity for fame and the furthering of political agendas, too often at the expense of the common good. In this sense, post-objective journalism could be seen as a hijacking of the public discourse through its new, expanded and digitally-based manifestation.

Here again, it is the traditional journalists themselves who are partly to blame for the situation, especially by increasingly removing original reporting from journalism and replacing it with opinion. The lure of highly-profitable and high-profile discussion programs presented as journalism has proven too great, leading many journalists to jettison objectivity for participation in partisan squabbling. As Downie and Kaiser (2003) wrote:

> The talking heads are not covering news, they are commenting on news. Early versions of these programs—the original *Meet the Press*, for example—used reporters to perform their proper role, asking questions. But the modern television talk show wants answers more than questions. So the reporters are expected to pass judgment.... Journalists who once were careful with facts often wind up performing like professional wrestlers, tossing around rumors, conjecture and opinions in verbal combat that amounts to playacting [pp. 231–232].

The temptation for ambitious non-journalists to climb into the ring has also proven just too great. Self-promotion and the generation of opinion have replaced too much journalistic work; journalistic reputations can be made in the talk arena by people who have never done any real reporting.

At the same time, post-objective journalists want to claim a connection to the journalism profession. O'Keefe's "Project Veritas" maintains that it tries to "teach others how to become modern-day muckrakers" (*About Project Veritas*, 2011, para. 2). Breitbart has said, "I'm kind of the Upton Sinclair of the mainstream media" (Ratigan, 2011). Through statements like these, the pseudo-journalists try to legitimize their activities by claiming them to be part of a tradition going back over a century, one that includes not only Sinclair, but Nellie Bly, Ida B. Wells, Jacob Riis, and Lincoln Steffens. Like the new post-objective journalists, the muckrakers certainly were often outside of the mainstream, even when published in established commercial venues. Some of their descendants, such as I. F. Stone, became independent watchdogs of the media, a role Breitbart claims for himself. Breitbart and O'Keefe, however, are perhaps instead most influenced by people like Bly, who willingly turned to deception in order to get a story.

The difference between the muckrakers and contemporary post-objective journalists is that the muckrakers sometimes spent months or more building a story, while these self-proclaimed descendants rely more on creating imagery—through words and videos—than on actual investigative research. Like the traditional muckrakers, the pseudo-journalists want to expose what they believe is deceptive or duplicitous activity, but the muckrakers generally wanted to find evidence while the post-objective journalists often turn to creating it. For them, the presentation of image and opinion as reality *are* the story.

Breitbart and O'Keefe first came to national attention through a series of videotapes that O'Keefe and Hannah Giles made during visits to offices of the Association of Community Organizations for Reform Now (ACORN) during the summer of 2009 and that were subsequently edited and published on Breitbart's website BigGovernment.com (one of his chain of "Big" websites). The videos featured ACORN employees providing unethical and illegal advice. According to a report compiled by the California Attorney General:

> In each of the ACORN offices they visited together, Giles posed as a prostitute fleeing an abusive pimp, and O'Keefe posed as her boyfriend, trying to help her, and, in some instances, attempting to benefit from the proceeds of the prostitution trade.... Although their story morphed over time, the couple requested advice from ACORN employees related to Giles' prostitution business, including obtaining a mortgage, reporting income and taxes from the illicit business, avoiding law enforcement scrutiny, smuggling young girls into the country to serve as prostitutes, and obtaining documentation and voting privileges for them ... O'Keefe wore a hidden camera and secretly recorded audio and video of the conversations [California Department, 2010, pp. 8–9].

The report concluded that

> O'Keefe stated he was out to make a point and to damage ACORN and therefore did not act as a journalist objectively reporting a story. The video releases were heavily edited to feature only the worst or most inappropriate statements of the various ACORN employees and to omit some of the most salient statements by O'Keefe and Giles. Each of the ACORN employees recorded in California was a low-level employee whose job was to help the needy individuals who walked in the door seeking assistance. Giles and O'Keefe lied to engender compassion, but then edited their statements from the released videos [California Department, 2010, pp. 23–24].

In other words, for the sake of undermining a politically-oriented organization with a clearly sloppy structure, O'Keefe was willing to distort events and conversations to make them appear different from the actuality. Though the deception was quickly uncovered, the damage had been done: ACORN had been destroyed and a new model of activist, post-objective journalism created — for O'Keefe, Breitbart and others had now realized that it did not matter if the truth is eventually disclosed. What mattered was a presentation that offered believable imagery and immediate impact.

Another successful operation of a similar nature was an edited videotape released in 2010 by Breitbart of a speech by Shirley Sherrod, Georgia State Director of Rural Development for the United States Department of Agriculture in the Obama administration. The tape appeared to show Sherrod praising her own actions in refusing to aid a white couple in need (Sherrod is African-American). Breitbart, in his post along with the edited video, wrote:

> We are in possession of a video ... in which Shirley Sherrod, USDA Georgia Director of Rural Development, speaks at the NAACP Freedom Fund dinner in Georgia.

> In her meandering speech ... this federally appointed executive bureaucrat lays out in stark detail, that her federal duties are managed through the prism of race and class distinctions ... Sherrod describes how she racially discriminates against a white farmer. She describes how she is torn over how much she will choose to help him. And, she admits that she doesn't do everything she can for him, because he is white. Eventually, her basic humanity informs that this white man is poor and needs help. But she decides that he should get help from "one of his own kind." She refers him to a white lawyer [Breitbart, 2010, para. 17].

Under pressure, Sherrod quickly resigned her position, her career destroyed, though Breitbart's real target was the NAACP. Within days, however, the full videotape of her speech, along with statements from the white family involved (whom Sherrod had, in fact, helped), had vindicated her. Though she received an apology from the White House, she refused to return to work for the administration.

The pattern of deceptive but initially objective-looking stories continued in 2011, with O'Keefe setting up a sting against National Public Radio (NPR), orchestrating what appeared to be an Islamic organization attempting to give a large donation. This time he edited and released a video of a meeting with Ronald Schiller, a leading NPR fundraiser. The video led to Schiller's resignation and that of the organization's CEO, Vivian Schiller. That video

> made it appear that [Ronald] Schiller had laughed and commented "really, that's what they said?" after being told that the fake Muslim group advocates for sharia law. In fact, the longer tape shows that [Ronald] Schiller made that comment during an "innocuous exchange" that had nothing to do with the supposed group's position on sharia law [Memmott, 2011, para. 4].

Once again, revelation of the deceit did not change the result. In fact, the only impact seems to have been on NPR. Since then, O'Keefe has continued to operate in much the same vein, presenting a similar sort of deceptively-edited videos online concerning visits to Medicaid offices (Reilly, 2011). Though his penchant for dressing himself and others in costume for his stings has even gotten him arrested, his successes have outweighed negatives enough for him to want to continue.[3]

To illustrate just how major a change this represents, one need only to view O'Keefe against Stephen Glass, erstwhile writer for *The New Republic*. In 1998, Glass was discovered to have fabricated all or part of a large number of stories over several years. He was fired and *The New Republic*, having determined that over half of his stories that it had published were suspect, issued an apology. Unlike the magazine's, Glass's reputation never recovered, and he left journalism. O'Keefe, who has also produced distorted and semi-fictionalized news accounts, was able to continue his activities long after exposure of his faked stories.

Neither Breitbart nor O'Keefe is dependent on the backing of a traditional news organization. Skilled at manipulation of the tools of the digital age, they have added an element of real independence that Gannon, for example, did not have. They exhibit an autonomy that allows them to ignore failure and to move past accusations of fraud without the necessity of response. At the same time, however, the impact of their work is magnified through a traditional news media that does not question their framing/editing of the stories, presents them as commentators, and allows them to assume the aura of a news worker that is still associated with real reporters.

Because he did not work for a legitimate news organization, Gannon's failure was not like that of the rogue's gallery of scandalous journalists of the previous decade, one that includes Glass, Jayson Blair of *The New York Times*, Jack Kelly of *USA Today*, Brian Walski of *The Los Angeles Times*, and *The Boston Globe*'s Patricia Smith. In each of these instances, an institution with its own reputation to protect ousted their employee upon investigation. What the Gannon case showed people like Brietbart and O'Keefe was that an independent operative needn't fear the consequences of exposure. The profession of journalism cannot rely on government oversight to enforce ethical standards, given the strictures of the First Amendment. Instead, it must rely on the ability of the specific journalistic entities to police themselves, protecting their reputations (which once had real financial value) by enforcing standards internally. This is not something journalists are used to doing outside of their own houses; in the past, outliers in the profession, such as supermarket tabloids, were clearly separate from the serious business of news. Their "reporters" would not be expected to show up at a White House press briefing. When the lines are blurred, as has happened in the digital age, the traditional news venues find that they are no longer perceived as the sole and necessary part of the news profession. They are no longer even in any position to act as gatekeepers (if they ever could) and it becomes easier than ever before for savvy operators to present the appearance of journalism without responsibility for the stories they produce. Breitbart and O'Keefe are cases in point.

Calling what pseudo-journalists do "post-objective" may be accurate, descriptively, but it does not alone offer a picture of progress beyond objectivity. Instead, it references an attitude towards objectivity, towards journalism and its past, and towards the public discourse. To the post-objective journalist, these are all merely tools for achieving personal and political goals. In a subjective world, objectivity can be argued away as simply a myth, after all. Journalism, too often, has shown itself to be self-serving and hypocritical these past decades, so it, in the minds of its critics, deserves only what it gets. And, too often, the public discourse has become little more than the quest for celebrity.

One of the prime components of post-objective journalism is the understanding that the accuracy of a story is likely to be secondary to a story's impact. If the story does what it was intended to do (destroy or harm an organization, generally), it does not matter if it is later shown to have been a fabrication. Alternatively, if the news account fails to have impact, accuracy still may not have ever played a significant role. There is no traditional organization behind the post-objective journalist, no venue whose reputation is on the line, and this kind of journalist has learned from experience that even being exposed as having manipulated a story helps, instead of hindering a career.

So, how does one respond? As a profession, journalism should seriously question its increasing proclivity for using material from this particular iteration of post-objective, self-described journalists. Traditional news outlets need to not only ask whether or not an agenda is being furthered when Breitbart and O'Keefe (and those like them) are prime sources for news accounts, but how journalism's credibility may be at risk when such pseudo-journalists actually become the media stories. To address these concerns more specifically, what does an individual do in the face of an attack by a post-objective journalist?

Judy Ancel, Director of The Institute of Labor Studies at the University of Missouri–Kansas City, who was herself a target of a Breitbart attack in April of 2011, provided a list, one she developed out of her own experiences fighting a Breitbart video edited to distort how she conducted herself in an online course she had co-taught. Included with her list is a call to move from the reactive to the proactive — advice that real journalists, in reporting on post-objective journalism activities such as Brietbart's, might heed. She made the decision to not be passive about Brietbart's news framing by going to the original, uncut video. From that original source material she, with the cooperation of her "fair-minded provost" surfaced the rest of the story (para. 6). She wrote, "Breitbart's attacks depend on institutions reacting fearfully and doing the wrong thing" (para. 5). Breitbart and O'Keefe, she wrote, "post their product first on one of their 'Big' websites and then use Fox.net to push it into more legitimate media outlets" (para. 8) This was the process that was used to bring down Anthony Weiner, a member of Congress who had posted inappropriate sexual comments and pictures on Twitter. Weiner's actions were certainly wrong, and he was a naïf compared with Breitbart, who knows how to use the tools of contemporary media much more skillfully than the hapless and foolish Congressman. From the Ancel, Sherrod and Weiner cases one can see that no one can count on the mainstream media to take a pseudo-journalist's representations at face value and expect a "fair" presentation. Therefore, citizens and mainstream journalists should take the time to learn how pseudo-journalists operate. This will have to become part of our basic education as citizens of a democracy where almost any information about anyone has the possibility not only of becoming public but also of become grist for the mill that is another's specific agenda.

In the past, callous abuse aimed at crumbling institutions and vulnerable individuals has sometimes been checked by legal systems and cultural beliefs that force activities back within certain constraints. This may be what brought American journalism from its "yellow" days to its heyday or professionalism in the 1960s. However, the unique position of American journalism under the first amendment is that is exists outside of many legal constraints, making a movement toward constraining pseudo-journalists difficult to achieve. As a result, it may even be likely that post-objective journalism, rather than remaining a side-show on the public scene, will one day become the mainstream itself, the Breitbarts and O'Keefes becoming the Edward Murrows and Walter Cronkites of a new media age. Without, of course, the journalistic integrity of the latter pair.

Shortly before he died, David Halberstam (2007) described his own optimistic view of the best of journalism:

> Even as I write, there are ... young men and women going out every day and doing something difficult and complicated, something that takes a surprisingly varied array of talents ... and, of course, a certain kind of courage, the courage to stand up to powerful people who are always trying to bend you and intimidate you [pp. 16–17].

What is lacking in Breitbart and O'Keefe, what made Morrow and Cronkite and even Halberstam so great is a commitment to fostering deliberation. As described by Buzz Merritt (1998), deliberation is a "part of human cultures over the centuries, as in the Roman forum, in American colonial town meetings, and, in many nations, the gathering of tribal chiefs" (p. 108). Such gatherings, ideally, took the time to carefully prepare and to make sure they contributed to deliberation without undercutting it. Breitbart, O'Keefe, and other post-objective journalists, on the other hand, set out to make deliberation impossible, to spark reaction, not thought or incisive discussion. Their work, then, by centering on allegation, spectacle and falsification too often endangers both the institutions and individuals they target.

And journalism as a force for deliberative democracy? It is possible for news workers to prompt a resurgence in public dialogue, but only with a better realization of the power of the pseudo-journalist in a post-objective world. Without such contemplation within journalism, sparking deliberation may simply be a lofty mission statement. And those can be easily forgotten when the pseudo-journalist calls the next press conference.

Chapter Notes

1. Objectivism is a philosophy of knowledge encompassing a belief in the possibility of really "knowing." According to Rand, it is a stance that touts every man as "an end in himself," and that the best way to pursue the realization of such an end is through *laissez-faire capitalism*. See http://www.aynrand.org/site/PageServer?pagename=objectivism_intro.

2. Consider recent trends in survey results offered by the Pew Research Center for the People and the Press. They find that the public is increasingly unwilling to rely on the traditional press, and a chief reason is that the public does not find news reports to be accurate and credible. See http://people-press.org/

3. In May 2010, U.S. District Judge Sanwood Duval Jr. sentenced O'Keefe to probation, a fine, and community service for entering a federal building under false pretenses.

References

About Project Veritas (2011). Retrieved July 15, 2011, from http://theprojectveritas.com/about.

Ancel, J. (July 2011). What doesn't kill you ... A guide to surviving right-wing media assaults. *Dollars & Sense*. Retrieved July 19, 2011, from http://www.dollarsandsense.org/archives/2011/0711ancel.html.

Bagdikian, B. H. (2004). *The new media monopoly*. Boston: Beacon Press.

Breitbart, A. (2010). Video proof: The NAACP awards racism — 2010. *Big Government*. Retrieved July 19, 2011, from http://biggovernment.com/abreitbart/2010/07/19/video-proof-the-naacp-awards-racism2010/

_____. (2011). *Righteous indignation: Excuse me while I save the world*. New York: Grand Central.

California Department of Justice. (2010). *Report of the attorney general on the activities of ACORN in California*. Sacramento: Office of the Attorney General.

Downie, L., & Kaiser, R. G. (2003). *The news about the news: American journalism in peril*. New York: Vintage Books.

Fallows, J. M. (1996). *Breaking the news: How the media undermine American democracy*. New York: Pantheon Books.

Fenton, T. (2005). *Bad news: The decline of reporting, the business of news, and the danger to us all*. New York: Regan Books.

Halberstam, D. (2007). *Breaking news: How the Associated Press has covered war, peace, and everything else*. New York: Princeton Architectural Press.

Jenkins, H. (2006). *Convergence culture: Where old and new media collide*. New York: New York University Press.

Kitty, A. (2005). *Outfoxed: Rupert Murdoch's war on journalism*. New York: Disinformation.

Memmott, M. (2011). NPR: O'Keefe "inappropriately edited" video; exec's words still "egregious." *National Public Radio*. Retrieved March, 14, 2011, from http://www.npr.org/blogs/thetwo-way/2011/03/14/134528545/npr-okeefe-inappropriately-edited-video-execs-words-still-egregious

Merritt, D. (1998). *Public journalism and public life: Why telling the news is not enough*. Mahwah, NJ: Erlbaum.

Nyhan, B., & Reifler, J. (2010). When corrections fail: The persistence of political misperceptions. *Political Behavior, 32*(2), 303–330.

Palfrey, J. G., & Gasser, U. (2008). *Born digital: Understanding the first generation of digital natives*. New York: Basic Books.

Ratigan, D. (2011, April 19). Breitbart: "I am misunderstood by the mainstream media."

The Dylan Ratigan Show. Retrieved April 25, 2011, from http://www.msnbc.msn.com/id/31510813/#42669495

Reilly, R. (2011). James O'Keefe's latest "terrorist" medicaid sting goes after woman for following law. *Talking Points Memo*. Retrieved July 20, 2011, from http://tpmmuckraker.talkingpointsmemo.com/2011/07/james_okeefes_latest_terrorist_medicaid_sting_goes_after_woman_for_following_law.php?ref=fpb

Savage, C., & Wirzbicki, A. (2005). White House-friendly reporter under scrutiny. *Boston.com*. Retrieved February 2, 2011, from http://www.boston.com/news/nation/washington/articles/2005/02/02/white_house_friendly_reporter_under_scrutiny?pg=full.

Sheppard, N. (2011). Chris Wallace strikes back at Jon Stewart: Hannity and O'Reilly's viewers better informed than Daily Show's. *News Busters*. Retrieved July 15, 2011, from http://m.newsbusters.org/blogs/noel-sheppard/2011/06/26/chris-wallace-strikes-back-jon-stewart-hannity-and-oreillys-viewers-b.

3

A New Model of Objectivity

Investigative Reporting in the Twentieth Century

Gerry Lanosga

In the introduction to a recent collection of highlights from three centuries of American investigative reporting, the authors made an intriguing assertion about the practice of journalism: "Journalists wear disguises," wrote Judith and William Serrin, "and one of them is the disguise of objectivity." Objectivity — one of the most influential ideals of modern journalistic practice — a mere disguise? The Serrins continued:

> No reporter goes into journalism saying he or she wants to be objective, yet journalists continue to say that they write only what people say and do, that they, professional journalists, have no agendas. This is fiction. All good journalists have agendas. They wish to put the crooked sheriff in jail. They wish to unveil the patent medicine fraud. They wish to free the innocent man from jail.... The driving force of unobjectivity is not mentioned in journalism schools or newsrooms but it is the truth [2002, p. xxi].

These forceful sentences written by a pair of former journalists are striking in their outright rejection of the long-revered principle of journalistic objectivity. As the Serrins suggested, most journalists, even that self-assured breed who call themselves *investigative* journalists, are disinclined to renounce allegiance to objectivity. Indeed, one suspects that the reporters whose work is excerpted in the Serrins' book might not agree with the authors' blunt assessment that their work is compelling precisely because it is unobjective.

Either way, the pursuit of agenda implicit in investigative reporting sets this particular journalistic genre apart from, if not in opposition to, traditional notions of objective reporting. Investigative reporting by definition involves taking positions on matters of public concern, and that act stands in direct conflict with the formulation of objectivity as neutrality. Yet even as this neutrality model of objectivity served as the dominant professional paradigm for twentieth-century American journalism, decidedly non-neutral investigations took hold and endured as part of a competing tradition for journalistic practitioners (and despite unwillingness by those practitioners to acknowledge their work as a departure from objectivity). The role taken on by these journalists is far from that of passive observers of news; rather, the journalists cooperatively *create* news and quite frequently become participants acting to remedy the problems they unearth.

Moreover, as this chapter shows, this is not a recent development. For as long as objectivity has helped to shape American journalism, investigative reporters have resisted the restrictions required by the classic conception of objectivity. This "unobjectivity," as the Serrins characterize it, actually reflects an alternate view of what constitutes objectivity. That is, investigative reporting rests not on a feeble reading of objectivity-as-neutrality — the he-said-she-said version in which all sides carry equal weight — but on a robust re-conception of objectivity built upon a systematic examination of facts that allows journalists to draw conclusions. This competing model of objectivity offers insights for both the ongoing practice of investigative reporting and for new modes of journalistic production in a news landscape that some scholars believe signals the beginning of an era of "post-objectivity."

This chapter first examines ways that journalists and scholars have defined objectivity and conceived its practice and then explores investigative reporting as a competing ideology within the objectivity framework using examples from journalism prize entries.

Formulating the Concept of Objectivity

Defining objectivity has proven to be a somewhat slippery task for scholars, journalists and the public alike. As a trade journal editor observed, "Ask ten journalists what objectivity means and you'll get ten different answers" (Cunningham, 2003, p. 2). Journalism historian David Nord said, "[T]he most characteristic convention of modern journalism — a style of relativism that journalists call objectivity — can be both puzzling and annoying to even the most faithful reader" (2001, p. 247). Nord himself defined objectivity as a turn toward impartiality and "facticity" (p. 258). Similarly, sociologist Michael Schudson wrote of objectivity as "a faith in 'facts,' a distrust of 'values,' and a commitment to their segregation" (1978, p. 6). In theory, this separation of facts and values affords a journalist the ability to report from a neutral stance, thus allowing audience members to make up their own minds about events and issues in the news.

According to Robert Miraldi, there are five conventions of objectivity: balance, evidence for each side of an issue, attribution of facts, an external "newspeg" justifying a story and use of the inverted pyramid story structure (1990, p. 15). Other writers have offered their own parameters. In a recent attempt to "parse through the divergent definitions," Andrew Porwancher concluded that, despite some differing terminology, historians largely agree that objectivity encompasses accuracy, fairness, impartiality, independence, and responsibility to the public (2011). A tighter definition can be inferred from the title of journalism historian David Mindich's book on objectivity, *Just the Facts* (1998).

Scholars generally place the beginning of the objectivity paradigm around the turn of the twentieth century, when journalists were confronted with new concerns about public relations agents and the propaganda of World War I (Schudson, 1978). These developments gave rise to the realization that facts did not always speak for themselves — Schudson called this "the subjectivization of fact"—and that an objective journalistic rendering of events and data was necessary. In a seminal and oft-quoted work, sociologist Gaye Tuchman (1972) characterized the embrace of objectivity as a strategic move that provided journalists with insulation against accusations of bias.

Abandoning Objectivity-as-Neutrality

This move to neutrality would seem to preclude genres of journalism, namely investigative reporting, that entail taking a position. Investigations, however, have maintained a significant presence throughout the history of American journalism. While some historical accounts treat the Muckrakers as the progenitors of investigative reporting in America, there is evidence of episodic investigative journalism beginning with the very first colonial newspaper in 1690 (Aucoin, 2005). In fact, the crusading exposé became an ingrained practice in daily newspapers in the latter decades of the nineteenth century (Hofstadter, 1955; Miraldi, 1990). Interpretive reporting also developed around this time and into the early 20th century, as a means of dealing with factual subjectivity. However, as Schudson pointed out, most journalists were daily reporters who were not free to write interpretive articles: "They needed a framework within which they could take their own work seriously and persuade their readers and critics to take it seriously, too. This is what the notion of 'objectivity' ... tried to provide" (p. 151).

Miraldi drew a notable association between the decline of muckraking in the years leading up to World War I and the rise of the objectivity norm (Miraldi, 1990), arguing that investigative reporting was later re-awakened in the 1960s. Others have echoed that assertion and contended that investigative reporting was essentially dormant after the muckraking era (Aucoin, 2005).

Investigative reporting did, nevertheless, flourish between the muckraking era and the 1960s, especially at the local level. A study of Pulitzer Prize entry materials found that about 14 percent of the prize nominations from 1917 to 1960 were investigative in nature (Lanosga, 2010). Though the term "investigative reporting" didn't surface until the late 1940s, investigations were conducted with regularity by newspapers of all sizes from all regions of the country. The study further found that newspaper exposés were explicitly encouraged by the Pulitzer establishment.

This continuity in investigative reporting is significant in that it shows the endurance of a competing paradigm of professional journalistic practice during a lengthy period of dominance by the traditional objectivity norm. That is, despite the weight given to the practice of objectivity by the professional journalistic establishment (industry groups, trade journals, codes of ethics), reporters and their newspapers have continually supported significant and high-profile investigative works that involved the abandonment of neutrality. While the classic notion of objectivity might have worked well for the daily report, investigative reporting was another matter. Protess et al. (1991) identified one key distinction between investigative reporting and daily reporting: "[T]he hallmark of daily journalism is its reactiveness. Most journalists lack the time or commitment to investigate the richest dimensions of breaking news events" (p. 4). Investigative journalism, on the other hand, is defined as proactive reporting of important matters that, often, someone wants to keep secret (Houston, Bruzzese, & Weinberg, 2002, p. viii). It is this active seeking and ferreting out of hidden information that takes investigative reporting out of the realm of traditional objectivity.

As Stein and Harrison (1973) have argued, a journalistic investigation is "inevitably non-neutral" because it "denounces or praises specific individuals, conditions, or values, and exhorts its audience, explicitly or by tone, to take action or to support specific remedies" (p. 14). "Objectivity observes; muckraking intrudes," argued Miraldi (1990, p. 10). He distinguished the earlier activist Progressive Era muckraking from modern investigative reporting, suggesting that the latter is rendered less effective by its practitioners' loyalty to objectivity and corresponding unwillingness to become active partners in trying to change society. Still, it is clear that the act of investigation itself involves shedding the mantle of neutrality that a devotion to classic objectivity demands. "Implicit in the decision to write an exposé is the belief that something needs to be done about the problem or person being exposed," Miraldi wrote. "This, of course, represents a point of view," he said (p. 6).

However, Miraldi's distinction between the Progressive Era magazine muckrakers and later newspaper investigators becomes less clear in light of the aforementioned study of Pulitzer nominations. The study showed a high degree of active involvement by reporters in shepherding results of investigations:

> [I]nvestigative reporters not only prompted official reaction to matters that previously were ignored, often they acted as more than just passive recipients of information from official sources. In fact, journalists sometimes acted in near-official capacity [Lanosga, 2010, p. 5].

Nord (2001) hinted at this in his study of newspaper readers, refuting the idea that the job of journalism is merely to inform while avoiding any overt role in community politics. "[N]ewspapers have always crossed that line," he wrote. "They have always been thoroughly enmeshed in the political and cultural lives of their communities" (p. 11).

In spite of the demonstrably activist position occupied by investigative reporters and their news organizations, however, most journalists are loathe to acknowledge any departure from the concept of objectivity. This is so even though, as Schudson (2003) observed, objective detachment is not necessarily expected in areas of journalistic practice such as sports, human interest features and investigative reporting, the latter which "presumes a capacity for moral indignation" (p. 51).

Ettema and Glasser (1998) probed this disjuncture in journalistic thinking in their perceptive study of contemporary investigative reporters:

> The essential energy of investigative reporting is still best characterized as righteous indignation.... But this unmistakable tone of moral engagement stands in apparent opposition to the presumed objectivity of news. How can journalists function as the custodians of conscience and at the same time claim to be mere observers of fact? That is, how can they expose wrongdoing without making moral judgments? [p. 61].

The reporters that Ettema and Glasser interviewed did not have a satisfying answer for this. They constantly made judgments in finding, choosing, interpreting, and applying standards of conduct in pursuit of their stories of failure or wrongdoing — all of which clearly involved a contribution to "the crafting of the moral order" (p. 185). Ettema and Glasser claimed that news workers have not resolved the apparent incongruity between neutrality and investigative reporting; journalists have simply found a way to live with their "simultaneous embrace of active adversarialism and objective detachment," they said (p. 70).

With this stance, these journalists mirror the views of famed investigators Bob Woodward and Carl Bernstein, who, Schudson said, believed they were following a true objectivity as opposed to the "counterfeit conventions justified in its name" (1978, pp. 186–187). That is, they seem to exhibit allegiance to a different, assertive notion of objectivity, one that emphasizes a scientific or positivistic seeking after the "true" facts versus Tuchman's conception of an anemic, relativistic objectivity that deals with subjective facts by simply assigning them all equal weight.

Investigations with a View

In investigative stories, journalists push against this relativistic objectivity in various ways: by simply making an accusation of failure or wrongdoing, by using the loaded rhetoric of victimization and irony, and by explicitly advocating official action or a suggested solution to the problem identified in the story. Not all investigative stories have all of these elements — for instance, some journalists are careful *not* to suggest solutions while others go so far as to offer remedies. However, every investigative story must make a claim that something or someone has gone wrong.

The claim of wrongdoing relies not on statements attributed to others, as in ordinary news stories, but rather on reportorial fact-finding. An accusation can be made in an authoritative tone because it has originated from research conducted by the journalist, who takes a position by asserting the "true facts" of the story and implicitly urging those in charge to do something about them. For instance, *New York Sun* reporter Harold Littledale spoke with authority in his stories exposing abuses in New Jersey's prison system because he had visited all of the state's prisons — even getting himself locked up so he could report what it was like to be inside. His efforts prompted statewide prison reform and won him the Pulitzer Prize for reporting in 1918.

Washington Post reporter John Singerhoff provided another illustration of this reportorial authority with his 1947 story reporting that the Metropolitan Police Department hid more than 600 robbery cases by leaving them out of official reports. He wrote: "Failure to list these offenses has kept knowledge of many lawless acts from the police force as a whole, from the public and from formal statistics of crimes committed and cases solved" (p. 1). Singerhoff did not need to qualify his findings because they were based on his own "exhaustive survey" of police records. An internal police investigation of the matter quickly followed.

Marshall Hail of the *El Paso Herald* opened a 1943 series on the looting of a public park in similar straightforward fashion, writing:

> El Paso County's Ascarate Park, supposedly a public playground, has been turned into a private truck farm and a private hog ranch, with little visible benefit to the

taxpayers. This has been done either with the consent or through the negligence of the Commissioners Court [p. 1].

Hail's article was paired with an editorial calling for a grand jury investigation, and a grand jury later returned three felony indictments.

A final example of the confident accusation of an investigative reporter appeared in the *Washington Post* and *Times Herald* in 1954. Five years after a voter referendum legalized slot machines in Charles County, Maryland, the newspaper found major problems and illegalities in the slot machine industry there. Reporter Ed Koterba spent weeks on documentary research, interviews and firsthand observations. His research yielded a confidently-written, six-part series that began with a sweeping accusation. "Charles County — where the slot machine is king — may best be described as the place where the gambler winks at the law while the public official keeps his eyes closed," he wrote (p. 1). The sentence could have been crafted to top an editorial, yet it is the lead for a page-one news story written at the height of the objectivity paradigm.

Koterba's work also highlights the second way that investigative reporting pushes against the restrictions of the traditional objectivity norm. His framing of the slot machine exposé demonstrates how the rhetorical construction of an investigative story — with its villains, victims and ironic juxtaposition — transforms the reporter from a neutral observer to a morally-engaged advocate. Protess et al. (1991) suggested that journalists use the rhetoric of victimization to stimulate public outrage in hopes of prompting reform. Ettema and Glasser (1998) expanded on the notion, arguing that the victim-villain narrative is an ironic device that "transfigures the conventions of journalistic objectivity into a morally charged vocabulary for condemnation of the villains to whom we have foolishly entrusted our public affairs" (p. 12). Through this framing of objective, fact-based reporting, investigative reporters subtly engage the moral outrage of their audience.

In the following passage, for instance, Koterba drew a fine portrait of victims — children lured in by the temptation of gambling — and villains, the tavern operators willing to take their money and the incompetent inspector willing to look the other way:

> Two newsmen in a random check of a dozen places found violations of the law at more than a third of them. In two places they saw youngsters 10 to 12 years old playing the slots.
>
> Above the machines were large signs warning: "Children under 16 years not allowed to play these machines."
>
> In a crowded tavern-dance hall in Waldorf, one of the county's two major communities, a 12-year-old boy who had earned $2 singing with a hillbilly band poured his meager salary into a penny machine.

The bartender made change for the boy — 25 pennies at a time. Twice the machine jammed and the proprietor obligingly repaired it.

A few doors away, another boy at a penny machine was told by the bartender: "Here, young fellow, let me move the machine back of this pillar where they can't see you from the highway."

The penalty for conviction on a charge of permitting children to operate the machines is [a] $1000 fine or six months in jail.

County officials boast that only one arrest — for a minor violation — has been made in the last five years.

Slot Machine Inspector Richard H. Stubbs said, before the survey was made, "By God, if we didn't keep this thing clean, the State would wipe out the machines tomorrow."

After the tour, Stubbs insisted, "As far as I know, everything and everybody is proper" [1954, p. 1, 16].

The image of taverns taking pennies from minors alongside signs that prohibited gambling by children — juxtaposed with the criminal penalties that are never enforced — amount to a powerful irony sure to create outrage in any reasonable reader. This is, in Ettema and Glasser's words, a "carefully documented 'web of facticity,'" an incisive selection of direct quotations, and a conscientious attempt to balance the story (that is, get the villain's side) ... all essential tools of journalistic ironists" (p. 92).

Investigative stories are balanced only in the sense that they usually allow their targets the courtesy of a response. The "other side" is told, most often through a villain's admission or dodge, because the nature of the accusation — backed with evidence and confirmed well before a decision is made to publish — is such that there is no refuting it. In Koterba's story, Stubbs' denial is incongruous and silly when set against the violations that are plain for anyone to see. As Ettema and Glasser pointed out, by the time the response comes, "it is difficult to read anything [the target] might have to say without that sense of ironic knowingness" (p. 99). The slot machine stories spurred two grand jury investigations, and for his expertise, Koterba was called before one of the panels, where he testified for ninety minutes.

The reporter's involvement in an official investigation brings us to a third way that investigative reporters have resisted the conventions of objectivity-as-neutrality — personal involvement in a solution to the problem identified in a story. Koterba's involvement — providing compelled testimony before a grand jury — was relatively minimal in light of other kinds of advocacy that have been practiced by some investigative reporters. Case studies by Protess et al. (1991) demonstrated that investigative journalism may have the most impact not when the public becomes outraged and lobbies for change, but when journalists actively collaborate with policy-makers, often before publication. They noted that investigative journalists may share their findings with policy makers whom they know to be interested in the subject matter of their exposé, even prior to its publication, in the hope that official action will be taken. They may spotlight particular programs, or policy arenas, where reform initiatives are languishing. They may point to models of "how to do it right" that have worked elsewhere [p. 21].

Serrin and Serrin (2002) went further, suggesting some journalistic investigators became even more closely involved. They cite the case of William English Walling, who wrote about race riots in Illinois and then went on to help establish the National Association for the Advancement of Colored People. "Some journalists, particularly in decades gone by, stepped back and forth between writing about problems and working in or heading up groups that tried to deal with the problems," they said (p. xxi).

Lanosga (2010) tracked the development of an investigative press that is involved not just in pushing for publicity about failures and wrongdoing but also in actively advocating for and working on solutions to those problems. In these efforts, journalists have also become intimately enmeshed with officials in positions of power, indeed, sometimes acting as virtual officials themselves.

For example, the *Los Angeles Times* worked with officials to tackle the problem of smog. Reporter Ed Ainsworth (1947) produced a series of reports that, among other things, identified top polluters in the county. And the newspaper engaged the services of an expert from St. Louis to prepare an exhaustive report on the sources of smog and possible solutions. "This newspaper," Ainsworth wrote, "has taken the lead in co-ordinating and guiding the campaign — which it initiated — for a united community-wide attempt to eradicate the harmful smog" (p. A1).

The *Times* entered Ainsworth's series on smog for a Pulitzer Prize in local reporting. Though it did not win, the newspaper considered the degree of reporter involvement in the story as a fact to be touted to the jury. According to the description of the story in the Pulitzer office's index of entries: "Mr. Ainsworth ... named the offenders, wrote factual stories, fought for needed legislation, helped frame a needed State law, wrote all dovetailing editorials for the campaign and helped in selection of administrator of the clean-up job" (Pulitzer Prize Office, 1948, p. 1). This would seem to be a remarkable degree of engagement for a journalist in the age of objectivity, and a remarkable stamp of approval from one of journalism's most prestigious institutions. Fighting for legislation, writing the law, helping choose the administrator — these are activities that fly in the face of detachment. Yet Ainsworth's level of participation in his story was not without precedent among his fellow Pulitzer competitors from the 1920s onward.

The same year Ainsworth was documenting polluters, for instance, reporters at the *Kansas City Star* were nominated for a Pulitzer for their work investigating voter fraud. When they were done, according to the Pulitzer jury judging the entry, they put their evidence directly "in the hands of the FBI, the department of Justice, a congressional elections committee and the prosecuting attorney of Jackson County, Mo" (Kirchhofer & Sterling, 1947, p. 2).

Similarly, two decades earlier, James W. Mulroy and Alvin H. Goldstein of the *Chicago Daily News* won the Pulitzer Prize reporting award for their stories on the Leopold and Loeb murder case. A lengthy summary of their accounts by the Pulitzer jury emphasized the fact that their reporting led directly to evidence used in the criminal case. Their cause was helped by a laudatory letter from Cook County state's attorney Robert E. Crowe, who credited the reporters for systematic interviewing of potential witnesses and other detective work. As the prize jury recounted, "This evidence was very material in helping to break down the alibi of Leopold, he being confronted with the evidence produced solely by Goldstein and Mulroy" (Cooper, Beazell, & Crist, 1925, p. 2).

In 1927, the reporting prize went to John T. Rogers of the *St. Louis Post-Dispatch* for his investigation of misconduct by federal judge George W. English. But Rogers' work did not end with the publication of stories. He gave his materials to the Judiciary Committee in the U.S. House of Representatives, which promptly appointed a subcommittee to investigate. Then came an astonishing display of press-government collaboration, according to the account of the Pulitzer jury:

> Counsel furnished by the *Post-Dispatch* conducted the examination of witnesses, Rogers sitting at his side throughout the two weeks of the hearings to direct his questioning, and spending much of each night in coaching him for his next day's work. Nine hundred pages of the Congressional Record were filled with the testimony so taken. Even at hearings held in camera the sub-committee required the presence of Rogers for their guidance [Beazell, Rukeyser, & Cummins, 1927, p. 1].

Later, Rogers even participated with House investigators in gathering a confession from English's co-conspirators. The jury wrote: "After the House had voted to impeach and managers had been appointed to prosecute the case before the Senate, special agents of the Department of Justice ... placed their entire dependence on Rogers" (Beazell, Rukeyser, & Cummins, 1927, p. 2). The jury notes also contain excerpts of letters written by numerous government officials praising Rogers for his cooperation.

It is clear from the decision to award a prize to Rogers that the Pulitzer establishment — made up of journalism professors and top newspaper executives — saw no problem with this extraordinary participation in a story by a reporter. This is a significant fact, given the prize board's role in helping to define accepted standards of journalistic practice.

James English has written of the "economy of prestige" created by cultural prizes like the Pulitzers. Winners often receive money, of course, but more importantly, the prestige that accompanies a major prize can be treated as cultural capital. In the journalism milieu, the Pulitzers amount to the highest of professional affirmations. Because the prizes are so sought-after, the culture that grew up around them helped define standards of journalistic quality and professionalism. While the prizes recognized regular daily reporting, the Pulitzer juries also put a premium on the exposé, including tactics that clearly conflicted with the norms of classic objectivity. The reporting prize, for instance, was not created just to recognize a reporter's work in informing the public. More importantly, it emphasized "the accomplishment of some public good commanding public attention and respect"—the phrase Joseph Pulitzer used to describe the prize in his will, which was included in the contest documents put together by the faculty at Columbia University (Pulitzer, 1904, p. 6).

Thus, in keeping with Pulitzer's wishes, the juries showed a keen interest in enterprise reporting as opposed to the straight collection of facts. For example, the 1921 public service prize went to the *Boston Post* for its exposure of the Ponzi financial swindle. The public service jury chose it over a *New York Evening Post* exposé of failings in government rehabilitation of war veterans because the latter "consisted mainly in gathering and verifying the mass of soldiers' complaints that were lying ready on every hand" (Cunliffe, 1921, p. 2).

The Pulitzer record is filled with cases of journalistic investigators who were praised not just for writing good stories, but for their active advocacy and collaboration with authorities in bringing about resolution of the problems they had identified. That the Pulitzer juries and board recognized and rewarded such behavior is a strong testament to the existence of a competing view of the objectivity norm.

Looking Beyond Neutrality

What all this suggests for the changing world of today's journalism is that there is more than one model of journalistic objectivity to use as a guide in charting a course forward. While journalists, as shown by Ettema and Glasser, are reluctant to acknowledge that they are anything but neutral, it is clear that investigative reporting does not rest — and never has rested — on a foundation of relativistic objectivity.

Investigative reporting by its very nature is journalism with a viewpoint, albeit a viewpoint backed by a rigorous examination of facts. Contemporary journalists and their observers certainly recognize this reality. As *The Investigative Reporter's Handbook* noted:

> Many journalists are transmission belts for official proceedings. They attend a city council meeting, write on a notepad or tape the meeting and then edit their material to fit the space or time allotted. Such journalists are not investigators: They follow somebody else's agenda; they fail to capture what took place in private among city council members, staff and interest groups; and they do not check land records, contracts or other potentially revealing documents on which the council's decisions are based [Houston, Bruzzese, & Weinberg, 2002, p. vii].

The authors of this practical guide for reporters asserted that every journalist can be an investigative journalist if he or she has curiosity "accompanied by skepticism stopping short of cynicism or nihilism, abetted by undying outrage that expresses itself through comforting the afflicted and afflicting the comfortable" (p. vii). They did not mention objectivity; instead, they emphasized qualities — outrage, skepticism, empathy for victims — that tend to be incompatible with notions of neutrality and he-said-she-said objectivity.

The standard journalistic conception of objectivity is really a pseudo-objectivity, argued Phil Meyer (2004), a former reporter and author of a seminal practical handbook for journalists. He suggested that journalists have always had opinions but have simply had to conceal them because of the reality of mass media economics. But today, with more diffused audiences and more opportunities for spin, there is a need for a more rigorous objectivity. "True objectivity is based on method, not result," Meyer wrote. "Instead of implying that there is an equal amount of weight to be accorded every side, the objective investigator makes an effort to evaluate the competing viewpoints. The methods of investigation keep the reporter from being misled by his or her own desires and prejudices" (p. 54).

Meyer is not alone in his wish for a more nuanced understanding of objectivity. Stephen Berry (2005) called for reclaiming the objectivity Walter Lippmann advocated, which "does not exclude 'aggressive analyzers and explainers.' Nor does it ban investigative journalism or interpretive reporting" (p. 16). Franklin Foer (2005) said journalists need to be freed of the shackles of balance. "Reporters should have greater latitude to point out distortions without worrying that they have violated the laws of objectivity," he wrote (p. 6). And journalism professor Robert Jensen (2000) asserted that reporters need more, not less, bias — a bias toward analysis and truth-telling. "The journalistic norms of neutrality and objectivity so constrain reporting that much of the news ends up seeming — or actually being — contradictory or incoherent," Jensen said (p. A41).

Columbia Journalism Review's managing editor Brent Cunningham (2003) recounted a story about Jason Riley, a young journalist at the *Louisville*

Courier-Journal who spent half a year investigating his city's dysfunctional court system. When Riley was done, he turned in a story that noted the loss of hundreds of felony cases and called the system flawed. It seemed natural; after all, he had just spent six months investigating and was drawing a reasonable conclusion based on his research. Yet the story came back to him with a note from his editor: "Says who?" Cunningham reflected:

> Riley discovered a problem on his own, reported the hell out of it, developed an understanding of the situation, and reached some conclusions based on that. No official sources were speaking out about it, so he felt obliged to fill that void. Is that bias? Good reporters do it, or attempt to do it, all the time. The strictures of objectivity can make it difficult [p. 28].

What Cunningham and others want is for journalists to acknowledge they "are far more subjective and far less detached than the aura of objectivity implies" (p. 31). In this, these critics echo Michael Schudson (1978), who offered for would-be enterprise reporters the concept of "mature subjectivity ... tempered by encounters with, and regard for, the views of significant others in the profession; and subjectivity aged by encounters with, and regard for, the facts of the world" (p. 192).

Mature subjectivity sounds very much like what investigative reporters have been doing for a century and even farther back in the United States. And they continue to do it today for both new and old news platforms. Witness the most recent round of the Pulitzer Prizes, which saw old-line newspaper investigations capturing the prizes for Public Service and Investigative Reporting but also a non-profit online investigative operation called ProPublica winning for a series of investigative reports in the National Reporting category.

ProPublica's prize was for a series of reports by Jake Bernstein and Jesse Eisinger (2010) about questionable financial practices by Wall Street investment firms. Like the investigative reports examined here, the series had some of the same attributes that represent challenges to the conventional notion of objectivity, such as a refusal to rely solely on traditional sources. Instead, they pursued rigorous research that allowed them to confidently make tough, unattributed accusations like this:

> Over the last two years of the housing bubble, Wall Street bankers perpetrated one of the greatest episodes of self-dealing in financial history. Faced with increasing difficulty in selling the mortgage-backed securities that had been among their most lucrative products, the banks hit on a solution that preserved their quarterly earnings and huge bonuses: They created fake demand [para. 1–3].

Though the prominence of objectivity-as-neutrality may have made it difficult to discern over the decades, there is an alternate model of an assertive objectivity that can serve as a guide for the future of journalistic practice in the 21st century. Schudson (2003) and others remind us that news is about manufacturing, not harvesting. Investigative reporting, with its zeal for documenting, verifying and contextualizing facts rather than simply disseminating them, has perhaps best underscored that reality. But its example can be instructive for news workers trying to make sense of the changes being wrought by advancements in communications technologies. The neutrality model of objectivity doesn't make much sense in a world where "just the facts" can be accessed and even generated by audiences through countless channels on an increasing number of information platforms.

On the other hand, the sheer number of available sources cries out for assertive news work that decodes, explains, interprets and even offers conclusions and advocacy to consumers bewildered by the enormity of the information economy. For instance, a rapidly-growing flood of public data is now available to anyone — not just journalists, officials or analysts — and in many cases, it's free for the downloading. As *The Economist* noted in 2010:

> According to one estimate, mankind created 150 exabytes (billion gigabytes) of data in 2005. This year, it will create 1,200 exabytes. Merely keeping up with this flood, and storing the bits that might be useful, is difficult enough. Analysing it, to spot patterns and extract useful information, is harder still ["The data deluge," 2010, para. 2].

There will be some media consumers who will tap into this surfeit of data and make their own meaning of it. But for the many others who will not or cannot, it spells meaning-making opportunities for today's journalists, both traditional and emerging.

To function successfully in this new atmosphere journalists need to embrace a more vigorous and useful conception of objectivity. Specifically, news workers would do well to question traditional notions of objectivity-as-neutrality. As the investigative journalists have shown, journalists can contextualize facts so as to make the public aware of wrongdoings, the victims involved, and who is responsible for such egregious action. Moreover, these journalists move past dated notions of objectivity-as-detachment by advocating remedies to address our society's failures. In an increasingly post-objective news landscape, investigative reporters show how a sincere allegiance to facts often compels a journalist to abandon neutrality and assume a point of view.

References

Ainsworth, E. (1947, September 28). Smog drive set to get under way. *The Los Angeles Times*, p. A1.

Aucoin, J. L. (2005). *The evolution of American investigative journalism*. Columbia: University of Missouri Press.

Beazell, W., Rukeyser, M., & Cummins, A. (1927). Letter to Nicholas Murray Butler. Pulitzer Prize Office, Columbia University, New York.

Bernstein, J., & Eisinger, J. (2010, August 26). Banks' self-dealing super-charged financial crisis. *ProPublica*. Retrieved May 16, 2010, from http://www.propublica.org/article/banks-self-dealing-super-charged-financial-crisis

Berry, S. J. (2005, Summer). Why objectivity still matters: "Precisely because we understand our [human] frailties, we insist upon maintaining the pursuit of objectivity." *Nieman Reports, 59*(2), 15–16.

Cooper, C., Beazell, W., & Crist, H. (1925). Report of the jury on the reporter's prize. Pulitzer Prize Office, Columbia University, New York.

Cunliffe, J. (1921). Letter to Nicholas Murray Butler. Pulitzer Prize Office, Columbia University, New York.

Cunningham, B. (2003, July/August). Re-thinking objectivity. *Columbia Journalism Review, 42*(2), 24-32.

The data deluge: Businesses, governments and society are only starting to tap its vast potential. (2010, February 25). *The Economist*. Retrieved August 5, 2010, from http://www.economist.com/node/15579717.

English, J. (2005). *The economy of prestige: Prizes, awards, and the circulation of cultural value*. Cambridge, MA: Harvard University Press.

Ettema, J. S. & Glasser, T. L. (1998). *Custodians of conscience: Investigative journalism and public virtue*. New York: Columbia University Press.

Foer, F. (2005, December 26). Bad news. *The New Republic, 233*(26–28), 6.

Hail, M. (1943, October 26). County park, employes used for private profit. *El Paso Herald-Post*, p. 1.

Hofstadter, R. (1955). *The age of reform: From Bryan to F.D.R.* New York: Vintage Books.

Houston, B., Bruzzese, L., & Weinberg, S. (2002). *The investigative reporter's handbook: A guide to documents, databases and techniques*. Boston: Bedford/St. Martin's.

Jensen, R. (2000, October 11). Journalists actually need *less* objectivity. *Newsday*, p. A41.

Kirchhofer, A., & Sterling, D. (1947). Report of the A.S.N.E. jury on public service nominations for 1947 Pulitzer Prizes in journalism for work done in 1946. Pulitzer Prize Office, Columbia University, New York.

Koterba, E. (1954, August 24). One-armed banditry: "Legal slots" make Charles County hum. *The Washington Post and Times Herald*, p. 1.

Lanosga, G. (2010). *The press, prizes and power: Investigative reporting in the United States, 1917-1960*. Unpublished doctoral dissertation, Indiana University, Bloomington, Indiana.

Meyer, P. (2004, Winter). The next journalism's objective reporting. *Nieman Reports, 58*(1), 54.

Mindich, D. T. Z. (1998). *Just the facts: How "objectivity" came to define American journalism*. New York: New York University Press.

Miraldi, R. (1990). *Muckraking and objectivity: Journalism's colliding traditions*. New York: Greenwood.

Nord, D. P. (2001). *Communities of journalism: A history of American newspapers and their readers*. Urbana: University of Illinois Press.

Porwancher, A. (2011). Objectivity's prophet: Adolph S. Ochs and the *New York Times*, 1896–1935. *Journalism History, 36*(4), 186–195.

Protess, D. L., Cook, F. L., Doppelt, J. C., Ettema, J. S., Gordon, M. T., Leff, D. R., & Miller, P. (1991). *The journalism of outrage: Investigative reporting and agenda building in America*. New York: The Guilford Press.

Pulitzer, J. (1904) Extracts from the will of Joseph Pulitzer. Joseph Pulitzer Papers, Box 60. Rare Book & Manuscript Library. Columbia University Library, New York.

Pulitzer Prize Office. (1948). Local reporting entries for 1948 Pulitzer prizes in journalism for work done in 1947. Pulitzer Prize Office, Columbia University, New York.

Schudson, M. (1978). *Discovering the news: A social history of American newspapers.* New York: Basic Books.

_____. (2003). *The sociology of news.* New York: W.W. Norton.

Serrin, J., & Serrin, W. (2002). *Muckraking! The journalism that changed America.* New York: The New Press.

Singerhoff, J. (1947, June 30). Concealed from public: 600 robbery cases never properly listed by D.C. police. *The Washington Post,* p. 1.

Stein, H. H., & Harrison, J. M. (1973). Muck-raking journalism in twentieth-century America. In J. M. Harrison & H. H. Stein (Eds.), *Muckraking: Past, present, and future* (pp. 11–22). University Park: Pennsylvania State University Press.

Tuchman, G. (1972, January). Objectivity as strategic ritual: An examination of newsmen's notions of objectivity. *American Journal of Sociology,* 77(4), 660–677.

PART II

Contemporary Examinations

4

Conversational Journalism and Journalist-Audience Relations

New Rules, New Voices

DOREEN MARCHIONNI

Thorson and Duffy's (2006) Media Choice Model tells us news consumers have myriad choices in news "voice" these days. In addition to traditional "objective" news, audiences may attend to opinionated news formats, such as Fox TV News, news blogs and so-called "collaborative" stories — those in which professional journalists collaborate intensely with ordinary citizens to tell more complete, human stories.

Of those, collaborative stories, or what some call conversational journalism, may hold great promise. Thanks to the Web, almost anyone these days with online access and a few tools can create and distribute news and/or work with professional journalists in real time. But what exactly *is* journalism as a conversation? Curiously, little empirical research has developed around it to help us recognize it when we see it, including how to measure it, or how to apply it to journalism's most treasured values — credibility and expertise. Using a series of online news experiments, I have found that conversation is both a real and powerful phenomenon in the experience of online news consumers. But it is also complicated and fickle, and doing journalism-as-a-conversation haphazardly can lead to loss of audience trust.

Conversation also is not a departure from facts-based reporting, though much confusion persists. Since completing my research, I have taken the data on the road, sharing it with academics and journalists alike, including the professional journalism school at The Poynter Institute, the Associated Press Media Editors association, the Association for Education in Journalism and Mass Communication, and the annual South by Southwest arts and technology conference in Austin, Texas. Almost without fail, I get some variation of these two questions: How does conversation square with objective news? Is this the end of objectivity? The short answer to both: It depends on what you mean by "objective." The long answer, as this chapter reveals, is that conversational news points to the need to rethink objectivity, and that is a complicated challenge. However, despite the lack of empirical research on conversational news, one point is clear: It represents a departure from the paradigm of the journalist as elusive, all-knowing, data-distributing automaton in favor of the journalist as co-collaborator, partner, and ordinary human. And for many, that is revolutionary.

Objectivity Redux

Objectivity occupies both hallowed and maligned territory in modern journalism. It is also easily one of the most misunderstood concepts in our field (Kovach & Rosenstiel, 2007). It was never meant as a description for journalists *themselves* because, as even a child knows, humans have biases. That is what makes them different from machines. Objectivity referred only to the *methods* journalists use to help overcome those biases, much like the procedures and stances scientists employ. In other words, objectivity in the field refers not to the absurd notion that *humans* are objective creatures but that journalists' *practices* or *methods* of gathering evidence can be free of human bias. In fact, the soundness of journalistic objectivity should allow an independent observer to re-trace a journalist's steps and ultimately see things as the journalist presented, something akin to replication in science (Kovach & Rosenstiel, 2007). This objective orientation arose, not surprisingly, during the Industrial Revolution of the last century, a time of intense public interest in all things scientific.

Even assuming a correct understanding of "objectivity" in the field, important questions remain. Can journalists employing objective methods with the best intentions ever reveal anything about the *journalist-as-person* behind the news? And would that make a difference in perceived credibility? It is the central question behind conversational news because conversation essentially asks journalists to foreground themselves. News that invites broad public participation in professional news processes suggests not only a change in journalists' traditional source of power — only they had access to means of distribution — but an emphasis on relationships, as does any form of collaboration in the human experience, from marriage to corporate teamwork. News goes from *product* or commodity delivered to passive consumers to *process*, where the lines between content creator and audience blur in a constant give-

and-take. Easier said than understood, though. The story of how journalism moved in this direction, at least in the media-saturated United States, begins in some ways with the American Revolution and in democratic theory.

Journalism by the People, for the People

As most of us first learned in elementary school, the United States was born in a crucible of revolt against a British monarchy that squelched expression, including that of the press. The Founding Fathers went to great pains to ensure that would not happen again, enshrining those freedoms in the First Amendment, arguably the most powerful statement of its kind in the history of modern civilization. It provides broad rights to journalists to conduct news free of interference from the government so that the press can operate as a kind of watchdog for the people. But what role do the people themselves play in that process? The right of the press to express itself on behalf of the people is not quite the same as the right of the people to be *heard* by the press. And yet that is what conversational journalism is about. This is an important dynamic to investigate because, at a minimum, we can infer that the First Amendment confers upon the public its right to be heard.

Journalism — from Revolutionary to Pragmatic

Thomas Jefferson, James Madison and Thomas Paine recognized expressive freedoms as central to American democracy. And that idea took inspiration from the French *philosophes* Francois Voltaire and Jean-Jacques Rousseau (Altschull, 1990). Indeed, those philosophers and American revolutionary Paine implicitly captured the earliest spirit of conversational journalism. Though Voltaire was contemptuous of the masses as a barbarous rabble, he argued human understanding is not advanced in the compilation of facts on the histories of kings but in the painstaking attention to the customs and behaviors of *ordinary* people. Not only is this supposed to be the "bread" of much journalism today, as Altschull (1990) noted, but it elevates the idea of turning to ordinary people instead of elites to capture a community's stories, an idea central to the concept of conversation. Even more than Voltaire, Rousseau (1953) insisted lawmakers and writers, including journalists, reject the lofty language of the elite in favor of the plain speech of the people so that everyone, including the "Kansas City milkman," as Altschull (1990) suggested, can grasp their ideas. To write *in* the words of those people, conversation advocates argued, is a key step to writing *of* their stories and ideas. For

Rousseau, the voice of the private citizen can be heard perhaps best through the press (Altschull, 1990). Paine similarly saw the American journalist's role as capturing public opinion, which Rousseau (1968) argued is instrumental for popular sovereignty in his vision of the General Will. If information exists for the benefit of the governed and not the government, as Paine argued, journalists who engage in a two-way conversation with citizens are in an ideal position to capture that opinion. In short, Paine and the French philosophers celebrated the average person's stories. Together, they tell us the voices of ordinary people in everyday discourse count — they represent the construction of community knowledge and they reify democratic rule. Journalists, themselves citizens, have the unique responsibility in a democracy as facilitators of discourse because of their work within a mass medium. Perhaps nowhere is that clearer than in 19th-century Pragmatism, the United States' greatest contribution to philosophical thought and the philosophy most closely associated with the objective, scientific impulse of modern American journalism (Altschull, 1990).

Pragmatism draws its strength from experience and observation, not thought, and makes no attempts to answer cosmic questions (Altschull, 1990). The Pragmatist who best gave expression to what we now think of as conversational journalism? American philosopher John Dewey. He spoke of community, communication via the symbols of language and public education all as forces for democracy. Unlike journalist and media scholar Walter Lippmann, Dewey held the public in high esteem, and the two scholars' debates in the 1920s about the role of the public in democratic processes should be required reading for all journalism students.

For Dewey, democracy is an ideal to work toward and literally begins at home and in the neighborhood. Democracy relies on the social intercourse of everyday life; it thrives on the distribution and the acquisition of community knowledge. Public schools and the press perform a powerful role in this scenario, "for a thing is fully known only when it is published, shared [and] socially accessible," wrote Dewey. "Record and communication are indispensable to knowledge" (1927, p. 176). Perhaps not coincidentally, no index entry for "reporter," "journalist" or "news" can be found in his seminal volume *The Public and its Problems*. But discussions abound on all three under various entries for "public," suggesting he viewed the public and the journalist as somewhat synonymous, or at least acting in concert. Lippmann (1922) argued that democracy should be left in the hands of ruling elites, who have the time and intellect to understand issues of public importance. Dewey, in contrast, elevated the over-the-backyard-fence neighborly chitchat of ordinary citizens as the basis for community and, ultimately, democracy. Further, he suggested personalized, socially-relevant news could approximate interpersonal communication and stimulate conversation that fuels community life (Dewey, 1927).

In other words, he eschewed trust in authoritative elites for a pragmatic trust in the genuine reasoning and informed rationality of common people.

Power (Back) to the People

If conversation can be seen as a metaphor for news, its champion in contemporary times was the late James Carey (1992). He urged journalists and journalism scholars to reject traditional notions of the craft as the mechanical transmission of information to the ignorant masses and instead embrace a ritualistic notion of journalism as a culture's conversation with itself. Carey maintained that all citizens, including journalists, were on equal footing and shared a stake in improving democratic self-governance. He attacked what then had become a decades-long infatuation with elite sources in the news — public officials, politicians, bureaucrats, pollsters — at the expense of ordinary citizens and their concerns. Those kinds of critiques, in turn, helped fuel a reform movement in journalism in the 1990s known as public journalism, or civic journalism, most closely associated with New York University Professor Jay Rosen.

Reform efforts ranged from newsroom-sponsored focus groups with citizens to public surveys, town-hall-style meetings and other efforts aimed at engaging citizens in a public dialogue about community issues (Eksterowicz & Roberts, 2000). From the beginning, though, traditional journalists attacked public journalism, many of whom complained it depleted valuable resources in already cash-strapped newsrooms and pandered to readers (Eksterowicz & Roberts, 2000; Hoyt, 1995). Yet while public journalism has been criticized in some corners as a marketing ploy by the media to become the community's "pal" (Hoyt, 1995), thereby abdicating the press's traditional role as detached observers of the polity, its underlying concept of journalism as conversation is well-geared toward the expectations of today's online news consumer. Indeed, the Web is rewriting the rules of the news business, and traditional media giants are trying to make sense of it all: "We're in the middle of a revolution, and revolutions offer both challenges and opportunities," Paul Steiger, managing editor of *The Wall Street Journal*, said at a 2006 conference. "The business models are being totally destroyed and reordered every day" (Peterson, 2006, para. 10).

Conversation: New Rules, New Relations

Also being destroyed are traditional relationships and boundaries between content creators and audiences. In some ways, it is a return to our roots — to ordinary people owning the means of distribution (a computer and Web access these days) and to free-wheeling discussions in and around the news in the town square (the virtual squares of blogs, chat rooms, social media and the like). The revolutionary, democratic impulses of colonial America today can be seen in everything from *Asbury Park Press'* "coffee house newsroom" in New Jersey, where everyday citizens and journalists mix freely, to "live chats" with journalists on various news sites around issues of the day.

My interest in citizen participation in the news started years ago in the newsroom with so-called "lobby calls." Readers routinely showed up in the newspaper's lobby unannounced, sometimes in what look like faded pajamas or in camping gear, to share tips or seek coverage of some kind. Sometimes they arrived clutching crinkled manila envelopes packed with papers and yellowing documents. I always wondered what motivated them to try to participate in the news. With the rise of the Web and my return to graduate school, it became a scholarly question. The concept of journalism as a conversation seemed most apt to describe highly collaborative journalism between professional journalists and interested audience members. Rich, descriptive studies on the concept filled the literature. However empirical research, including measurement of the phenomenon for the purposes of explanation and prediction, was lacking. My mission was set: identify the variables that theoretically measure the phenomenon of conversational journalism, then run them through a pair of news experiments. In short, find the science, if any, behind conversation.

Even before that work began, I had a suspicion about at least two potential features or variables of conversation from previous experiments I worked on. Those early studies explored how audiences judged various types of online news by examining the role of social presence (Wackman, 1973), or perceived humanness of a journalist, and coorientation (Gunawardena, 1995; Swan, 2002), or perceived audience similarity to a journalist. The studies also examined whether those variables hurt or help the perceived credibility and expertise of the news worker. Those "types" or "voices" addressed how the journalist comes across in the news and are key to Thorson and Duffy's (2006) Media Choice Model mentioned earlier. That model extends uses and gratifications theory to online contexts to understand why and how audiences choose certain types of online news over others (among those types: traditional, collaborative, Fox-News-style opinionated and blogs). The model itself recognizes a profound shift away from traditional, objective news toward emerging, post-objective news types.

As it turned out, these studies offered ample evidence for the power of social presence and particularly coorientation affecting how the audience perceived the journalist as a regular person. Study participants perceived the journalist's social presence most powerfully in opinionated news blogs, though credibility ratings suffered there. Coorientation, meanwhile, was a primary predictor of perceived credibility and expertise in traditional and collaborative stories.

Among the more intriguing findings in those early studies was the strength of traditional, objective news. The first study compared perceived social presence and coorientation within the four story modes (Meyer, Marchionni, & Thorson, 2010). The second study tested those same variables in politically slanted blogs and traditional stories (Marchionni, Meyer, & Thorson, 2008). In convenience samples of undergraduates and graduate students, or what some might describe as the Web Generation, participants across these studies found traditional stories as the most credible and expert, though collaborative texts were a close second in the first experiment. The second study provided some particularly notable findings as well, including evidence that participants with self-disclosed political biases still found traditional stories more credible than blogs with which they politically agreed.

Together these early studies suggested traditional, just-the-facts reportage should not go away anytime soon. However, given the collaborative story's strong showing on credibility in the first experiment how well might it do in a more focused test of journalism as a conversation? The first step was determining, at least theoretically, what variables index conversation in online news from the audience perspective. That involved a broad look at literatures as disparate as computer-mediated communication, interpersonal communication, and social psychology, where conversation is discussed or tested, often as an embedded or implied concept. From that literature, with key citations listed below, came these five variables:

• Coorientation/homophily — Two types of perceived similarity to journalist: intellectual (Wackman, 1973) and demographic (McCroskey, Richmond, & Daly, 1975).
• Interactivity — Perceived use of the Web by journalist to interact with citizens (Rafaeli, 1988).
• Social presence — Perceived humanness of journalist (Gunawardena, 1995; Swan, 2002).
• Friendliness — Perceived openness and accessibility of journalist to citizen collaboration (Norton & Pettegrew, 1977).
• Informality — Perceived relaxed, casual tone with audience (Althen, 1992).

Of these features, perhaps three offer the most insight into the question of objectivity in the news: coorientation/homophily, social presence, and friendliness. These socio-psychological features of conversation best reveal how online audiences relate to journalists as *humans*. Research into these variables began in earnest with a pair of online news experiments and relied on new or pre-existing, Likert-style scales informed by the literature review.

Two Experiments, One Big Concept

EXPERIMENT 1

The first experiment used a 2 (story type) by 2 (video or no video) by 4 (story topics) within-subjects design. It compared traditional, Associated Press-style news stories with collaborative texts from the earlier studies, and some of the stories featured personal videos of the journalist addressing the audience to help convey a sense of humanness (Marchionni, 2010a). Collaborative, or what some might call conversational, news included human-interest ledes and more citizen quotes than traditional stories. It also featured information both in the body of the stories and in a box atop the stories that indicated the reporter was talking to citizens in the community as part of the reporting. Each story itself also included several references to readers who provided information in the reporting via threads of e-mail exchanges or chat-forum conversations with the writer. The point of view of the story essentially was that of the reader most likely impacted by the news and included minimal references to official sources, such as public officials, agency leaders, and bureaucrats. These collaborative stories also ended with a tagline on how to reach the reporter by e-mail. Despite these features, the accounts remained detail-oriented, the information vetted by professional journalists but free of opinion. In other words, though the reader might get a greater sense of the journalist as a human being, the stories still highlighted verified, fact-based reporting. Perhaps the best example of such journalism today is Minnesota Public Radio/American Public Media's Public Insight Journalism reform initiative. In the early 2000s, the St. Paul radio station developed software and protocols that allow everyday citizens to routinely and systematically contribute their experiences and expertise to story coverage, putting the newsroom at the vanguard of conversational news practices in the United States. That program has since expanded into several dozen newsrooms, mostly in public broadcasting, said Public Insight (PIN) Director Linda Fantin, and the network of citizen contributors to PIN numbers around 100,000, from scientists to accountants (personal conversation, May 17, 2011).

Traditional news stories, by contrast, contained no language about the writer or the writer's connection with readers. The pieces upheld the standards and format of traditional inverted-pyramid news stories, conveying objectivity, balance and authority; accounts largely relied on quotes from official sources, such as government leaders or bureaucrats.

In this study (N = 66), I hypothesized that collaborative stories would score higher on the conversation variables than the traditional stories, and highest when personalized videos accompanied stories. I also hypothesized that participants would view the more conversational stories (collaborative with or without videos) as most credible and expert, particularly because of high scores expected for coorientation. The larger theoretical groundwork for examining credibility and expertise stems from related research, namely that people seek a human presence in the news and judge credibility accordingly (Newhagen & Nass, 1989), communicate through and with various electronic media as though they were human (Reeves & Nass, 1996) and consider ordinary citizens as credible news sources (Hamman, 2006; Meyer, Marchionni & Thorson, 2010). I tested two types of credibility, one for the actual article and one for the Web site on which it appeared. Both scales largely relied on Meyer's (1988) definition of news credibility as essentially the believability and accuracy of the reporting. The expertise scale relied heavily on Perloff's (2003) conceptualization of information that conveys authority, or specialized know-how.

EXPERIMENT 2

The second experiment (N = 67) used a used a 3 (story type) by 4 (story topics) within-subjects design (Marchionni, 2010b). It compared three *types* of conversational journalism from the real world, none with videos this time: a Wikinews story written by ordinary citizens for citizens without the help of professional journalists; the same collaborative story condition from Experiment 1 as described in Thorson and Duffy's (2006) Media Choice Model; and a story derived from the crowd-sourcing tool, Twitter. (Participants first read a brief exchange between a reporter on Twitter and some followers, then read a story in part aided by that exchange.) The study tested the same dependent variables as the previous experiment: the five conversation processing variables — most notably coorientation/homophily, social presence and friendliness — and the outcome measures of article and website credibility and expertise.

KEY FINDINGS

The first experiment hypothesized, among other things, that conversation variables would be significant in collaborative news conditions, especially with a reporter's personalized video, but not in traditional texts. As shown in Table 1, analyses of co-variance (ANCOVAs) followed by Bonferonni post-hoc comparisons found that was the case for some but not all conversational variables. Social presence, or the sense of a journalist's humanness, generally required the presence of a video to register with study participants in *any* condition, as did friendliness. Similarly, coorientation/homophily, or the perception of similarity with another, showed no differences in comparisons of story texts,

Table 1

	Coor/Homo	Social	Friendly Credibility	Article Credibility	Web Site	Expertise
Experiment 1						
Collaborative/no video	3.41	2.32	3.46	3.54	3.54	3.25
Collaborative/with video	3.47	2.97	3.96	3.58	3.58	3.12
	(−.07)	(−.64)**	(−.50)**	(−.05)	(−.04)	(.14)
Collaborative/no video	3.41	2.32	3.46	3.54	3.54	3.25
Traditional/no video	3.42	2.12	3.42	3.64	3.64	3.49
	(−.01)	(.20)	(.04)	(−.11)	(−.10)	(−.25)
Collaborative/no video	3.41	2.32	3.46	3.54	3.54	3.25
Traditional/with video	3.58	2.96	3.83	3.66	3.62	3.44
	(−.17)	(−.64)**	(−.37)**	(−.12)	(−.08)	(−.20)
Collaborative/with video	3.47	2.97	3.96	3.58	3.58	3.21
Traditional/no video	3.42	2.12	3.42	3.64	3.64	3.49
	(−.05)	(.85)**	(.54)**	(−.07)	(−.06)	(−.28)*
Collaborative/with video	3.47	2.97	3.96	3.58	3.58	3.21
Traditional/with video	3.58	2.96	3.83	3.66	3.62	3.44
	(−.11)	(.01)	(.13)	(−.08)	(−.05)	(−.23)
Traditional/no video	3.42	2.12	3.42	3.64	3.64	3.49
Traditional/with video	3.58	2.96	3.83	3.66	3.62	3.44
	(−.16)	(−.85)**	(−.41)**	(−.01)	(.01)	(.05)
Experiment 2						
Twitter	3.23	2.59	3.62	3.35	3.16	3.00
Wikinews	3.25	2.31	3.41	2.94	2.64	2.92
	(−.02)	(.27)	(.22)*	(.41)**	(.53)**	(.18)
Twitter	3.23	2.59	3.62	3.35	3.16	3.00
Collaborative	3.29	2.46	3.72	3.60	3.45	3.18
	(−.06)	(.13)	(−.10)	(−.25)	(−.29)*	(−.18)
Wikinews	3.25	2.31	3.41	2.94	2.64	2.82
Collaborative	3.29	2.46	3.72	3.60	3.45	3.18
	(−.04)	(−.13)	(−.32)**	(−.66)**	(−.82)**	(−.36)*

*p < .05   **p < .01

Bonferroni post-hoc comparisons for conversational indices (coorientation,/homophily, social presence, friendliness) and outcome variables (article credibility, Web site credibility, expertise) for all pairwise conditions in two experiments. (Means and mean differences rounded up to nearest hundredth.)

meaning audiences respond equally well to cues of similarity across story types. The study also hypothesized participants would view collaborative stories as more credible and expert than traditional accounts, especially when accompanied by videos, but that was not the case. Participants rated both types of news stories as equally credible, with or without videos.

Regressions in this experiment, meanwhile, generally showed that as conditions became more conversational — first adding video to traditional texts, then altering the text to be collaborative, then eventually adding video to that — the conversational variables generally became operant and predictive of credibility and expertise in the manner expected. Coorientation proved to be one of the strongest predictors of both types of credibility and expertise in the more conversational conditions, meaning the extent to which participants perceived themselves as similar to the journalist predicted how much they trusted stories or found them expert.

Specifically, as Table 2 shows, in the case of perceived article credibility, friendliness predicted the measure for collaborative stories without videos (β = .51, p < .05), while coorientation/homophily predicted article credibility for collaborative stories with videos (β = .57, p < .01). In the case of perceived website (source) credibility, different conversational variables became operant, though some in the opposite manner predicted: coorientation/homophily (β = .40, p < .01) and social presence (β = -.25, p < .05) for collaborative stories without videos; and coorientation/homophily (β = .58, p < .01) for collaborative stories with videos. In the case of perceived expertise, conversational variables were operant in this way: coorientation/homophily (β = .29, p < .05) for traditional stories without videos and coorientation/homophily (β = .57, p < .01) for collaborative stories with videos.

The second experiment attempted to shed light on some of these findings but also determine any differences in how people view *types* of conversational news. In that experiment, I hypothesized the conversational variables would be operant in various degrees depending on the actual type of story/tool. For instance, because the individuals who wrote the Wikinews story were ordinary citizens just like the experiment participants, I expected to see high scores on coorientation/homophily, or perceived similarity.

As it turned out, participants perceived no differences across conditions for coorientation/homophily and social presence (Table 1). As with the first experiment, regressions also proved illuminating. Most intriguing was coorientation/homophily's role as a key predictor of perceived credibility and expertise in almost every story condition (Table 2) and yet the variable's weak showing in ANCOVAs. In other words, though coorientation/homophily predicted credibility and expertise for most story types, participants did not perceive significant differences on coorientation/homophily among those story

Table 2

Blocks of Independent Variables by Condition		Article Credibility	Website Credibility	Expertise
Experiment 1				
Traditional/No video	Coorient/Homophily	.12	.06	-.23
	Social Presence	.03	-.03	.03
	Friendliness	.08	.12	.12
Traditional/Video	Coorient/Homophily	.20	.24	.29*
	Social Presence	.13	.29	.27
	Friendliness	.13	.09	-.08
Collaborative/No Video	Coorient/Homophily	.12	.40**	.19
	Social Presence	-.14	-.25*	-.03
	Friendliness	.51*	.24	.30
Collaborative/Video	Coorient/Homophily	.57**	.58**	.57**
	Social Presence	-.04	-.15	-.15
	Friendliness	-.16	.10	-.12
Experiment 2				
Twitter	Coorient/Homophily	.51**	.49**	.17
	Social Presence	.05	-.03	.03
	Friendliness	-.19	.06	.11
Wikinews	Coorient/Homophily	.37**	.39**	.36**
	Social Presence	.06	.05	.08
	Friendliness	.08	.02	-.02
Collaborative	Coorient/Homophily	.21	.25	.38**
	Social Presence	.18	.06	.06
	Friendliness	-.18	-.30*	.11

*p < .05   **p < .01

Hierarchical Linear Regressions: Impact of conversation variables reported in standardized betas (coorientation/homophily, social presence, friendliness) on dependent variables of article credibility, website credibility and expertise across all conditions for two experiments.

types, or the experimental groups. This requires fleshing out in future studies but suggests, among other things, that coorientation/homophily might work best *in concert* with the other variables that index conversation.

Friendliness, meanwhile, proved somewhat problematic. The journalist's perceived friendly openness in collaborative stories hurt website credibility in Experiment 2, as Table 2 shows, while friendliness helped predict article credibility and expertise in collaborative texts in Experiment 1. The issue may be a matter of how much friendliness news consumers find acceptable, which in turn may depend on other stories in the mix, traditional versus non-traditional.

Regressions again shed some light on the matter. Again looking at Table 2, in the case of article credibility, coorientation/homophily predicted the measure for the Twitter condition (β = .51, p < .01) and for Wikinews (β = .37, p < .01). In the case of website credibility, predictors in each condition varied somewhat. In the Twitter condition, coorientation/homphily (β = .49, p > .01) predicted the measure; in Wikinews, coorientation/homophily (β = .39, p < .01) predicted the measure. For collaborative stories, friendliness (β = -.30, p < .05) predicted the measure, though in a manner that was the opposite of what was expected. Finally, in the case of expertise, coorientation/homophily alone predicted the measure in Wikinews stories (β = .36, p < .01) and in collaborative stories (β = .38, p < .01).

RESEARCH RECAP

The news experiments attempted to measure the phenomenon of conversational journalism and determine if it hurts or helps journalists assert, through conversational approaches, two of their most treasured values — perceived credibility and expertise. The results indicated journalism-as-a-conversation is a real, multi-dimensional phenomenon that can vary across story types but with some predictability. It is also somewhat fickle. For news managers, the results suggest above all that you cannot simply tell a journalist "to write more conversationally," given the complexity of the phenomenon. Conveying humanness, for instance, likely requires more than textual cues, perhaps videos, as scores for social presence indicated. Those videos also provide crucial information on questions of perceived similarity, and similarity is a powerful predictor of credibility and expertise. If the Web has provided any advantage to print media, it is the ability to convey two-dimensional information about print and audio reporters in videos, as broadcast journalists always have. The research also adds further support to Newhagen and Nass' findings (1989) that credibility is not just a rational but a social construct. Here is how: Researchers had struggled for years to understand why TV news consistently outpaced newspapers in credibility ratings, despite newspapers' relative comprehensiveness. The Stanford pair discovered news audiences appear to evaluate credibility differently for television and newspapers. In the case of TV, they judge credibility based on the human delivering the news, to whom they respond positively, while in the case of newspapers, they judge credibility based on the institution *behind* the journalist, which they view as cold, hard and distant. In short, when it comes to trust, the human behind the news matters to news consumers.

Re-thinking Objectivity

So what does this all mean for objectivity in the news? If by objectivity we mean the *method* of verified, vetted, fact-based reportage that aims to be inclusive of key stakeholders, conversational journalism as tested upholds the standard. In some ways, conversation both broadens and deepens reporting by drawing on the experiences and expertise of audience members previously ignored. That clearly aids fairness in reporting and possibly accuracy. You cannot work in a newsroom for long without audience members upbraiding you for getting *something* wrong they know more about. Cases in point: cherry blossoms and birds. At *The Seattle Times* where I work as the Sunday metro editor, I recently learned that photos of cherry blossoms and birds frequently get the paper into deep trouble with audience experts. The pale-pink blossoms of plum trees look a lot like cherry-tree blossoms in the spring, at least to many in the newsroom. And photojournalists can certainly have a tough time distinguishing certain song birds by appearance. The conversational solution would be to routinely draw on audience mavens to help vet photos and publicly praise these experts for their help in creating more accurate journalism. My research suggests audiences respond quite well to such efforts, the most successful being Minnesota Public Radio/American Public Media's network of some 100,000 everyday citizen sources mentioned earlier.

Tapping citizens for their experiences to tell a more complete story is one thing. Asking journalists to step out from behind the curtain to reveal the *person* behind the news, particularly at newspapers, is quite another. Again, this refers not to reporters sharing their opinions but essentially showing themselves as human as they report and share the news. I had no idea how uncomfortable this is for some journalists until I took my data on the road. I now realize it has much to do with the confused notions of objectivity I discussed at the beginning of this essay. Most of us were trained to keep ourselves out of the news, taking that to mean not just our personal biases but what I call our "personness." Now, as journalists, we are urged to get comfortable with voice and a slightly more casual tone, to be friendly and accessible to audiences, and to unabashedly tap citizens for their expertise where appropriate. We are encouraged to talk transparently about the news process, sometimes in short biographical videos — in essence, to form a social, human connection to readers and viewers. This is a form of news that centers on relationships and processes, not products and power, and there is little in traditional J-School training that suggests any of this is appropriate, or effective. Complicating matters is the subtlety of some of the features of conversation. Getting some of this wrong can mean loss of perceived credibility among both the public and a journalist's peers.

I tell journalists and scholars alike that we are living in an era of extraordinary transition, but that it also harkens back to our democratic roots. It seems unfamiliar but it should not. As we continue to experience the repercussions of the Web on traditional news, we ought to take a closer look at bloggers, among them political commentator Andrew Sullivan ("The Daily Dish") and productivity expert Merlin Mann ("43 Folders"). Though some bloggers are highly opinionated, all of the successful ones seem to excel at one of the most powerful conversation variables in my studies — coorientation/homophily (perceived similarity). The voice and approach of the writer is clear and distinct and reveals something about the person behind the post. If news is moving in any direction, it appears to be going this way, certainly in terms of online audience preferences. For example, when *The New York Times* snatched up private blogger Nate Silver and his popular, statistics-laden political blog after the 2008 presidential election, the paper made clear that it wanted plenty of writerly voice, revealing the blogger's personality and perhaps humor, but no opinion (Tenore, 2011).

This evolution in news suggests wholesale changes in how we teach journalism. Online audience engagement in the form of citizen-journalist collaboration should be central to all news sequences, be they print- or broadcast-focused. A story about the impacts of an economic recession on student enrollment, for instance, might begin with a student journalist's call-out to Twitter followers for student perspectives on the issue, in an effort to tell a more complete, accurate story beyond the usual official sources. That means student journalists must be trained in how to use social media to do their jobs in the 21st century. The "social" part of that equation is crucial. It means more than just using Twitter or Facebook or Tumblr to distribute news through a headline and story link reminiscent of last century's we-talk-you-listen communication model. To be a part of social media means to be social, to engage and to interact with audiences. And that means revealing yourself as a living, breathing, trustworthy person. The variables I used to index conversation essentially represent a unique measurement of online audience engagement, with heavy emphasis on socio-psychological dynamics. But it is a metric whose experimental tests keep perceived credibility and expertise at the heart of the enterprise. That is important because my research suggests online audiences are still looking for fact-based, verified, comprehensive reporting they can rely on.

In addition to training students on social-media practices for purposes of audience engagement, we may need to eliminate traditional print and broadcast sequences (many schools already have done so) because they have outlived the times: Online news instruction, or what some refer to as multimedia convergence, ought to form the core of journalism education, not merely another sequence or elective. Does any of this mean the death of news? Or the death of objectivity? Not really. There is plenty of support in all of my studies for verified, fact-based reporting. My research points to the public's continuing view that traditional news stories are more credible (even as compared to blogs with which they personally agreed). But conversational news does mean a different approach from the past 100 years or so, one that is more social, more transparent and more human. When it comes to unease about making the transition to conversational journalism, twenty years from now we may be shaking our heads wondering what all the fuss was about.

References

Althen, G. (1992). The Americans have to say everything. *Communication Quarterly, 40*(4), 413–421.

Altschull, J. H. (1990). *From Milton to McLuhan: The ideas behind American journalism.* New York: Longman.

Carey, J. W. (1992, Winter). The press and the public discourse. *Kettering Review,* 9–22.

Dewey, J. (1927). *The public and its problems.* Denver: Alan Swallow.

Eksterowicz, A. J. & Roberts, R. N. (Eds.). (2000). *Public knowledge and political knowledge.* Lanham, MD: Rowman & Littlefield.

Gunawardena, C. N. (1995). Social presence theory and implications for interaction and collaborative learning in computer conferences. *International Journal of Educational Telecommunications, 1*(2/3), 147–166.

Hamman, B. (2006). *Two voices: Social presence, participation, and credibility in online news.* Unpublished master's thesis, University of Missouri-Columbia, Columbia, MO.

Hoyt, M. (1995, Sept./Oct.). Are you now, or will you ever be, a civic journalist? *Columbia Journalism Review, 34,* 27–34.

Kovach, B., & Rosenstiel, T. (2007). *The elements of journalism: What newspeople should know and the public should expect.* New York: Crown.

Lippmann, W. (1922). *Public opinion.* New York: Free Press.

Marchionni, D. (2010a, August). *Conversational journalism: An experimental test of traditional and "collaborative" online news.* Paper presented at the Newspaper /Multimedia Practices Division of the Association for Education in Journalism and Mass Communication (AEJMC) conference, Denver, CO.

_____. (2010b, August). *Explicating journalism-as-a-conversation: An experimental test of wiki, "Twittered" and "collaborative" news models.* Paper presented at the Civic and Citizen Journalism Division of the Association for Education in Journalism and Mass Communication (AEJMC) conference, Denver, CO.

Marchionni, D., Meyer, H. K., & Thorson, E. (2008, August). *When newspaper reporters blog: The credibility of news and blogs that match or mismatch people's socio/political leanings.* Paper presented at the Newspaper/Multimedia Practices Division of the Association for Education in Journalism and Mass Communication (AEJMC) conference, Chicago, IL.

McCroskey, J. C., Richmond, V. P., & Daly, J. A. (1975). The development of a measure of perceived homophily in interpersonal communication. *Human Communication Research, 1*(4) 323–332.

Meyer, H., Marchionni, D., & Thorson, E. (2010). The journalist behind the news: Credibility of straight, collaborative, opinionated and blogged "news." *American Behavioral Scientist, 54*(2), 100–119.

Meyer, P. (1988). Defining and measuring credibility of newspapers: Developing an index. *Journalism Quarterly, 65,* 567–588.

Newhagen, J., & Nass, C. (1989). Differential criteria for evaluating credibility of newspapers and TV news. *Journalism Quarterly, 66*(2) 277–284.

Norton, R. & Pettegrew, L. (1977). Communicator style as an effect determinant in attraction. *Communication Research, 4*(3), 257–282.

Perloff, R. (2003). *The dynamics of persuasion: Communication and attitudes in the 21st century*. Mahwah, NJ: Lawrence Erlbaum.

Peterson, K. (2006, September 27). News brought to you by the average Joe. *The Seattle Times*. Retrieved December 8, 2008, from http://seattletimes.nwsource.com/html/businesstechnology/2003277355_citjournalism26.html.

Rafaeli, S. (1988). Interactivity: From new media to communication. In R. P. Hawkins, J. M. Wiemann & S. Pingree (Eds.), *Advancing communication science: Merging mass and interpersonal process* (pp. 110–134). Newbury Park, CA: Sage.

Reeves, B., & Nass, C. (1996). *The media equation: How people treat computers, television, and new media like real people and places*. Cambridge: Cambridge University Press.

Rousseau, J. (1953). *The confessions* (J. M. Cohen, Trans.). London: Penguin.

_____. (1968). *The social contract* (M. Cranston, Trans.). London: Penguin.

Swan, K. (2002). Building learning communities in online courses: The important interaction. *Education, Communication & Information, 2*(1), 23–49.

Tenore, M. (2011, February 21). FiveThirtyEight's Nate Silver adjusts to New York Times, six months after joining the newsroom. *The Poynter Institute*. Retrieved April 4, 2011, from http://www.poynter.org/latest-news/top-stories/120212/fivethirtyeights-nate-silver-adjusts-to-new-york-times-as-a-blogger-6-months-after-joining-the-newsroom/

Thorson, E. & Duffy, M. (2006). *A needs-based theory of the revolution in news use and its implications for the newspaper business* (Tech. Rep.). Columbia: University of Missouri-Columbia, Reynolds Journalism Institute at the School of Journalism.

Wackman, D. B. (1973). Interpersonal communication and coorientation. *American Behavioral Scientist, 16*(4), 537–550.

5

The Sociality of News Sociology

Examining User Participation and News Selection Practices in Social Media News Sites

SHARON MERAZ

Changes within the mass media industry over the last 40 years have further eroded the notion of an unbiased, objective press. According to audience data, partisan news programs during prime time hours on MSNBC and Fox news have higher ratings compared to the more-objective tone of CNN news programming (Carter, 2009). Though audiences seem aware of the dangers of partisan bickering, they are using the Internet more than ever to connect to others of like-minded viewpoints in the political arena (Lawrence, Sides, & Farrell, 2010; Mutz, 2006; Smith, A., 2011), causing scholars to worry about the deleterious effects of partisan dialogue on deliberative democracy and civil political discussion within online spaces (Sunstein, 2000, 2001, 2002, 2008, 2009).[1] As technology continues to advance at a breathtaking pace, enabling customers to choose from more web-based news sources (Anderson, C., 2006, 2009a; Gourville & Somon, 2005; Hoch, Bradlow, & Wansink, 1999; Schwartz, 2005), print newsrooms across the U.S. are witnessing declines in circulations (Plambeck, 2010). News publics are consuming content from political blogs in growing numbers, particularly during U.S. political campaigning cycles (Smith, A., 2011).

This collapse in the singular authority of traditional mass media to dictate the public news agenda of active, news selecting Web publics has been due in no small part to the relentless development of social media Web technologies (Meraz, 2009a, 2011a, 2011b). Successful bloggers can now command audiences that rival news media entities across all news-specific genres (Meraz, 2008). Web 2.0 data storage technologies enable individuals to house and

78

share their multimedia content on the Web for free (Anderson, C., 2009b; Gillmor, 2004) through such applications as YouTube, Vimeo and Flickr. Web users also flock to social networking applications like Facebook, posting status updates and sharing links in a river of news to their friends. The success of Twitter has made us connect to others in an always-on fashion (Hermida, 2010). Twitter is also a breaking news platform, as seen in its use regarding Osama Bin Ladin's death (Smith, C., 2011) and during the political change/unrest in Iran (Beilin, Blake and Cowell, 2009), Mumbai (Zuckerman, 2008), and Egypt (McCarthy, 2011).

These rapid changes in media technologies have been summed up through the concept dubbed Web 2.0 (O'Reilly, 2005). Though there is definitional ambiguity in Web 2.0, critics highlight its meaning as connected to specific techniques of improving software architecture. Enhancements include software production that offers more agile, rapid development timeframes (software in permanent beta), new business models of software architecture (for example, AJAX, Web services, and open APIs), and greater user-driven participation in software development and content creation, the latter creating network effects that create a more intelligent Web platform (Allen, 2008; Scholtz, 2008).[2] Web 2.0 applications are "architected for participation," designed from inception to encourage user participation (O'Reilly, 2004).

Arguably, most Web 2.0 applications only gain utility and meaning through user contribution and participation. Within these sites, monetary compensation is not the driving force, and most users are motivated by such non-monetary impulses as ego-seeking, gift-giving and altruism, or forging collaboration and community (Benkler, 2006; O'Reilly, 1999; Raymond, 1999). Though critics have decried aspects of Web 2.0 as an exploitation of free labor (Carr, 2009; Postigo, 2003), active Web publics continue to participate and populate these sites with Web content possibly due to the gratifications they receive from its network effects. That is, Web 2.0 applications have made it easier to communicate, form community, and collaborate with others in group-forming networks (Boyd, 2007). These networks are often held together by the glue of shared interests and perspectives. Emphasis is on the social experience, leading many to also describe these Web 2.0 applications as "social media" applications or "social software."

This paper focuses on one such enduring strand of social media applications, social media news aggregators, which began appearing on the Web around 2004 (Lerman, 2007; Meraz, 2008). Within these sites, members scour and curate the Web for interesting news stories, submitting accounts for collective voting. Site-specific algorithms collate the voting tallies and, in conjunction with other site specific metrics, promote the most popular, submitted stories to their home/front pages. These top news stories, unlike pieces used by traditional media newsrooms, are arguably derived in a more egalitarian fashion because of the involvement of more individuals in the news selection process. Unlike traditional media newsrooms which depend heavily on bureaucratic, elite sources (Gans, 1979; Shoemaker & Reese, 1996; Sigal, 1973), members of these sites also have the option to scour the long tail of media on the Web to include both citizen and traditional media sources. The selection of news within these sites is undeniably part of a social, collaborative experience, as members can vote on stories that their friends have selected, making the selection of news more open to "sociality" and viral effects.[3]

This chapter examines the general contribution of social media news aggregators such as Digg, Mixx, Netscape (now defunct), Newsvine, and Reddit to the development and dissemination of news as a product and service. This chapter addresses how these various sites question and interrogate traditional media effect theories founded on the relative dominance of traditional media entities as selectors and disseminators of objective news to an atomized, disconnected, largely consumptive audience (Friedson, 1953). This paper makes reference to data culled from social media news aggregators over two separate time points in June 2007 and June 2008 in an effort to explore how these sites are changing how we conceive of news as a product in the collaborative Web 2.0 environment.

Crowdsourcing, Collaborative Filtering, Algorithmic Decision-Making

Shoemaker (1991) defined gatekeeping in traditional media effects theory as mainstream news operations selecting, from a large number of messages, those news items that will be transmitted to one or more receivers. Before the onset of Web-influenced changes in the news industry, scholars described traditional media operations as holding virtually absolute power on message creation and message transmission. Scholars articulated five broad factors affecting news sociology, or the influences on traditional media content: journalists' individual level factors (for example, a journalist's personality, background, values, and professional role conception), media routines, organizational-level factors, extramedia factors, and ideological factors (Shoemaker, 1991; Shoemaker & Reese, 1996). In such an environment, scholars of agenda setting predicted that traditional news media had the power to determine the salience of issues and their attributes (McCombs, 2004; McCombs & Shaw, 1972). Given that gatekeeping theory was articulated when mass media audiences were atomized and disconnected from each other due to a largely, one-way media industry (Friedson, 1953), it is not surprising that sociality was not articulated as a driving factor in the news selection process. Instead, newsrooms' influences on each other were conceived as intermedia agenda setting (McCombs, 2004); concurrently, the impact of citizens on the news and on each other remained largely irrelevant. Within traditional mass media, information was held in check by newsroom personnel. Throughout most of the 20th century there were almost no free technologies that could enable horizontal citizen connections that could countervail newsrooms' gatekeeping effects.

Now, in the age of Web 2.0 media, the viability of traditional gatekeeping theory is questionable. News flows on the Internet in distributed, decentralized modes, with content increasingly created to be platform/channel agnostic and liquid/mobile across different mediums. Active Web publics now play a gatekeeping role. They help determine the popularity of news on the Internet through each mouse click, Web search, and website visit. Network effects reveal an engaged audience at all levels of participation that elevates or makes significant the concept of sociality in message production and distribution.[4] Shoemaker and Vos (2009) argued that gatekeeping theory can be revised and reconceptualized to take into account this active media climate. The Internet allows anyone to be a gatekeeper through passing news items along and commenting on news stories. Readers now have their own "gate" as they send along news items to their friends or indicate story importance via email lists and links in blog posts. This ability of active, "produser" Web publics to share and pass along preexisting news stories was dubbed "gatewatching," suggesting that traditional media is not alone in controlling what becomes popular on the Internet (Bruns, 2005). One scholar has suggested movement towards the term "network gatekeeping" (Barzali-Nahon, 2008).

It remains doubtful that the rigid metaphors reflective of gatekeeping theory can be extended to the shareable Web 2.0 environment because social media news aggregators reveal different concepts and processes at work in the selection of news items. Indeed, what better explains the processes at work within social media news aggregators are concepts that center on social effects and networked, connected Web publics.

Crowdsourcing: This term, coined by Howe (2006, 2008), is defined as an open work call by a corporation/business entity on the Web. The entity attempts to outsource the creation of a product/service to a pool of self-selected, qualified participants in an effort to create a for-profit solution (Brabham, 2008a). Crowdsourcing is the creation of products/services through distributed, collaborative acts and is visible in the production processes of sites like iStockphoto (Brabham, 2008b), Threadless, and Mechanical Turk (Kittur, Chi, & Suh, 2008). Crowdsourcing has become a buzz word to describe projects that involve distributed labor on the Internet among participants who have their actions aggregated and/or amalgamated towards the creation of an end product or service. The idea that products built through this mechanism can be superior to deliverables created in a hierarchical form of production is often supported through successful open source projects like Linux (Benkler, 2002). However, scholars now acknowledge that crowd wisdom is only assured when the crowd is diverse in skill and independent in the decision-making process (Sunstein, 2008; Surowiecki, 2005). Without independence in decision making, the danger of the herd effect, also called "informational cascades" can bias crowd wisdom toward popular or existing choices (Bikhchandani, Hirshleifer, & Welch, 1992).[5]

Within social media news aggregators, no formal studies have been conducted on the motivation of members who participate within these sites. Reference to other communities that depend on free labor suggest that pleasure in collective problem solving appears to be a strong motivational factor (Bradham, 2008a). In fact, crowdsourcing-supported sites tend to benefit from the services of white, educated, relatively affluent contributors who possess high-speed Internet connections (Bradham, 2008b). Other studies have found a power law to participation. Similar to a Pareto law, a few users tend to be responsible for the majority of content created (Adamic & Huberman, 2000; Barabasi, 2002, 2003; Barabasi & Albert, 1999; Barabasi, Albert, Jeong, & Bianconi, 2000; Faloutsas, Faloutsas, & Faloutsas, 1999), while the majority of users trail with a "long tail" of small contributions (Anderson, 2006).[6] This finding appears to be common across all large-scale networks on the Web, evidenced in the blogosphere and Web 2.0 systems like Wikipedia (Panciera, Halfaker, & Terveen, 2009). The power law also operates at the level of attention: greater productivity among individuals is positively associated with more attention to those individuals and less attention to individuals who are less productive (Huberman, Romero, & Wu, 2009).

Social media news aggregators promise an opening of the news selection process to a wider variety of diverse Web publics. In such a scenario, do all members of these sites have the same level of power? Or, put another way, do all members of these sites choose to participate at the same level? If only a core group of users drive top news within these sites, it can be argued that these sites are actually driven by an elite core of gatekeepers, similar to the mass media model of news production and distribution.

Recommendation Systems and Collaborative/Social Filtering: Given the large amount of data now available in Web 2.0 applications, scholars point to concerns about information overload and overburdened choices on selective outcomes (Anderson, 2009b; Davenport & Beck, 2002; Goldhaber, 1997; Jackson, 2009; Schwartz, 2005).[7] Recommendation systems are burgeoning in an effort to improve satisfaction with online information search results within virtual communities (Hill, Stead, Rosenstein, & Furnas, 1995; Melville & Sindhwani, 2010). These systems also enable users to make the most of information abundance within the Web 2.0 environment (Davenport & Beck, 2002; Goldhaber, 1997). Web 2.0 systems have improved on former content-filtering techniques, which had automatically assumed that users' tastes were similar, based on attributes or characteristics of the item they were interested in consuming (Mooney & Roy, 1999). Now, many Web 2.0 systems like Amazon and Netflix depend on collaborative filtering algorithms to help users navigate large troves of data.

Collaborative filtering mechanisms give suggestions to users based on ratings that point to user similarities (Schafer, Frankowski, Herlocker, & Sen, 2007). One of the earliest examples of collaborative filtering usage included Firefly (previously known as Ringo), where users rated music CDs. The site used such ratings to provide music recommendations to users who had similar interests (Oakes, 1999). Another early example was GroupLens, which employed collaborative filtering techniques to highlight UseNet news stories (Resnick, Iacovou, Suchak, Bergstrom, & Reidl, 1994). Collaborative filtering techniques enable a personalized experience while allowing users who share interests to locate interesting content based on their tastes and similarities (Linden, Smith, & York, 2003).

In collaborative filtering systems, items that have not been rated cannot be part of the filtering mechanism. As such, utilizing collaborative filtering for steering choice and limiting options can perpetuate homogeneity because only content rated by the user base will be available for recommendations (Mooney & Roy, 1999). Items unrated by users are inaccessible to algorithms that search for overlapping interest among users.

Social media news aggregators employ a form of collaborative filtering known as social filtering. Social filtering postulates that people's tastes are not randomly distributed (Shardanand & Maes, 1995), and that sociality and the subjective judgments among friends can improve the filtering of information (Resnick, Iacavou, Suchak, Bergstrom, & Reidl, 1994). Social filtering is informed by the principle of homophily (McPherson, Smith-Lovin, & Cook, 2001). That is, the underlying homogeneity in friendship choice makes it more likely that we would like the stories our friends like. Within these sites, community members can see what their friends have voted as popular (Lerman, 2007), and this metric is visible as a primary filtering mechanism. Prior studies on the social media news aggregator Digg have found that members are more prone to like Digg stories that their friends have dug (Lerman, 2007; Lerman & Galstyan, 2007).

This study questions whether collaborative filtering, fueled by this phenomenon of social filtering, can also enable the production of quality news items within social media news aggregators. To date, very little is known about the types of news and sources of news shared within these communities (Meraz, 2008), and virtually no research published to date examines these news items through a longitudinal timeframe.

Research Questions

This study questions whether social media aggregators' efforts to foster crowdsourcing and collaborative/social filtering enables Web publics to have a voice in the selection of top news items within these sites. In particular, this study advances the following research question:

> RQ1: Over a longitudinal time frame, to what extent is there a power law in user activity for those users that gain top news stories on these sites?

Given the different mechanics that operate to drive story selection and emphasis within social media news aggregators, it is questionable to what extent both traditional media and citizen media leverage influence within these sites. A related question examines whether the story items are driven by traditional media's agenda, and whether story items reflect the choices common in traditional newsrooms. Therefore, this study also advances the following two research questions:

> RQ2: Over a longitudinal time frame, to what extent do social media news aggregators reflect a curation of the long tail of social media?
>
> RQ3: Over a longitudinal time frame, to what extent do social media news aggregators share emphasis of the same story genres that are popular in top news items selected by traditional media entities?

Methodology

In an effort to provide descriptive analysis of the significance of social media news aggregators over a longitudinal time frame, this study compared data collected over two different time points in 2007 and 2008. For both of these years, three social media sites remained consistently popular among active Web-reading publics: Digg (created in 2004), Reddit (created in 2005), and Newsvine (created in 2005). In 2007, the Netscape social media news aggregator was also existent, but by 2008 the site became defunct. In 2007, a new site, Mixx, became a source for social sharing of news and information, utilizing a model similar to the preexisting sites Digg, Reddit, and Newsvine.

In order to assess the top news content within these social media news sites, the top 10 news stories on these sites at three separate times each day (morning, afternoon, and night), were downloaded for a week-long period in June 2007 and in June 2008. Given the importance of observing how these sites operate on a daily basis, a random time point was selected in 2007, and emphasis was placed on replicating the time period one year later in an effort to compare samples from similar time frames. Across both time periods, 1200 stories were assessed: In 2007, 600 top news stories were downloaded in total from social media news sites Digg, Reddit, Netscape and Newsvine, while in 2008, 600 top news stories in total were downloaded from social media news sites Digg, Reddit, Newsvine, and Mixx. To automate the download of top news content in 2007, Firefox was utilized to take automated snapshots of social media news site home pages. In 2008, a Web script was written to automate the selection of top news content from these sites via their RSS feeds. For both 2007 and 2008, user data, story source, and story characteristics (news genre and story content) were accessible via the RSS feeds.

Upon automating the extraction of the aforementioned data, manual content analysis was subsequently conducted to tag URL sources as well as to consolidate story genres across the disparate sites. In terms of coding for story source (traditional media or citizen media), URLs for each story were extracted and reduced to the parent URL for each story (for example cnn.com versus cnn.com/story) and manually coded. Among the many URL categories created for tagging URLs, interest was directed at the URL categories for mainstream media news entities (newspapers, television, radio, newsmagazines, news blogs attached to another professional news outlet, and AP/wire syndicated content), and citizen media entities (liberal blog, conservative blog, moderate blog, and other citizen media, including video-sharing sites). Other URL categories included organizational entities (partisan or nonpartisan), media conglomerates, governmental sites, educational sites, niche media entities (for example, entertainment media, hobby media, technology sites), and nontraditional media entities (portal news sites and Web-only news media entities).

Across both disparate time frames, intercoder reliability between two coders for URL coding via Krippendorf's alpha ranged from .85 to .95. Similarly, across both time frames, intercoder reliability between two coders for story genre recoding via Krippendorf's alpha ranged from .92 to .98.

User Involvement in Social Media News Aggregators

In 2007, all social media news sites examined (Digg, Reddit, Newsvine, and Netscape) displayed a clear power law: The top 20 percent of the users were responsible for between 28 to 73 percent of the content on the top news pages. For some sites, the power law was steeper than others for the top 20 percent of users: the least democratic community was Newsvine (73 percent) followed by Netscape (72 percent), Reddit (50 percent), and then Digg (28 percent).

But do these networks show greater egalitarianism over time? Examining data from 2008 reveals that for all of the mature networks (Digg, Reddit, and Newsvine) there remained a persistent superstar effect such that a small core group of users gained an inordinate degree of front page, top news hits. In Digg, five percent of users attained more than three front page stories and posted 18 percent of content in total during the time period examined. In Reddit, eight percent of users attained more than three front page stories and posted 29 percent of the content. In Newsvine, 15 percent of users were able to receive more than three front page stories, and were responsible for 47 percent of the content. As of 2008, a relatively new social media site, Mixx, showed the greatest egalitarianism. In Mixx, approximately 63 percent of users attained three home page stories or more, and were responsible for 42 percent of the content.

Reinterpreting this content through the lens of long-tail user participation provides support for the competing hypothesis of enhanced user participation. In Digg, 95 percent of users posted two stories or less, but these small levels of home page contributions accounted for 82 percent of overall content. Similarly, in Reddit, 92 percent of users posted two stories or less but accounted for 71 percent of overall content. Likewise, in Newsvine, 85 percent of users posted two stories or less but accounted for 53 percent of overall content. In Mixx, long-tail user contribution is less dramatic: 37 percent of users who posted two stories or less were responsible for 58 percent of overall content. In sum, within most of the sites the majority of content was driven by small levels of participation among an engaged, active Web public. That is, across all sites, the sum total of stories from all users who posted two stories or less was responsible for a larger percentage of top news content than the total of stories posted by select, elite users (even when those elite users posted more than two stories to a site's top news pages). As long tail theory predicts, there is indeed an A-list cadre of users who are able to get inordinate front page attention, but their total story contributions to the top news pages was less than the sum total of all the small contributions from the remaining members that frequented each site. After accounting for those elite users, a large number of users were able to achieve some success at getting their submitted stories elevated to front/top news status.

It is also instructive to examine the nature of relationships among those that show a heavy level of engagement, primarily because of the role of social filtering in information dissemination within these sites. In 2008, data from the social media news site Digg also permitted further analysis of the user relationships. Examining network connections within this social site reveal a dense core/subset of users who know each other, and a fair amount of isolates or disconnected members from the social system (those with no ties). Status homophily and the power of social filtering accurately accounts for that fact that those users who posted three stories or more were in strong, reciprocal relationships with each other. Unlike these dense interconnections, users who posted two stories or less had fewer connections. Disconnection was visible in the Digg social system such that some members appeared as isolates, completely disconnected from other members.

These findings support a few broad conclusions. It is evident that within these systems, a few elite users can hold an inordinate degree of power. However, as forecasted by long-tail economic theory, a few posted stories by contributors can, over time, generate the bulk of subsequent story submissions on the home page. These sites are indeed avenues for the democratic crowdsourcing of news. Similarly, these sites also enable a few users to attain inordinate power over the bulk of members. The few users that gain inordinate power share a strong friendship network, which arguably enhances their reputation as drivers of content within the system.

News Sources in Social Media News Aggregators

In 2007, all four social media news aggregators examined showed consistent dependence on a few traditional media outlets as sources (BBC, the *Daily Mail,* and the *Washington Post*). Yet, within these aggregators, the long tail influence of citizen media surpassed traditional media in two of the four social media news sites.

As Figure 1 shows, for Digg and Reddit, citizen media was depended upon more heavily than traditional media as a source for top news stories. However, this was not the case in Newsvine and Netscape, which both showed heavier dependence on traditional media as sources for its top news content. In relation to Newsvine, its heavy reliance on traditional media could be explained by its ownership by MSNBC and partnerships with traditional media entities.

In 2008, the overall dependence on citizen media strengthened within those social media sites that were independent of traditional media newsrooms. Aggregating home page links across all social media entities revealed that citizen media (M = 55.5, SD = 8.8) were much more heavily depended upon than traditional media (M = 30.1, SD = 4.4). At the level of the individual sites, three of the four examined social media sites, relied much more heavily on citizen media in comparison to traditional media. Only the social media news site Newsvine cited traditional media more heavily as a source than citizen media. Similar to 2007, these findings could be due, in part, to Newsvine's ownership by traditional media sources.

These findings highlight that social media news sites, and its members, see their function as indexers or curators of the long tail of citizen media. Unlike traditional media entities, which heavily depend on bureaucratic sources for information, social media news entities are less reliant on mainstream, elite authorities. Their crowdsourcing efforts clearly encourage more citizen contributions that can be used as sources for shared media content. Indeed, social media news aggregators function as filters and gateways into the best of the citizen media world. These sites' use of content filtering over a larger mass of individuals allows more citizens to become gatewatchers to the richness of citizen media content.

Story Genre and Story Characteristics of Popular, Top News Items

Table 1 presents data on top story news genres in 2007 and 2008. The data reveals that news topics were fairly stable across the entire two-year period. Further examination reveals that this community was a highly-political crowd, with strong interests in technology and science. This data shows that politics, technology, science, and U.S./International News were top news genres enjoyed by these communities. Additionally, the users' strong focus on entertainment is undeniable, as the publics who flocked to these platforms seemed to enjoy humor and odd news. However, these Web publics did not exhibit a marked interest in sports or business news as evidenced by the low percentage total of this type of news shared within this community.

Examining the content of the actual stories within popular genres reveals even more information about these Web publics. Within technology, stories were published on gadgets like the iPhone release, software programming, and social media tools like Facebook (for example, "Is Facebook the New Ning?"). There was also a strong focus on science, particularly discoveries that revealed strange or uncommon phenomenon (for example, "Scientist Find Monkeys Who Know How to Fish" or "The World's First Bionic Hand"), or provided do-it-yourself projects (for example, "How to Run Your Car on Free Vegetable Oil" or "Teaching Your Kids to Make Games").

Political stories that ascended to top news within these sites also revealed a left-leaning slant, with a strong criticism of Republican politics. For example, in 2007, top news stories included then-U.S. President George W. Bush's commuting of Scooter Libby's prison sentence, and the nature of presidential executive privilege. In 2008, top political news stories included Dennis Kucinich's "Articles of Impeachment" against President Bush (a news story that got scant traditional media coverage, save on CSPAN), the rights of Guantanamo detainees and the closing of that prison, and John McCain's computer illiteracy. Several positive stories were run about Barack Obama, such as his stance on taxes and his speech to black fathers on Father's Day. These sites not only enabled a discussion on stories that received little traditional media coverage, but in many cases, provided a forum for critiquing how political news was presented in traditional media circles (for example, Fox News's reporting of Michelle Obama's and Barack Obama's fist bump as a "terrorist fist jab"). Unlike traditional media, most political stories were overtly partisan — positive in tone toward left-leaning positions and politicians.

Like other genres, entertainment stories shared an offbeat or odd news characteristic, highlighting the playfulness and humor of these Web publics who crowdsource the news along the long tail of citizen media. Entertainment stories ran the gamut of images, with textual commentary placed on the actual multimedia piece (similar to the approach for "Lolcats: I Can Haz Cheezburger,"), or links to stories that are unusual and different (e.g., "Dead Man Wakes Up as Doctors Prepare to Remove His Organs" or "Feds Say Man Wore Diaper Full of Heroin"). Many of these stories featured citizen media sources (e.g., "The 5 Most Ridiculous SkyMall Products Money Can Buy"). Vulgar and sexual material often rose to top news spots in these sites, possibly suggesting a larger male membership demographic within these sites.

Conclusion

Social media news aggregators present an unusual challenge to the former articulated theory of media gatekeeping (Shoemaker, 1991; Shoemaker & Reese, 1996; Shoemaker & Vos, 2009). Social media news aggregators enable socially-connected Web publics to troll the Web for interesting news stories that can be submitted to these sites for collective member voting. Selection is impacted by social/collaborative filtering, as the majority of these sites enable members to see what their friends find interesting. Unlike the former, articulated theory of media gatekeeping, social media news aggregators exploit sociality as a mainstay factor to ease the burden of information overload and permit more crowd-relevant news items to emerge in the selection of top news stories for home page display.

It is easy to understand why sociality was not formerly considered as a significant factor impacting media sociology in the pre–Web 2.0 media climate. Traditional media entities were the only gatekeepers regarding news, information, and public opinion due to their ownership and control of the news production and dissemination process. In the former media climate, citizens lacked the technologies to build an information-sharing community and remained atomized, with little entrance into the news creation and dissemination process.

Flash-forward to the 21st century and Web 2.0 now allows many more individuals the opportunity to act as gatewatchers or produsers (Bruns, 2005). Citizens now create content via blogs, Twitter, and social networking sites. Data storage on the Web permits citizens to host their content at no, or low cost, without seeking the authority or permission of traditional media entities to rebroadcast their content. Most importantly, Web 2.0 applications enable group-forming networks, gatherings of connected citizenry who may coalesce in either an ad-hoc, emergent fashion, or for specific purposes. Social media news aggregators bring together connected, news-reading Web publics who curate the long tail of media options on the Web. Unlike traditional news organizations, the social act of sharing and filtering information reveals different news norms than ones that drive professional, objective motives of traditional media entities. Unlike the objective norms of traditional media newsrooms, the emphasis in these sites is on the social act of sharing, often through a process of story curation and story promotion. Within this sociality norm, friendships and collaboration drive story selection. There is no formal attempt to apply objective news norm criteria to the selection of top stories for home page display within these social sites. Instead, these Web publics seek richness and diversity in their news content, eagerly trolling the Web for unusual, often opinionated stories that capture the attention and interest of their news communities.

Though a small percentage of the members of these sites exhibited an inordinate degree of power, the majority of the sites' home page or top news content came from small levels of contributions from a wider array of users. Indeed, these sites allowed more voices to affect the news selection process, unlike traditional media agenda setting which is only open to select gatekeepers. Though it is arguable that these sites' strong focus on entertainment may have marred the quality of what rose to the top news page, the Web publics that flock to these outlets sought humor, playfulness, and entertainment within their daily news. Much of this humor, generated from active content creation and DIY multimedia projects, showcased the talent and creative energy of site members. Unlike the past where "all the news that's fit to print" was an apt slogan for traditional media news gatekeeping, the phenomenon in the 21st century media climate is more akin to "all the news that's fit to share." Shelf space on the Internet is unlimited. Media options now abound on the Internet. Anyone can now be a source, and any source can now be responsible for shaping public opinion on niche subject matter.

Table 1: Comparison of News Genres across Social Media News Aggregators in 2007 and 2008.

News Genres	2007	2008
Technology	17 (3)*	18 (3)
Science	3 (7)	5 (6)
U.S. Politics	32 (1)	24 (1)
World/International	8 (5)	17 (4)
Business	2 (8)	4 (8)
Health	4 (6)	3 (9)
U.S. other	14 (4)	8 (5)
Sport	2 (8)	5 (6)
Entertainment	18 (2)	20 (2)

*Number in parenthesis represents the rank order of the news genre based on its percentage weighting among all other news genres.

However, though the sites boast a more open news selection process, it is important to remain cautious about the process by which these sites promote top news and information. These sites deliberately utilize sociality and social filtering to help them see what their friends have submitted in an effort to suggest value and credibility of news items. Prior studies on group decision-making warns of the dangers of informational cascades (Sunstein, 2006), and of poor decision making outcomes when individuals cannot make independent, objective decisions and, instead, choose to depend on earlier choices.

Figure 1

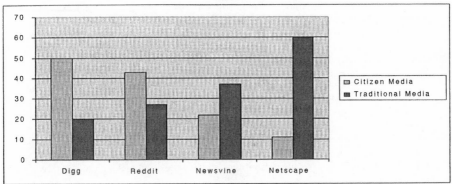

Percentage Links to Traditional Media and Citizen Media in Social Media News Sites in 2007.

Social filtering can bias the selection and sharing of news and information, specifically if news decisions are made based on friendship criteria.

It is yet to be seen whether social media news aggregators morph into a product/service that further develops/exploits sociality in news production and selection. This social process enables some Web publics to become powerful, and the approach exploits friendship as a metric to improve the relevance of news creation and distribution. Moreover — and this is crucial — what is certain is that news creation and production has now become a social process that far transcends both objectivity and the cultural boundaries of a professional newsroom.

Chapter Notes

1. The breakup of Web publics into social networks of like-minded perspective has often been called "cocooning." The phenomenon has also been referred to as "echo-chambers." Scholars fear that one-sided dialogue limits argument diversity, resulting in more extreme viewpoints.

2. AJAX, an acronym for Asynchronous Javascript and XML, refers to a way of using existing programming standards to exchange data with a server and update parts of a Web page without reloading the page. It has been used to create more timely and responsive, interactive Web pages in the Web 2.0 era. Web services are Web-based software applications that enable the exchange of data with other Web-based applications. It facilitates the linking of applications that operate on different network platforms, allowing software and services provided by different companies to be combined. API is an acronym for Application Programming Interfaces, and refers to the interface through which an application interfaces with other applications. In the Web 2.0 era, applications like Twitter and Facebook have made their API open so that developers can create third-party applications to run on their sites.

3. The growing impact of social influence in decision making within the Web 2.0 era is due to the growth of applications that encourage group-based activity, collaboration, conversation, and community. Sociality, or the tendency to form social groups, is thus a significant force in the creation and distribution of news in the 21st century. Sociality is heightened in applications like social media news aggregators which harness the social groupings of its members in the curation and selection of top news stories on their sites. The impact of sociality is currently unaccounted for in former models of media sociology.

4. Network effects refer to the magnified effect of a Web public that is connected. Within group-forming networks, Reed's law predicts that the utility of large networks scale exponentially with the size of the network (2^N, where N is the number of people). This law captures the value, or network effects, of group forming networks, which suggest that each person's potential multiplies exponentially due to the range of expanded potential connections facilitated by a group-forming network.

5. The term "informational cascades" refers to the social effect of biased decision-making as a result of members being able to see the choices of those that preceded their decisions. Previously made choices, visible to later members, bias decision making towards those former choices.

6. The term "long tail" refers to the expanded media options, and growth of niche marketplaces, that has resulted due to the development of Web 2.0 applications that facilitate easy media creation and distribution, Unlike the pre-21st century media marketplace,

which was dominated by limited media options and large, traditional media entities, the long tail captures the expansion of the media marketplace to include media options that command smaller audiences. The total effect of audience attention to this "long tail" of niche media offerings is said to outnumber audience attention to these large media entities.

7. The term "selective outcomes" addresses an individual's attention, perception and retention as it relates to stimuli. There are growing concerns that selective outcomes are frustrated by the extent of choices on the Internet. This imbalance in signal to noise is frustrated by Web 2.0 applications which permit easy media creation such that anyone can be a news producer. In such an environment, Web publics are overburdened by choice, with the potential to make poor selective outcomes in their news decision-making process.

References

Adamic, L.A., & Huberman, B.A. (2000, March 24). Power-law distribution of the World Wide Web. *Science, 287*(5461), 2115.

Allen, M. (2008). Market ideology and the myths of Web 2.0. *First Monday, 13*(3). Retrieved September 1, 2011, from http://www.uic.edu/htbin/cgiwrap/bin/ojs/index.php/fm/article/view/2139/1946

Anderson, C. (2006). *The long tail: Why the future of business is selling more of less.* New York: Hyperion.

_____. (2009a). *Free: The future of a radical price.* New York: Hyperion.

_____. (2009b). In defense of distraction. *New York Magazine.* Retrieved April 1, 2010, from http://nymag.com/news/features/56793/

Barabasi, A.L., (2002). *Linked: The new science of networks.* Cambridge, MA.: Perseus.

_____. (2003). *Linked: How everything is connected to everything else and what does it mean.* New York: Plume.

Barabasi, A.L., & Albert, R. (1999, October 15). Emergence of scaling in random networks. *Science, 286*(5439), 509–512

Barabasi, A.L., & Albert, R., & Jeong, J. (2000). Scale-free characteristics of random networks: The topology of the World Wide Web. *Physics A, 281,* 69–77.

Barabasi, A.L., & Albert, R., Jeong, H., & Bianconi, G. (2000, March 24). Power law distribution of the World Wide Web. *Science,* 287, 2115.

Barzali-Nahon, K. (2008). Toward a theory of network gatekeeping: A framework for exploring information control. *Journal of the American Society for Information Science and Technology, 59*(9), 1493–1512.

Beilin, J., Blake, M., & Cowell, M. (2009). The Iranian election on Twitter: The first eighteen days. *The Web Ecology Project.* Retrieved September 1, 2011, from http://www.webecologyproject.org/studies/

Benkler, Y. (2002). Coase's penguin, or linux, and the nature of the firm. *Yale Law Journal, 112*(2), 369–446.

_____. (2006). *The wealth of networks: How social production transforms markets and freedom.* New Haven: Yale University Press.

Bikhchandani, S., Hirshleifer, D., & Welch, I. (1992). A theory of fads, fashion, custom, and cultural change as information cascades. *The Journal of Political Economy, 100*(5), 992–1025.

Boyd, D. (2007). The significance of social software. In T. Burg and J. Schmidt (Eds.), *Blogtalks reloaded: Social software: Research and cases* (pp. 15–30). Norderstedt, Germany: Books on Demand.

Brabham, D. (2008a). Crowdsourcing as a model for problem solving. *Convergence, 14*(1), 75–90.

_____. (2008b). Moving the crowd at iStockPhoto. *First Monday, 13*(6). Retrieved September 1, 2011, from http://firstmonday.org/htbin/cgiwrap/bin/ojs/index.php/fm/article/viewArticle/2159/1969

Bruns, A. (2005). *Gatewatching: Collaborative online news production.* New York: Peter Lang.

Carr, N. (2009). *Big switch: Rewiring the world from Edison to Google.* New York: W.W. Norton.

Carter, B. (2009). CNN drops to last place among cable news networks. *Media Decoder.* Retrieved September 1, 2011, from http://mediadecoder.blogs.nytimes.com/2009/10/26/cnn-drops-to-last-place-among-cable-news-networks/

Davenport, T.H., & Beck, J.C. (2002). *The attention economy: Understanding the new currency of business.* Boston: Harvard Business School Press.

Faloutsas, M., Faloutsas, P. & Faloutsas, C. (1999). On power law relationships of the Internet topology. *Computer Communications Review, 29*(4), 251–262.

Freidson, E. (1953). Communications research and the concept of the mass. *American Sociological Review, 18*(3), 313–317.

Gans, H. (1979). *Deciding what's news: A study of CBS Evening News, NBC Nightly News, Newsweek, and Time.* New York: Random House.

Gillmor, D. (2004). *We the media: Grassroots journalism by the people, for the people.* Sebastopol, CA: O'Reilly.

Goldhaber, M.H. (1997). The attention economy and the net. *First Monday.* Retrieved September 1, 2011, from http://www.firstmonday.org/issues/issue2_4/goldhaber/

Gourville, J.T., & Somon, D. (2005). Overchoice and assortment type: When and why variety backfires. *Marketing Science, 24*(3), 382–395.

Hermida, A. (2010). Twittering the news: The emergence of ambient journalism. *Journalism Practice, 4*(3), 297–308.

Hill, C.W., Stead, L., Rosenstein, M., & Furnas, G. (1995). Recommending and evaluating choices in a virtual community of use. *Proceedings of the SIGCHI Conference on Human Factors in Computing Systems,* New York, NY, 194–201.

Hoch, S.T., Bradlow, E.T., & Wansink, B. (1999). The variety of an assortment. *Marketing Science, 18*(4), 527–546.

Howe, J. (2006). The rise of crowdsourcing. *Wired.* Retrieved September 1, 2011, from http://www.wired.com/wired/archive/14.06/crowds.html

_____. (2008). *Crowdsourcing: Why the power of the crowd is driving the future of business.* New York: Crown Business.

Huberman, B.A., Romero, D.M., & Wu, F. (2009). Crowdsourcing, attention, and productivity. *Journal of Information Science, 35*(6), 758–765.

Jackson, M. (2009). *Distracted: The erosion of attention and the coming dark age.* Amherst, NY: Prometheus Books.

Kittur, A., Chi, E.H., & Suh, B. (2008). Crowdsourcing user studies with mechanical turk. *Proceedings of the Twenty-Sixth Annual SIGCHI Conference on Human Factors in Computing Systems,* New York, NY, 453–456.

Lawrence, E., Sides, J., & Farrell, H. (2010). Self-segregation or deliberation? Blog readership, participation and polarization in American politics. *Perspectives on Politics, 8*(1), 141–15.

Lerman, K. (2007). Social information processing in news aggregation. *IEEE Internet Computing: Special Issue on Social Search, 11*(6), 16–28.

Lerman, K., & Galystan, A. (2007). Analysis of social voting patterns on Digg. *Proceedings of the ACMSIGCOMM Workshop on Online Social Networks,* New York, NY, 7–12.

Linden, G., Smith, B., & York, J. (2003) Amazon.com recommendations; Item to item collaborative filtering. *IEEE, 7*(1), 76–80.

McCarthy, C. (2011). Egypt, Twitter, and the rise of the watchdog crowd. *CNET News.* Retrieved September 1, 2011, from http://news.cnet.com/8301-13577_3-20031600-36.html

McCombs, M. (2004). *Setting the agenda: The mass media and public opinion.* Cambridge, England: Polity Press.

McCombs, M., & Shaw, D. (1972). The agenda-setting function of mass media. *Public Opinion Quarterly, 36*(2), 176–187.

McPherson, M., Smith-Lovin, L., & Cook, J.M. (2001). Birds of a feather: Homophily in social networks. *Annual Review of Sociology, 27*(1), 415–444.

Melville, P., & Sindhwani, V. (2010). Recommender systems. In C. Sammut & G. Webb (Eds.), *Encyclopedia of machine learning* (pp. 829–838). New York: Springer.

Meraz, S. (2008). The many faced "you" of social media. In Z. Papacharissi (Ed.), *Journalism and citizenship: New agendas in communication* (pp. 123–148). New York: Routledge.

_____. (2009). Is there an elite hold: Traditional media to social media agenda setting influence in blog networks. *Journal of Computer Mediated Communication, 14*(3), 682–707.

_____. (2011a). The fight for "how to think": Traditional media, social networks, and issue interpretation. *Journalism: Theory, Practice, and Criticism, 12*(1), 107–127.

_____. (2011b). Using time series analysis to measure intermedia agenda setting in traditional media and political blog networks. *Journalism and Mass Communication Quarterly, 88*(1), 176–194.

Mooney, R.J., & Roy, L. (1999). Content-based book recommending: User learning for text categorization. *Proceedings of the SIGIR-99 Workshop on Recommender Systems: Algorithms and Evaluation.* Berkley, CA, 195–204.

Mutz, D. (2006). *Hearing the other side: Deliberative versus participatory democracy.* New York: Cambridge University Press.

Oakes, C. (1999). Firefly's dim light snuffed out. *Wired.* Retrieved September 1, 2011, from http://www.wired.com/culture/lifestyle/news/1999/08/21243

O'Reilly, T. (1999). *Open source: Voices from the open source revolution.* Retrieved September 1, 2011, from http://www.oreilly.com/catalog/opensources/book/toc.html

_____. (2004). *The architecture of participation.* Retrieved September 1, 2011, from http://www.oreillynet.com/pub/a/oreilly/tim/articles/architecture_of_participation.html

_____. (2005). *What is Web 2.0.* Retrieved September 1, 2011, from http://www.oreilly.com/pub/a/oreilly/tim/news/2005/09/30/what-is-web-20.html

Panciera, K., Halfaker, A., & Terveen, L. (2009). Wikipedians are born not made: A study of power editors on Wikipedia. *Proceedings of the ACM 2009 International Conference on Supporting Group Work,* New York, NY, 51–60.

Plambeck, J. (2010). More steep circulation declines at newspapers. *New York Times.* Retrieved September 1, 2011, from http://mediadecoder.blogs.nytimes.com/2010/04/26/more-steep-circulation-declines-at-newspapers/

Postigo, H. (2003). From pong to planet quake: Post-industrial transitions from leisure to work. *Information, Communication and Society, 6*(4), 593–607.

Raymond, E. (1999). *The cathedral and the bazaar: Musings on linux and open source by an accidental revolutionary.* Cambridge, MA: O'Reilly.

Resnick, R., Iacovou, N., Suchak, M., Bergstrom, P., & Reidl, J. (1994). GroupLens: An open architecture for collaborative filtering of NetNews. *Proceedings of the ACM 1994 Conference on Computer-Supported Cooperative Work,* Chapel Hill, NC, 175–186.

Schafer, J.B., Frankowski, D., Herlocker, J., & Sen, S. (2007). Collaborative filtering recommender systems. In P. Brusilovsky, A. Kobsa, & W. Nejdl (Eds.), *The adaptive Web* (pp. 291–324). Berlin: Springer-Verlag.

Scholtz, T. (2008). Market ideology and the myths of Web 2.0. *First Monday, 13*(3). Retrieved September 1, 2011, from http://www.uic.edu/htbin/cgiwrap/bin/ojs/index.php/fm/article/view/2138/1945

Schwartz, B. (2005). *The paradox of choice: Why less is more.* New York: Harper Perennial.

Shardanand, U., & Maes, P. (1995). Social information filtering: Algorithms for automating word of mouth. *Proceedings of the SIGCHI Conference on Human Factors in Computing Systems,* New York, NY, 201–217.

Shoemaker, P. (1991). *Gatekeeping.* Newberry Park, CA: Sage.

Shoemaker, P., & Reese, S.D. (1996). *Mediating the message: Theories of influence on mass media content* (2nd Ed.). New York: Longman.

Shoemaker, P., & Vos, T.P. (2009). *Gatekeeping theory.* New York: Routledge.

Sigal, L.V. (1973). *Reporters and officials: The organization and politics of newsmaking.* Lexington, MA: DC Heath.

Smith, A. (2011). The Internet and campaign 2010. *Pew Internet and American Life Project.* Retrieved September 1, 2011, from http://www.pewinternet.org/Reports/2011/The-Internet-and-Campaign-2010.aspx

Smith, C. (2011). Osama Bin Ladin's death leaked via Twitter. *The Huffington Post.* Retrieved September 1, 2011, from http://www.huffingtonpost.com/2011/05/02/osama-bin-laden-death-twitter-leak_n_856121.html.

Sunstein, C. (2000). Deliberative trouble? Why groups go to extremes. *Yale Law Journal, 110*(1), 71–119.

_____. (2001). *Republic.com.* Princeton, NJ: Princeton University Press.

_____. (2002). The law of group polarization. *The Journal of Political Philosophy, 10*(2), 175–195.

_____. (2008). *Infotopia: How many minds produce knowledge.* Oxford: Oxford University Press.

_____. (2009). *Going to extremes: How like minds unite and divide.* Oxford: Oxford University Press.

Surowiecki, J. (2005). *The wisdom of crowds.* New York: Anchor Books.

Zuckerman, E. (2008). Citizen voices and the Mumbai attacks. *My Heart's in Accra.* Retrieved September 1, 2011, from http://www.ethanzuckerman.com/blog/2008/11/29/citizen-voices-and-the-mumbai-attacks/.

6

Why Contribute?

Motivations and Role Conceptions among Citizen Journalists

DEBORAH S. CHUNG *and* SEUNGAHN NAH

With the emergence of information communication technologies and their implementation into online news presentation, there has been a growth in citizens as journalists and their participation in the production of news (Schaffer, 2007). Many news sites today offer features for local citizens to submit news stories or photos, allowing news consumers to also have a say in what they consider to be meaningful news. According to a report from the Pew Internet & American Life Project (2006), 35 percent of adults have created content online, and more than half of teenagers 12–17 post their own Web content. Another recent Pew study reports that video-sharing sites, such as YouTube and Vimeo, are used by fully 71 percent of Americans (Pew Internet & American Life Project, 2011). The report also found that rural Internet users and online African-Americans and Hispanics are now just as likely to make use of these video-sharing sites as their urban/suburban and white counterparts. Furthermore, among the 100 major daily newspapers in the U.S., 58 percent have integrated user-generated content (e.g., comments, photos, videos and articles) into their news-making processes (The Bivings Group, 2006).

It is evident that a diversity of citizens are using an increasing array of electronic tools to participate in news creation, and even news professionals are becoming progressively more aware of the roles of citizen journalists (Nah & Chung, 2009). Such participatory activities by citizens challenge fundamental notions regarding journalistic objectivity. The sacred distinction between news and opinion is deeply etched into professional journalistic norms, practices and culture (Lichtenberg, 1991/1996; Soloski, 1989). However, the relevance of the age-old ideal of objectivity may be gradually eroding. In fact, citizens who do not have this objectivity orientation have often proved to be competent sources for contributing fresh and meaningful stories where the mainstream press were sometimes not readily available or failed to provide meaningful coverage (Chung, 2010; Kenix, 2009).

Embedded within the objectivity stance is the belief that detached journalistic authority benefits the public. For example, news people are trained to be the authoritative distributors of news. They follow specified practices in order to cover stories in a systematic manner on a timely deadline. The trained, professional journalist exhibits the signs of objectivity: balancing the views of various sources, using primarily expert and official sources, and adhering to the inverted pyramid structure.

At the same time many scholars claim that the traditional transmission-like business model of mainstream media has failed to encourage the public to engage in democratic practices and decision-making processes (Christians, Ferre, & Fackler, 1993). As Glasser (1984) argued almost three decades ago, objectivity is rooted in a positivist view that stresses a commitment to the supremacy of facts. However, this commitment, he said, impinges on the day's news because objectivity is biased in favor of the status quo (e.g., relying on the prominent and the elite as sources of information), and biased against independent thinking (e.g., following a mechanical methodology of reporting).

In the age of digital, interactive, and participatory journalism, the objectivity stance needs reassessment and reevaluation in order to more appropriately address the current climate of story telling. As such, citizen journalists are pushing these boundaries as they often contribute subjective news accounts that may sometimes be closer to the truth. Such "truth telling" can spark discussion and further citizen engagement in our democratic society.

Because of the potential to facilitate audience deliberation and participation in society, there has been steady enthusiasm regarding citizens' abilities to contribute to news gathering and distribution. Research is growing on the characteristics of citizen journalism news sites, the perceived credibility of these sites and the sourcing practices of citizen journalism sites (Carpenter, 2008; Johnson & Wiedenbeck, 2009; Lacy, Riffe, Thorson, & Duffy, 2009). However, scholars have yet to examine what drives citizens to act as journalists. Moreover, research is lacking on how their motivations for contributing news content relate to the development of citizen journalist role perceptions.

The fact is that citizen journalists increasingly blur the boundaries between objectivity and subjectivity and news and opinion. Accordingly, this chapter examines citizen journalists' motivations for contributing content, their perceived role conceptions and the relationship between these two variables. In exploring these questions, we examine the uses and gratifications literature on motivations to direct our investigation into why ordinary citizens participate in such reporting activities online. Additionally, we incorporate the literature on journalism role conceptions to investigate how these citizens perceive their roles when contributing online news content.

Traditional Media Concerns and New Media Promises

Media critics have characterized the traditional press as a vehicle of expert transmission rather than a network of community discussion (Christians et al., 1993). The delivery of objectively-viewed, observable facts has been a foundation of professionally-trained journalists. Further, critics point out that objective journalism is often disconnected from its optimal role within a democratic society. That is, instead of being the adversarial watchdog, the press tends toward supporting the status quo (Glasser, 1984). Critics have argued that the public will only begin "to reawaken when they are addressed as a conversational partner and are encouraged to join the talk rather than sit passively as spectators before a discussion conducted by journalists and experts" (Carey, 1987, p. 14). Many today believe that the emergent interactive technologies of news online could provide greater opportunities for traditionally neglected news audiences to participate as actively involved and engaged citizens. Nip (2006) called the recent movement toward citizen participation the second phase of public journalism, largely facilitated through the emergence of interactive electronic communication tools.

Rise and Prominence of Citizen Journalists

The news industry is undergoing massive change with the emergence of various interactive communication technologies. This transformation within the news industry is evident particularly in recent years with century-old news publications folding and many news outlets choosing to move online exclusively. For example, in order to adapt to a media climate teaming with Web 2.0 applications, news publications offer increased opportunities for audiences to participate in both news consumption and production (Chan-Olmsted & Park, 2000; Kenney, Gorelik, & Mwangi, 2000; Massey & Levy, 1999; Rosenberry, 2005; Schultz, 1999). A growing number of ordinary citizens have contributed their views as citizen reporters, delivering information to other members of their communities through interactive media technologies (Nah & Chung, 2009). According to the Knight Citizen News Network (http://www.kcnn.org/citmedia_sites/), there are more than 1,000 citizen media sites throughout all 50 states in the U.S. and other parts of North America.

While there is much anecdotal concern and debate over the quality of citizen-produced content, scholarly research on online citizen journalism publications is minimal. There are only a handful of studies examining the venues and activities related to citizen journalism topics. For example, Carpenter (2008) analyzed differences between online citizen journalism publications and online newspapers' content and found online daily newspaper journalists are more likely to stick to traditional journalistic routines than citizen journalists, who used more unofficial sources. Johnson and Wiedenbeck (2009) examined factors affecting perceived credibility of citizen journalism websites. They found that hyperlinks and information about the writer enhanced perceived story credibility. In another investigation, Lacy, Riffe, Thorson and Duffy (2009) examined the policies, citizen participation features, and means of financial support of citizen journalism sites. They found that these sites did not take advantage of the interactive capabilities of the Internet so as to encourage citizen participation.

In sum, a limited number of studies have examined citizen journalism venues. However, even less is known about citizen journalists themselves. More importantly, existing scholarship does not track sufficiently the factors that prompt them to participate in the journalistic activity of news reporting. This chapter offers an empirical study that addresses who these individuals are, and sheds light on their perceived functions and motives for contributing often subjectively-formed news accounts. With this study, we aim to uncover what meaningful truths these citizens intend to share with society, pointing to larger changes in what is considered news in the contemporary climate.

Reengaging the Audience and Journalism Role Conceptions

Research examining how journalists view their functions in American society has documented both areas of stability and evolution over decades (Johnstone, et al., 1976; Weaver, Beam, Brownlee, Voakes, & Wilhoit, 2007; Weaver & Wilhoit, 1986, 1996). The evolving role conceptions reflect changes in the journalism climate over time. However, queries regarding perceptions about news reporters' roles have generally been directed toward professional journalists and rarely toward news audiences. Recognizing the importance of better understanding news audiences' needs and perspectives, Heider,

McCombs and Poindexter (2005) examined audiences' perceptions of the news media's roles in a metropolitan area. In their study, respondents were asked to rate the roles of local news media and characteristics of news coverage regarding (1) reporting the widest range of news; (2) concentrating on certain topics; (3) providing a forum for community views; (4) being a watchdog of powerful people and the government; (5) highlighting interesting people and groups in the community; and (6) offering solutions to community problems. Respondents were also asked to rate the most important characteristic of news coverage they wanted among (1) accuracy; (2) rapid reporting; (3) understanding the local community; (4) unbiased reporting; (5) caring about your community; (6) being inclusive of different points of view; and (7) providing explanation of issues and trends. These responses from Heider et al.'s study were then compared to Weaver et al.'s most recent study (2007) on American journalists. Four areas were compared specifically: offering solutions, providing a community forum, being a watchdog, and rapid reporting. Results of Heider et al.'s study indicate that the audience does not endorse traditional journalistic roles, such as watch dog and rapid reporting, and was more likely to say that civic journalism (e.g., providing a community forum) was extremely important.

News professionals are also becoming more aware of the role of citizen journalists. In their study examining community newspaper editors' role conceptions along with their views of emerging citizen journalists' roles, Nah and Chung (2009) found that the perceived roles of professional journalists are positively correlated with their perceived roles of citizen journalists. In other words, community newspaper editors perceived citizen journalists' roles to be similar to their roles as professional journalists — although editors generally rated their roles to be significantly more important than their counterparts. More importantly, Chung and Nah (2009) found that use of citizen content contributions (i.e., news stories and photos), led to audiences' perceived satisfaction when visiting a community news site. These findings reflect the growing prominence of citizen journalists and the positive outcomes related to their news contributing activities.

Motives for Media Use in Computer-Mediated Contexts

The uses and gratifications perspective starts with the audience as the point of departure. Rather than asking questions about what the media do to people (Katz, 1959; Swanson, 1979), this conceptual framework focuses on how individuals actively seek media and media messages to satisfy their needs.

It assumes that individuals consume media in an effort to meet individual needs and goals. The uses and gratifications approach has been considered an appropriate theoretical framework because its principles are generally applicable to various mediated communication situations (Lin, 1999). However, ever since Morris and Ogan (1996) identified that this conceptual framework is a meaningful approach to studying the Internet, there has been greater enthusiasm about the applicability of uses and gratifications perspectives to new media.

With the prevalence and rapid development of various information communication technologies, Ruggiero (2000) observed that the traditionally passive media audience can now play the role of active communicator. And several media scholars have applied the uses and gratifications approach to various different contexts online, including the use of home computers, the Internet, the World Wide Web, electronic bulletin boards, personal homepages, and virtual communities (Cho, Gil de Zuniga, Rojas, & Shah, 2003; Ebersole, 2000; Ferguson & Perse, 2000; Flanagin & Metzger, 2001; James, Wotring, & Forrest, 1995; Kaye & Johnson, 2002; Papacharissi, 2002; Papacharissi & Rubin, 2000; Sangwan, 2005).

Among various new digital technologies, the literature on the motivations of blogging has significantly improved the understanding of new media use. For example, Nardi, Schiano and Gumbrecht (2004) proposed five primary reasons for blogging motivations: updating others on individual's activities, expressing opinions to others, seeking others' feedback, organizing ideas through writing, and releasing emotional tension. Papacharissi (2004) conducted a content analysis of random blogs and found bloggers to be primarily motivated by personal communication/interaction purposes. Trammell, Tarkowski, Hofmokl and Sapp (2006) examined Polish blogs and found them to be driven more by self-expression purposes than by social interaction. Li (2005) also identified seven motivations for blogging: self-documentation, improving writing, self-expression, medium appeal, information, passing time and socialization.

In sum, the literature addresses motivations for using various media, including newer media. Additionally, the literature points to motivations of individuals who act as both consumers of information and sources of information, such as bloggers. In this study, we similarly investigate citizens — however, these citizens also function as amateur journalists.

Rationale for Study

This study uses the measurements developed by scholars examining motivations for new media use, including blogs. These motivations can, in essence, influence why certain citizens may perceive and then subsequently take on specific conceptions regarding the functions of the news media. Thus, examining citizens' reasons for participating in content contributions can shed light on their conceptions of the roles they play as citizen journalists.

Based on the above literature review, this study aims to not only describe citizen journalists, their motives for contributing news content, and their role conceptions, but also explore the relationships between these variables. Thus, the following research questions are proposed:

RQ1: What are citizen journalists' motives for contributing news content?

RQ2: What are citizen journalists' perceptions regarding their roles as citizen journalists?

RQ3: What are the relationships between citizen journalists' motives for contributing news content and citizen journalists' role conceptions, if any?

Method

In this study, the term "citizen journalists" refers to ordinary citizens who often do not have professional journalism training but can contribute to the conversation of democracy by writing news accounts, posting comments to news stories, or expressing opinions in online news forums (whether on citizen news sites or on professional news sites). This study employs Friedland and Kim's (2009) conceptualization that focuses on the act of participating in democratic conversations with less emphasis placed on the quality of those communications. While this definition is broad, it aims to focus on citizen deliberations and exchange — stressing that meaning emerges in the very act of citizen participation.

The data for this study came primarily from three sources as there is no single complete list of citizen journalists. For sampling, we first referred to the list available at the Knight Citizen News Network. At the time this study was conducted, its website included a list of about 800 citizen media sites. We excluded any site that was a news aggregator or sites that were not functioning at the time. To increase the generalizability of the sample, we also conducted a Google search using the keywords "citizen journalism sites." This search resulted in four sources that were included for the current study.[1] In addition, we recruited citizen journalists contributing content to the U.S.'s top 100 mainstream newspaper organizations (see The Bivings Group, 2006).

In compiling the list of individual citizen journalists, we visited every site on the Knight Citizen News Network's list and identified every available citizen journalist's email. We did the same for those news organizations identified through the Google search. In total we compiled a list of 1042 sites in which 102 were duplicate listings, 425 were either not functioning or were not qualified for the study (e.g., news aggregator), and 107 of these sites qualified but did not have any contact information (no e-mail, no contact form).

Based on the above information, we developed a final list of 408 sites, and we targeted 556 individual e-mail addresses gathered from the three sources: 181 general e-mail addresses from news organizations, contact form pages from 73 sites, and editor contact information from the top 100 mainstream newspapers in the U.S. We also employed snowball sampling by enlisting help from those who had contacted us individually about our survey (Babbie, 2002). Some individuals offered to circulate our request to other citizen journalist listservs and organizations. The survey invitation e-mail was sent weekly, and the data was also collected through Qualtrics, a Web-based survey software. The survey was kept active for five weeks.

Although the population examined was not a random or representative sample, this semi-purposive approach was considered appropriate for this project (Nah, Veenstra, & Shah, 2006). As it is virtually impossible to identify all citizen journalists — an unspecified population in this case — representative sampling and generalization factors are not applicable for this type of study.

The survey consisted of a self-administered questionnaire that asked respondents about their news contributing activities, including the duration that they contributed content to citizen media sources. We also asked participants about their perceptions regarding citizen journalists and citizen media roles, their motives for contributing news content, and questions related to demographic characteristics.

A total of 215 individuals participated in the survey, and after identifying incomplete responses, the final sample resulted in 130 cases yielding a final response rate of 14.3 percent. This response rate is similar to those reported in other Web surveys (Couper, 2000; Porter & Whitcomb, 2003).

Measures

INDEPENDENT VARIABLES

Motivations. Respondents were asked to indicate their levels of agreement toward 37 measures of motivation adopted and modified from prior uses and gratifications literature (Kaye & Johnson, 2002; Ko, Cho, & Roberts, 2005; Li, 2005; Papacharissi & Rubin, 2000). This literature examined motivations for surfing the World Wide Web, using the Internet for political information, and blogging motivations. The response scale ranged from "strongly disagree" (1) to "strongly agree" (7). The items were then factor analyzed to create indices for the motivations. The index scores for each motivation were constructed by taking the mean of the individual items (Cronbach α ranging from .59 to .84; see Table 1).

DEPENDENT VARIABLES

Citizen journalist role conceptions. Weaver et al.'s (2007) most recent survey battery of 15 questions was used to measure citizen journalists' role conceptions. The response scale ranged from "not really important" (1) to "extremely important" (7). After assessing reliability of emerging factor structures (Cronbach α ranging from .72 to .91; see Table 2), they were summed and then averaged to construct variables representing different citizen journalists and citizen media roles.

Civic journalism index. Four research questions assessed perceptions of civic journalism (Weaver et al., 2007). These items were (1) conduct polls to learn citizens' priorities on issues, (2) convene meetings of citizens and leaders to discuss public issues, (3) make special efforts to motivate citizens to participate in decision making on public issues, and (4) make special efforts to include ordinary citizens as sources in public affairs stories. The response scale was the same as that of the role conception questions. After assessing reliability (Cronbach α = .75), the scale was produced by summing the four questions and then averaging them.

In assessing relationships between citizens' motivations for contributing news content and their role conceptions, a series of hierarchical multiple regressions were employed to assess how motivations, after controlling for demographic features, contributed to specific role conceptions. We found no high correlations among the independent variables, indicating there were no multicollinearity issues.

Results

The Sample. About 67 percent of the sample was male with 88 percent consisting of white participants. Approximately 23 percent of the participants earned between $50,000 and $74,999, and another 16 percent earned between $75,000 and $99,999. Further, 19 percent earned between $100,000 and $199,999 and about three percent earned more than $200,000. However, 14 percent earned less than $25,000 and 25 percent earned between $25,000 and $49,999. The participants were highly educated with 40 percent having graduated from college and 41 percent having completed a graduate or professional degree. The mean age of the respondents was 44 years old (SD = 13.04).

Table 1: Motivations for Citizens Contributing News Content.

Factors				Factor Loadings					
	1	2	3	4	5	6	7	8	9
Factor 1: Alternative perspectives (N = 124)									
Offer alternative viewpoints	**.83**	-.06	.09	.05	.08	-.06	-.03	-.06	-.05
Make a difference	**.75**	-.05	-.05	-.15	.10	.05	.06	.20	.26
Seek/search for truth	**.70**	.02	-.15	-.02	.09	.22	.16	.03	.23
Get more points of view	**.66**	-.10	-.01	.04	.08	.06	.27	.44	-.03
Fresh perspectives	**.64**	-.02	.34	.04	.04	-.14	.25	.08	-.05
Contribute something meaningful as citizen	**.62**	-.04	.18	-.10	.28	-.40	.01	.14	.06
Factor 2: Expression (N = 120)									
Tell others about myself	-.11	**.77**	.07	.30	-.01	.10	.14	.15	-.10
Show my personality	-.12	**.76**	.94	.15	-.02	-.07	.22	.12	-.03
Get my name out	-.002	**.68**	.21	.03	.19	.32	-.09	.23	.06
Tell others what to do	.06	**.65**	-.02	.26	.19	.15	.06	.00	-.16
Practice my writing	.01	**.65**	.19	.09	.13	.11	-.20	-.01	.21
Refine my thinking	.49	**.59**	.08	.02	-.03	-.06	-.15	-.04	.25
I like seeing my byline	-.06	**.50**	.37	-.12	.26	.19	-.22	.22	-.07
Factor 3: Entertainment (N = 119)									
I just like to do it	.08	.18	**.83**	-.01	-.002	.07	.20	-.01	.07
It is enjoyable	.08	.12	**.76**	.06	.33	.08	.02	.12	.31
It is entertaining	.05	.01	**.75**	.23	.29	-.10	.01	.29	.05
It is fun to try out new things	.04	.13	**.65**	.16	.10	-.10	-.09	.36	.08
I enjoy answering questions	.48	.12	**.60**	-.03	-.10	.14	.20	-.21	.05
It is a place to publish myself	-.07	.38	.51	.12	.38	.25	-.10	-.03	.04
Factor 4: Habit (N = 123)									
When I have nothing better to do	.01	.11	.02	**.85**	-.10	-.01	.01	-.10	-.02
To pass time when bored	-.06	.20	.03	**.81**	-.03	.04	-.02	.08	.11

It is a habit	.07	.22	.20	.58	.33	.18	-.03	.08	-.03
Occupy my time	-.10	.22	.24	.53	.03	-.03	-.13	.26	.04

Factor 5: Community (N = 124)

Feel like I am part of a community	.21	.08	.11	-.06	**.73**	-.10	.17	.21	.10
Feel like an active participant	.48	.17	.24	.01	**.67**	.01	-.08	-.02	.06
I like writing	-.07	.26	.31	-.03	**.53**	.37	.24	-.08	.24
Express myself freely	.50	.20	.23	.16	**.52**	-.16	.09	-.13	-.03

Factor 6: Duty (N = 124)

It is my job	-.06	.11	.02	.03	-.08	**.82**	.04	.15	.11
For payment	.06	.34	.08	.10	.09	**.69**	-.07	.25	-.23

Factor 7: Accessibility (N = 126)

I can access it wherever I am	.09	-.03	-.02	.01	.02	-.06	**.84**	.12	.10
I can publish at any time	.27	.07	.21	-.09	.17	.09	**.81**	-.10	.04

Factor 8: Innovation (N = 126)

Learn about new technologies/skills	.06	.25	.18	.02	.03	.23	.16	**.69**	.16
Meet new people	.27	.24	.22	.09	.06	.17	-.11	**.66**	.09

Factor 9: Information (N = 125)

Present information on my interests	-.04	.27	.20	.19	-.01	-.06	.03	-.03	**.71**
Share information useful to other people	.37	-.15	.03	-.07	.13	-.05	.19	.25	**.62**
Provide information	.28	-.20	.16	-.05	.15	-.08	.05	.15	**.61**

Eigenvalues	4.44	4.00	3.83	2.43	2.37	2.06	2.03	1.95	1.88
Variance Explained	11.99	10.82	10.34	6.56	6.42	5.58	5.50	5.27	5.08
Reliability (Cronbach α)	.84	.83	.83	.78	.82	.72	.79	.59	.59
Mean (S.D.)	5.44	3.21	5.02	2.11	5.43	3.21	5.15	4.26	5.82
	(1.12)	(1.40)	(1.26)	(1.33)	(1.36)	(1.95)	(1.43)	(1.55)	(.85)

Participants reported contributing content to news publications for an average of three years and nine months, or 45 months (SD = 35.89). About 76 percent of the sample was represented by individuals contributing content to citizen media organizations. Twenty-three percent said they contributed content to both citizen and professional news organizations.

Motivations for contributing news content. In order to assess why citizens contributed news content (RQ1), a principles component factor analysis was employed using Varimax rotation. Individual items that cross loaded on multiple factors or items with factor loadings lower than .60 were eliminated from the analysis. This yielded 10 factors, but one factor was composed of a single item, so that factor was dropped resulting in a total of nine factors. All factors had eigenvalues of at least one. The factors accounted for 67.56 percent of the variance after rotation. Nine indices were then created. As illustrated in Table 1, the nine motivations were labeled alternative perspectives, expression, entertainment, habit, community, duty, accessibility, innovation, and information. The motivation for "habit" yielded the lowest mean score (M = 2.11, SD = 1.33) whereas "information" yielded the highest (M = 5.82, SD = .85).

Citizen journalists' role conceptions. In order to assess citizen journalism role conceptions (RQ2), a subsequent principles component factor analysis was conducted. We followed the same procedures as when identifying factors for motivation. The analysis yielded three factors that all had eigenvalues of at least one. The three factors accounted for 49.81 percent of the variance after rotation. Three indices were then created. In creating the index for the adversary role, the item "set the political agenda" was not included as it did not fit conceptually. As illustrated in Table 2, the three roles were labeled interpreter, adversary, and mobilizer. The "adversary" role resulted in the lowest mean score (M = 5.12, SD = 1.64) whereas the "mobilizer" role resulted in the highest mean score (M = 6.20, SD = 1.14). In addition, Weaver et al.'s four questions measuring civic journalism values were used to develop the civic role index (M = 4.70; SD = 1.42).

Relationships between motivations and role conceptions. The third research question sought to identify relationships between motivations and role conceptions among citizen journalists (RQ3). Using the indices created through the factor analyses, a series of hierarchical multiple regression analyses was conducted. Table 3 illustrates the regression analyses on the five role conception variables.

Predictors of the interpreter role. This model accounted for about 32 percent of the variance in the dependent measure. When the nine motivation variables were added to the regression equation, the model was significantly improved, R^2 change = .20, p < .01. Education (β = -.28, p < .01) was a sig-

Table 2: Citizen Journalists' Role Conceptions.

Factors	*Factor Loadings*		
Factor 1: Interpreter (N = 126)	*1*	*2*	*3*
Provide analysis and interpretation of international developments	.84	.14	.01
Provide analysis and interpretation of complex problems	.76	.27	.03
Investigate claims and statements made by the government	.73	.34	.06
Discuss national policy while it is still being developed	.69	.28	.02
Get information to the public quickly	.54	-.18	.20
Factor 2: Adversary (N = 128)			
Be an adversary of businesses by being constantly skeptical of their actions	.22	.82	.07
Be an adversary of public officials by being constantly skeptical of their actions	.23	.81	.10
Set the political agenda	.09	.70	.05
Point people toward possible solutions to society's problems	.27	.46	.37
Factor 3: Mobilizer (N = 129)			
Give ordinary people a chance to express their views on public affairs	-.07	.10	**.84**
Motivate ordinary people to get involved in public discussions of important issues	.14	.15	**.84**
Stay away from stories where factual content cannot be verified	.37	-.41	.41
Eigenvalues	3.00	2.65	1.82
Variance Explained	19.98	17.68	12.15
Reliability (Cronbach α)	.84	.91	.72
Mean (S.D.)	5.14 (1.45)	5.12 (1.64)	6.20 (1.14)

nificant negative predictor suggesting that individuals who had a higher education were less likely to perceive the interpreter function as important. However, three motivation items also surfaced as predictors: entertainment (β = -.26, p < .05), accessibility (β = .23, p < .05) and information (β = .31, p < .01). Among the four predictors, standardized beta coefficients indicate that the information motivation was the strongest predictor for perceptions of the interpreter role, suggesting that citizen reporters who sought to share content were most likely to highly rate the importance of the interpreter role.

Predictors of the adversary role. This model accounted for about 21 percent of the variance in the dependent measure. The demographic characteristics were not significantly related to the adversary role. However, the addition of the nine motivation variables yielded the expression motivation as the sole significant positive predictor (β = 33, p < .05). In other words, citizen reporters who were motivated to express their viewpoints were more likely to highly rate the importance of the adversary role of citizen journalists.

Predictors of the mobilizer role. This model accounted for about 18 percent of the variance in the dependent measure. Gender was a significant negative predictor (β = -.26, p < .05), with women more likely to highly rate the importance of the mobilizer role of citizen journalists. However, the nine motivation variables did not significantly improve the model nor yield significant predictor variables.

Predictors of the civic role. This model accounted for about 44 percent of the variance in the dependent measure, which is the highest compared to the other four role conceptions. Two predictors surfaced: the alternative perspectives motivation (β = .48, p < .01) and the habit motivation (β = -17, p < .05). The model was, thus, significantly improved, R^2 change = .34, p < .01. Overall, citizen journalists who were motivated to actively seek new content perspectives were more likely to highly rate the importance of the civic role. Habit was a negative predictor, which suggests that contributors based on merely habitual activity were not likely to rate the civic role as a prominent function.

Discussion and Conclusions

The findings point to the various motivations and the perceptions citizens develop regarding their journalistic roles as they participate in the sharing and production of information and news content. The factor analysis of motivations revealed numerous reasons that citizens contributed news information with content-related motivations yielding the highest mean scores (alternative perspectives, information) and routine-related motivations yielding the lowest mean scores (habit, duty). In other words, those variables that sprung from need for cognition were the most prominent motivations. The mobilizer role was perceived to be the most prominent role conception for citizen journalists, and the interpreter role was considered to be the next most prominent role, although a distant second. And citizens' role conceptions of their news-contributing practices yielded somewhat different roles than those of their professional journalist counterparts. For example, literature on professional journalists' role conceptions shows that the adversary function is consistently a minority attitude among professional journalists (Weaver et al., 2007). However, in this sample, citizen journalists appeared to champion the adversary role almost as much as the interpreter role. In addition, civic journalism values, such as mobilizing citizens to engage and discuss public issues and including

Table 3: Hierarchical Regression Analysis of Factors Influencing Citizen Journalists' Role Conceptions.

Predictor variables	Interpreter	Adversary	Mobilizer	Civic
Age	.02	.10	-.09	-.12
Gender	-.03	-.19	-.26*	-.18
Education	-.28**	-.11	.04	-.13
Income	-.19	-.21	-.08	-.15
Incremental R^2	.12	.06	.08	.10
Motivation 1: Alternative perspectives.	.11	.07	.24	.48**
Motivation 2: Expression	.11	.33*	.04	.04
Motivation 3: Entertainment	-.26*	-.08	-.07	-.06
Motivation 4: Habit	-.15	-.06	-.11	-.17*
Motivation 5: Community	-.01	-.11	-.12	-.15
Motivation 6: Duty	.07	-.05	.02	.02
Motivation 7: Accessibility	.23*	.21	.12	.15
Motivation 8: Innovation	-.10	-.22	-.01	.11
Motivation 9: Information	.31**	.19	.11	.12
Incremental R^2	.20	.15	.10	.34
Total R^2	.32	.21	.18	.44
Adjusted R^2	.21	.09	.06	.36
Sig. change	.01	.10	.36	.00

citizens as news sources in public affairs stories, were not rated as highly-endorsed roles among this sample compared with findings from professional journalists.

We found that citizen journalists' motivations predicted the citizen journalists' perceptions of their roles. For example, accessibility and information motivations were positive predictors of the interpreter role. That is, individuals who placed value on flexibility and analytical content sharing were more likely to rate the citizen journalist interpreter role as important. This indicates that those who were more goal-oriented to seek content were more likely to develop the interpreter role.

The alternative perspectives and habit motivations were positive and negative predictors respectively for the civic role of the citizen journalist. It appears that participants who were actively seeking different and fresh content viewpoints and not merely contributing content habitually, or to pass time, rated citizen journalistic roles as important. That is, citizens who were highly motivated to seek alternative perspectives saw citizen journalists as having a vital role in facilitating conversations among citizens.

As a whole, this study examined individuals who take on active content-contributing roles that are disseminated as information to the public. These individuals are not trained professionally but partake in the journalistic act of reporting. Such content may often not follow standard reporting practices that underscore the importance of fair and balanced reporting. There may be bias that creeps into the accounts that are disseminated. However, Glasser (1984) suggested that news is biased, and it must inevitably be. Subjectivity is, thus, unavoidable. At times, it is valuable. This is counterintuitive to the traditional ideal of objectivity. In today's media climate, news audiences understand that the participatory nature of society and culture warrants a discussion of news, and consumers (or prosumers — those who both produce and consume news) may choose from a diversity of perspectives offered by both professionally-trained individuals and ordinary citizens.

When ordinary citizens engage in both news making and news consuming, objectivity as a foundation of all news is no longer valid. This is even true for professional journalists who act as engaged citizens in their communities. Nah and Chung (2011) found that community newspaper editors also function and participate as citizens of a community. As such, they participate in their community activities (e.g., community building, integration, change, etc.) and are civically-engaged individuals. Therefore, the journalistic value of "objectivity" can no longer be valid when it comes to coverage of citizen voices. What community newspaper editors cover reflects, and are colored by, their participatory activities and interactions with community members. Citizens who participate in contributing journalistic content function somewhat similarly to engaged editors. Today's media climate features the blurring of the lines between producer and audience; and the validity and necessity of objectivity is becoming increasingly less apparent. A discussion and realization of post-objectivity perspectives may be more appropriate for the present media environment as news professionals increasingly witness the dissemination of news by citizens acting as part-time news producers.

Nonetheless, this study has several limitations. First, although every effort was made to create an inclusive sample, this study is still limited in its scope because of its rather small sample size and the inherent limitations of an online survey. Second, the regression models explain 18 to 44 percent of the variance, but even so, a large portion of the variance is left unexplained — especially for the mobilizer role conception. Future studies should work to identify predictors of this variable to better understand what leads to the formation and perception of distinct citizen journalism role conceptions. Finally, the role conception questions employed in this study are derived from traditional notions of journalism. Future studies should consider developing a new list of questions based on perspectives from citizen journalists to more appropriately understand the potentially growing role they may perform in their news production and consumption activities.

Still, this study provides a distinctive look into the activities of citizen journalists who merge the traditionally separate roles of senders and receivers of information. As the interactive digital media climate is constantly in transition, so are the boundaries of what defines journalism and who is considered a journalist. This study offers insight into newly-emerging content contributors and hopes to direct attention to them as viable informational sources. It documents the growing roles and responsibilities citizen journalists assume as they participate in journalistic reporting activities that may potentially contradict the traditional journalistic norms of objectivity. Rather than existing independently of the facts, citizen journalists have moved beyond the role of passive spectator toward being an integral part of the very stories they share.

Chapter Notes

1. The keyword search yielded the following five Websites:

    1. http://www.sourcewatch.org/index.php?title=List_of_citizen_journalism_websites [source: sourcewatch];
    2. http://www.dmoz.org/News/Media/Participatory// [source: open directory project];
    3. http://www.kcnn.org/citmedia_sites/ [source: kcnn, new voices];
    4. http://www.cyberjournalist.net/news/002226.php [source: cyberjournalist.net <http://cyberjournalist.net>]; and
    5. http://www.camcorderinfo.com/content/Top-citizen-journalism-sites-to-upload-video-34626.htm.

References

Babbie, E. (2002). *The basics of social research*. Belmont, CA: Wadsworth.

The Bivings Group. (2006). The use of the Internet by America's newspapers. Retrieved September 1, 2011, from http://www.bivingsreport.com/campaign/newspapers06_tz-fgb.pdf

Carey, J. (1987, March/April). The press and the public discourse. *The Center Magazine*, 5, 14.

Carpenter, S. (2008). How online citizen journalism publications and online newspapers utilize the objectivity standard and rely on external sources. *Journalism & Mass Communication Quarterly*, 85(3), 531–548.

Chan-Olmsted, S., & Park, J. (2000). From on-air to online world: Examining the content and structures of broadcast TV stations' websites. *Journalism & Mass Communication Quarterly*, 77(2), 321–339.

Cho, J., Gil de Zuniga, H., Rojas, H., & Shah, D. (2003). Audience activity among users of the World Wide Web. *IT & Society, 1*(4), 46–72.

Christians, C., Ferre. J. P., & Fackler, P. M. (1993). *Good news: Social ethics and the press*. New York: Oxford University Press.

Chung, D. S. (2010). The newspaper meets the Internet. In M. Cupito & M. Farrell (Eds.), *Newspapers: A complete guide to the industry* (pp. 185–200). New York: Peter Lang.

Chung, D. S., & Nah, S. (2009). The effects of interactive news presentation on perceived user satisfaction of online community newspapers. *Journal of Computer-Mediated Communication, 14*(4). Retrieved September 1, 2011, from http://www3.interscience.wiley.com/cgi-bin/fulltext/122530870/HTMLSTART

Couper, M. R. (2000). Review: Web surveys. *Public Opinion Quarterly, 64*(4), 464-494.

Ebersole, S. (2000). Uses and gratifications of the Web among students. *Journal of Com-*

puter-Mediated Communication, 6(1). Retrieved September 1, 2011, from http://jcmc.indiana.edu/vol6/issue1/ebersole.html

Ferguson, D., & Perse, E. M. (2000). The World Wide Web as a functional alternative to television. *Journal of Broadcasting & Electronic Media, 44*(2), 155–174.

Flanagin, A. J., & Metzger, M. J. (2001). Internet use in the contemporary media environment. *Human Communication Research, 27*(1), 153–181.

Friedland, L. A., & Kim, N. (2009). Citizen journalism. In C. H. Sterling (Ed.), *Encyclopedia of Journalism* (pp. 297–302). Thousand Oaks, CA: Sage.

Glasser, T. (1984, February). Objectivity precludes responsibility. *The Quill,* 13–16.

Heider, D., McCombs, M., & Poindexter, P. M. (2005). What the public expects of local news: Views on public and traditional journalism. *Journalism & Mass Communication Quarterly, 82*(4), 952–967.

James, M. L., Wotring, C. E., & Forrest, E. J. (1995). An exploratory study of the perceived benefits of electronic bulletin board use and their impact on other communication activities. *Journal of Broadcasting & Electronic Media, 39*(1), 30–50.

Johnson, K. A., & Wiedenbeck, S. (2009). Enhancing perceived credibility of citizen journalism websites. *Journalism & Mass Communication Quarterly, 86*(2), 332–348.

Johnstone, J. W. C., Slawski, E. J., & Bowman, W. W. (1976). *The news people: A sociological portrait of American journalists and their work.* Urbana: University of Illinois Press.

Katz, E. (1959). Mass communication research and the study of popular culture: An editorial note on a possible future for this journal. *Studies in Public Communications, 2,* 1–6.

Kaye, B. K., & Johnson, T. J. (2002). Online and in the know: Uses and gratifications of the Web for political information. *Journal of Broadcasting & Electronic Media, 46*(1), 54–57.

Kenix, L. J. (2009). Blogs as alternative. *Journal of Computer-Mediated Communication, 14*(4). Retrieved September 1, 2011, from http://onlinelibrary.wiley.com/doi/10.1111/j.1083–6101.2009.01471.x/full

Kenney, K., Gorelik, A., & Mwangi, S. (2000). Interactive features of online newspapers. *First Monday, 5*(1). Retrieved September 1, 2011, from http://firstmonday.org/htbin/cgi-wrap/bin/ojs/index.php/fm/article/view/720/629

Ko, H., Cho, C.-H., & Roberts, M. S. (2005). Internet uses and gratifications: A structural equation model of interactive advertising. *Journal of Advertising, 34*(2), 57–70.

Lacy, S. R., Riffe, D., Thorson, E., & Duffy, M. (2009). Examining the features, policies, and resources of citizen journalism: Citizen news sites and blogs. *The Web of Mass Communication Research,* 15. Retrieved August 30, 2011, from http://wjmcr.org/

Li, D. (2005). Why do you blog: A uses-and-gratifications inquiry into bloggers' motivations. Unpublished master's thesis, Marquette University, Milwaukee, Wisconsin.

Lichtenberg, J. (1991/1996). In defense of objectivity. In J. Curran & M. Guerevitch (Eds.), *Mass media and society* (pp. 216–231). London: Edward Arnold.

Lin, C. A. (1999). Uses and gratifications. In G. Stone, M. Singletary, & V. P. Richmond (Eds.), *Clarifying communication theories: A hands-on approach* (pp. 199–208). Ames: Iowa University Press.

Massey, B., & Levy, M. (1999). Interactivity, online journalism, and English-language Web newspapers in Asia. *Journalism & Mass Communication Quarterly, 76*(1), 138–151.

Morris, M., & Ogan, C. (1996). The Internet as mass medium. *Journal of Communication, 46*(1), 39–50.

Nah, S., & Chung, D. S. (2009). Rating citizen journalists versus pros: Editors' views. *Newspaper Research Journal, 30*(2), 71–83.

_____, & _____. (2011). News editors' demographics predict their social capital. *Newspaper Research Journal, 32*(1), 34–45.

Nah, S., Veenstra, A. S., & Shah, D. V. (2006). The Internet and anti-war activism: A case study of information, expression and action. *Journal of Computer-Mediated Communication, 12*(1), 230–247. Retrieved September 1, 2011, from http://jcmc.indiana. edu/vol12/issue1/nah.html

Nardi, B. A., Schiano, D. J., & Gumbrecht, M. (2004, November). Blogging as social activity, or, would you let 900 million people read your diary? *Proceedings of the ACM conference on Computer Supported Cooperative Work* (pp. 222–231). New York: ACM.

Nip, J. Y. M. (2006). Exploring the second phase of public journalism. *Journalism Studies, 7*(2), 212–236.

Papacharissi, Z. (2002). The self online: The utility of personal home pages. *Journal of Broadcasting & Electronic Media, 46*(3), 346–368.

_____. (2004, May). The blogger revolution? Audiences as media producers. Paper presented at the annual meeting of the International Communication Association, New Orleans, LA.

Papacharissi, Z., & Rubin, A. (2000). Predictors of Internet use. *Journal of Broadcasting & Electronic Media, 44*(2), 175–196.

Pew Internet & American Life Project (2006). *User-generated content.* Retrieved September 1, 2011, from http://www.pewinternet.org/Presentations/2006/UserGenerated-Content. aspx

_____. (2011). *71% of online adults now use video-sharing sites.* Retrieved September 1, 2011, from http://www.pewinternet.org/Reports/2011/Video-sharing-sites.aspx.

Porter, S. R., & Whitcomb, M. E. (2003). The impact of contact type on Web survey response rates. *Public Opinion Quarterly, 67*(4), 579–588.

Rosenberry, J. (2005). Few papers use online techniques to improve public communication. *Newspaper Research Journal, 26*(4), 61–73.

Ruggiero, T. E. (2000). Uses and gratifications theory in the 21st century. *Mass Communication & Society, 3*(1), 3–37.

Sangwan, S. (2005). Virtual community success: A uses and gratifications perspective. *Proceedings of the 38th HICSS Conference, Hawaii.*

Schaffer, J. (2007). *Citizen media: Fad or the future of news?* Retrieved September 1, 2011, from http://www.j-lab.org/citizen_media.pdf

Schultz, T. (1999). Interactive options in online journalism: A content analysis of 100 U.S. newspapers. *Journal of Computer Mediated Communication, 5*(1). Retrieved September 1, 2011, from http://jcmc.indiana.edu/vol5/issue1/schultz.html

Soloski, J. (1989). News reporting and professionalism: Some constraints on the reporting of news. *Media, Culture & Society, 11*(2), 207–228.

Swanson, D. L. (1979). Political communication research and the uses and gratifications model: A critique. *Communication Research, 6*(1), 37–53.

Trammell, K. D., Tarkowski, A., Hofmokl, J., & Sapp, A. M. (2006). Rzeczpospolita Blogów [Republic of Blog]: Examining Polish bloggers through content analysis. *Journal of Computer-Mediated Communication, 11*(3). Retrieved September 1, 2011, from http:// jcmc.indiana.edu/vol11/issue3/trammell.html

Weaver, D. H., Beam, R. A., Brownlee, B. J., Voakes, P. S., & Wilhoit, G. C. (2007). *The American journalist in the 21st Century: U.S. news people at the dawn of a new millennium.* Mahwah, NJ: Lawrence Erlbaum.

Weaver, D. H., & Wilhoit, G. C. (1986). *The American journalist: A portrait of U.S. news people and their work.* Bloomington: Indiana University Press.

_____, & _____. (1996). *The American journalist in the 1990s: U.S. news people at the end of an era.* Mahwah, NJ: Lawrence Erlbaum.

7

Morality, the News Media, and the Public

An Examination of Comment Forums on U.S. Daily Newspaper Websites

SERENA CARPENTER *and*
ROBIN BLOM

Psychologists seek to identify how people develop morals. Morals are internal regulators for humans, and humans apply moral guides when they interact with others (Bandura, 1977, 2002; Rest, 1979). The press plays a primary role in the socialization of humans including the shaping of one's values in the United States (Dhavan, McLeod, & Lee, 2009). Journalists have been shown to use moral reasoning; however they have been known to use low to mid-level moral language when reaching out to the public (Barger, 2003; Coleman & Wilkins, 2002). It has been said that the news media are enforcers of the status quo by identifying as deviant those who are not part of the mainstream (Blanks Hindman, 1998; Kessler, 1984; Shoemaker & Cohen, 2006). Geographic communities tend to reflect the morals of powerful classes and institutions, and smaller newspapers often align themselves with the prevalent viewpoints of community leaders (Janowitz, 1967; Schudson, 1999).

Published opinion articles in newspapers are meant to push the buttons of the public (Hynds, 1990) and "act as a catalyst to trigger an existing predisposition" (Sloan, Wray, & Sloan, 1997, p. 7). To help promote a constructive dialogue, newspapers publish opinion articles so as to allow a wide range of voices to speak on issues in the news. In particular, published letters to the editor and editorials in newspapers are argued to be indicators of public opinion, allowing and encouraging ordinary citizens to be involved in public debates (Hynds, 1976; Perrin & Vaisey, 2008; Tarrant, 1957; Thorton, 1998).

New media technologies can help researchers more precisely understand how people react when presented with moral issues. Reporters and their audiences, not surprisingly, can differ in their perceptions of reality. Online comment forums on newspaper websites provide a unique opportunity to research opinion expression in real-world settings.

This study investigates whether the moral focus of an article sparks variations in responses from newspaper readers within comment forums. Issues of morality can affect behavior and emotions (Glover, Garmon, & Hull, 2011). Comments reflect engagement of individuals with the news media including their thoughts concerning issues published in the news media. This work analyzes a sample of individual comments (n = 2103) adjacent to opinion articles (editorials written by the editorial staff and letters to the editor) featured in 15 online U.S. daily newspapers.

Literature Review

MORALITY

Within a news publication, the presence of a moral frame in an opinion article may affect opinions expressed in an adjacent comment section. Gert's (2011) definition of morality asserts that

> the term "morality" can be used either descriptively to refer to some codes of conduct put forward by a society or some other group, such as a religion, or accepted by an individual for his or her own behavior; or normatively to refer to a code of conduct that, given specified conditions, would be put forward by all rational persons [para. 1].

Morality fuses the individual with particular groups and the wider society. Morals serve as a guide for how one should behave and relate to others. Morals are typically taught to children in the form of do's and don'ts; as one grows older, society, peers, and mentors become more influential in guiding behavior (Janoff-Bulman, Sheikh, & Hepp, 2009).

A challenge to one's moral convictions can create self-inconsistency, which can lead to interpersonal conflict. To restore one's self-image, research has shown one will distance oneself from attitudinally-dissimilar people or react aggressively toward people who do not align with one's moral beliefs (Skitka, Bauman, & Sargis, 2005). In the comment section, morally-laden articles should, hypothetically, receive more hostile reaction. People who morally judge make quick, automatic justifications, known as moral stands, rather than offering thoughtful responses (Haidt, 2001; Skitka & Mullen, 2002).

Researchers in the field of communication have customarily focused on the examination of one moral issue at a time without fully attempting to dissect the construct of morality. Individuals' self-expressive stands tend to focus on specific issues, rather than broadly defining morality (Skitka & Mullen, 2002). Moral issues studied in the field of communication have included abortion, presidential elections, the environment, interracial marriage, whether children with AIDS should attend public school, equal rights for homosexuals, school prayer, genetically modified food, and whether the U.S. should declare English as the official language (Gonzenbach, 1994; Jeffres, Neuendorf, & Atkin, 1999; McDonald, Glynn, Kim, & Ostman, 2001; Neuwirth & Frederick, 2004; Salmon & Neuwirth, 1990; Scheufele, Shanahan, & Lee, 2001). Researchers have argued that an issue must be morally-laden in order for the spiral of silence theory to take effect (Noelle-Neumann, 1985). In this particular line of research, investigators have found people will contribute information to controversially moral conversations if they perceive that their contributions are in the majority; conversely, if they see that they are in the minority, they will remain silent and, perhaps, accommodate their opinions to those in the majority (Noelle-Neumann, 1984/1993).

Some framing researchers have looked at the presence of moral frames within articles. Moral frames are often defined by recording the presence of morals or social prescriptions present within an article (de Vreese, 2005; Neuman, Just, & Crigler, 1992). Communication researchers have also investigated how entertainment media influences moral reasoning. Exposure to sexual and violent content has been found to affect children's moral judgments. Most research in this area asks participants to rate whether acts by a character were justified or what aspects of characters influence perceptions (Glover, Garmon, & Hull, 2011; Hartman & Vorderer, 2010; Krcmar & Viera, 2005).

TRADITIONALIST VS. RIGHTS CONCERNS

Conflict occurs because people differ in their conceptualizations of moral behavior (Haidt & Graham, 2007; Janoff-Bulman, Sheikh, & Baldacci, 2008). Based on psychological and philosophical literature, morality can be divided into two broad categories: (1) traditionalists and (2) rights proponents. Some people perceive morality as adherence to traditions and norms, while others form judgments of morality based on principles of justice, fairness, and equal rights. Differences in whether one should emphasize community versus individual rights can result in conflict about what should be classified as moral behavior (Shweder & Haidt, 1993).

Traditionalists perceive moral behavior as acting to preserve values or ideals that society has handed down from previous generations. According to this group, the reestablishment of community cohesiveness is key in restoring morality. These duty-based believers are more concerned with challenges to status quo, divinity, community, sacredness, and authority. Traditionalists tend to idealize the ways of times past, and place a significant emphasis on local community and family values (Etzioni, 1993; Haidt & Graham, 2009; Putnam, 2000; Turiel, 2002). Social psychologist Jonathan Haidt (2008) stated, "We need to live in moral order that is created by shared stories and that offers beliefs about who we are, what we ought to do, and what is sacred" (p. 65). The traditionalist perspective emphasizes that interdependence and limitations of choice bind people to each other. In contrast, rights proponents are more concerned with human welfare and individualism. Rights proponents see morality in terms of equality and justice, emphasizing the need to deviate from traditional values when individuals are not given equal rights (Bellah, et al., 1985; Turiel, 2002).

Methodology

This study examined whether the presence of morality in opinion articles affects variations in comments within newspaper forums. Due to the vagueness and the culturally-bound perceptions of the concept of morality, opinion articles were coded for attributes related to the concept of morality. For the purposes of this study, articles were coded for whether the writer focused the opinion article on preserving (1) the rights of individuals or (2) tradition. Then, the study examined comment sections to see how people reacted to the presence of morality in these opinion pieces.

Dependent Variables

Online Comments. Comments adjacent to opinion articles present an opportunity for users to engage in interpersonal discussions on newspaper websites. In the past, the mass media represented "one-sided, indirect, public forms of communication, thus contrasting threefold with the most natural form of human communication, the conversation" (Noelle-Neumann, 1984/1993, p. 154). The mass media's approach to communicating made humans feel helpless, and loathe to speak out, said Noelle-Neumann.

Today, the presence of online comments allows researchers to examine users in naturally occurring, non-mass-media settings. Research comparing computer-mediated environments to face-to-face has shown people are more willing to speak out online than in interpersonal conversation (Ho & McLeod, 2008). The ability to cloak one's identity online has emboldened many people to voice their thoughts while often disregarding the etiquette usually present in face-to-face discussions (McDevitt, Kiouis, & Wahl-Jorgensen, 2003). Some newspaper editors have expressed concerns related to comments from citizens adjacent to articles. Online comment forums on news websites have been characterized as hostile opinion environments (Koop & Jansen, 2009; Memmott, 2011; O'Sullivan & Flanagin, 2003; Papacharissi, 2004). Commenting users can attack people for their opinions and, through negative textual comments, diminish participation from those in less extreme or vocal camps (Brauer, 2009; Nienaber, 2008).

Most online newspapers allow users to comment on articles (Domingo et al., 2008). Recent research has found that nearly 50 percent of U.S. newspaper editors monitor discussion forums daily (Lowrey & Woo, 2010). Comments can increase the number of page views, story tips, and accuracy (Kim, 2009). Hermida and Thurman (2008) interviewed United Kingdom news organization leaders in 2006 about their perceptions of user-generated content, which included comments on stories. They found news sites increased the number of opportunities to comment over an 18-month period and two-thirds of the 12 sites moderated comments before publication. Rosenberry (2010) found that the commenting users on U.S. daily newspapers are loyal readers, older, male residents of their community newspaper, and they perceive that participation in forums helps them understand community issues. However, Singer's (2009) study of comments on a Scottish newspaper found that only a vocal few participate.

Historically, the consumption of news media content has been used for social discourse (Scheufele, 1999). Opinion expression is important because it promotes the development of one's individual stances on issues. Citizens can process information better, and they are more likely to engage in participatory behavior, if they can share their thoughts with other people (Pitkin & Shumer, 1982).

Domingo et al. (2008) found that newspapers believe that their sites' comment sections should be oriented toward debates on current events. Interestingly, interviews with online political message board users found participants preferred to exchange information with people with dissimilar viewpoints (Galley-Stromer, 2003). In fact, online public discussions have several advantages over face-to-face situations. They can minimize status differences, promote honest expression, reduce fear of retribution, and encourage the exchange of new and more ideas among online users (Connolly, Jessup, & Valacich, 1990; Ho & McLeod, 2008; McKenna & Bargh, 1998; White & Dorman, 2001). However, the ability to cloak one's identity online has emboldened many people to disregard etiquette usually present in face-to-face discussions (McDevitt, Kiouis, & Wahl-Jorgensen, 2003). Collective behavior theorist Gustave Le Bon argued that the cloaking of an identity encourages people to behave as though they are in a crowd; in such a setting, disruptive behavior can be contagious (Le Bon, 1895/2002). Data analysis of this sample indicated that only five percent of the commenting users provided a full name, and those might be pseudonyms. Some news organizations are pushing commenting users to connect their true identities with their comments, rather than using fake identities. For example, some news outlets make users register their credit card information or connect comment registration with users' Facebook or Twitter IDs (Kiesow, 2010).

Comment Variations. Each posting was evaluated for the presence or absence of informational attributes. We coded for informational exchange, which is a distinct form of social support. Social support is a multifaceted concept (Wilcox & Vernberg, 1985). It is the idea that people give assistance to each other through emotional and tangible means during times of need. Social support research has focused primarily in the area of health communication and psychology especially in online health communities where users share information to cope with similar ailments (Buis, 2007, 2008; Cutrona, et al., 2007). So, we examined whether comments were informational — that is, whether they attempted to provide actual information to people in need of assistance.

This research also examined whether contributions were uncivil. Online comments on newspaper sites have been said to consist of mostly attacks (Nienaber, 2008). This research looked to literature on flaming to define uncivil information. Flaming consists of textual attacks intended to offend either people or organizations. They are often in the form of profanity and associated hostile language (O'Sullivan & Flanagin, 2003; Reinig, Briggs, & Nunmaker, 1998; Reinig & Megias, 2004).

HYPOTHESES

The goal was to determine how variations in the moral focus of an article are related to variations in online comments. Hypothetically, moral issues should lead to more uncivil online comments. It is difficult to be "correct" on a moral issue (Noelle-Neumann, 1985). The willingness to speak out in the face of opposition is related to whether a commenter perceives the other side as good or bad. People with strong moral convictions can treat their beliefs as matters of fact and, when faced with opposition, they tend to defend their beliefs (Bandura, 2002). Therefore, the hypotheses tested for this study are:

H1: Comments adjacent to opinion articles that are morally-laden will be significantly more uncivil than those comments adjacent to nonmoral articles.

H2: Comments adjacent to opinion articles that are morally-laden will be significantly less informational than those comments adjacent to nonmoral articles.

SAMPLE

The data came from 15 daily newspapers during a month-long period (April 7 to May 4) in 2009. Each night, between 8 P.M. and 11:59 P.M. eastern time (ET), two coders downloaded all opinion articles from the newspaper websites. Both the newspaper download schedule for the entire month and the download order each night were randomly selected.

SAMPLING PROCEDURE

Eighty newspapers were randomly selected from a list of 190 dailies for which the Audit Bureau of Circulations (ABC) provides statistical information regarding the number of newspaper website visitors. Newspaper outlets from the three largest metropolitan areas were removed (Chicago, Los Angeles, and New York) because those news media markets are atypical in potential audience size and competition level. The overwhelming majority of U.S. dailies are not published in such large metropolitan areas where multiple newspaper outlets — within the city and the suburbs — are competing for attention, while contending with a wide variety of broadcast organizations as well. Twenty newspapers were excluded because they did not have comments during the examined time period, leaving 60 dailies.

To make the project more manageable, three more steps were taken to reduce the number of opinion articles and comments to be analyzed. First, the newspapers were divided into categories based on circulation size: (1) more than 170,000 (large), (2) 50,001–170,000 (medium), and (3) 50,000 or less (small) (St. Cyr, Carpenter, & Lacy, 2010). Second, newspapers were selected that had *both* staff editorials and letters to the editor within the sampled time period. Third, we chose newspapers based on their geographical diversity. Each state was limited to one newspaper, and all of the U.S. regions were represented (U.S. Census Bureau, n.d.). We began by coding one randomly selected Northeast, South, West, and Midwest paper from the final sample; and continued to follow the same pattern when coding the remaining newspapers. This approach produced 15 U.S. online newspapers representing 15 different states (Norwich, CT; Des Moines, IA; Casper, WY; Lima, OH; Rochester, NY; Lakeland, FL; Boise City, ID; Vallejo, CA; Lebanon, PA; Detroit, MI; Spokane, WA; Greenville, NC; Nashville, TN; Boulder, CO; and Elizabethtown, KY). Each region was represented: Northeast (3), Midwest (3), West (5), and South (4). This sampling procedure resulted in 215 letters to the editor and editorials with 2,103 comments. The number of comments per newspaper ranged from 12 to 652. The mean number of comments per article was 37.5 with a standard deviation of 40.7 comments.

CODING CATEGORIES

Independent Variable. Coders were instructed to categorize articles as to their moral focus: traditionalist, rights-focused or "neither/can't tell." Traditionalists tend to idealize times past, and place a significant emphasis on local community and family values. Key terms included loyalty, community, tradition, respect, authority, and sanctity. For example, one reader of the *Des Moines Register* was furious that Governor Chester Culver did not "back a constitutional amendment to ban homosexual marriage in the state of Iowa" (Meyers, 2009). Another reader of the *Register* was opposed to legislation that would make it easier for teenagers to obtain contraception:

> How could it even be considered to make available such a pill without a prescription for girls as young as 17? That's just asking for trouble. I completely agree with the critics saying that Plan B will promote promiscuity because any girl can go to the nearest Walgreens to get these pills. Many teens have already started having sex, and this pill is an easy way out that could serve as an incentive to have sex more often [Cashman, 2009].

Rights advocates are more likely to deviate from traditional standards when individuals are not given equal rights. Key terms included fairness, justice, welfare, equal rights, individual, and access. For instance, the editorial board of the *Rochester Democrat and Chronicle* opposed torture and near-torture of detainees by the CIA during the George W. Bush administration. It stated that several terrorism suspects were denied "basic legal rights, to skirt international standards regarding prisoners of war" ("Memos show," 2009). Another example is a letter to the editor published by the *Vallejo Times Herald*, in which a writer wrote,

> I just don't understand what the big hoopla is with same-sex marriages! First of all I am not gay. And I am Christian by faith! People should be able to exercise a certain degree of freedom of choice, within considerable reason, especially in a country that so adamantly promotes separation of church and state [Napier, 2009].

Finally, coders categorized a piece as "neither/can't tell" if the article was not focused on a rights or traditionalist concern.

Dependent Variables. The researchers operationally defined informational exchanges based on research conducted on online communities (Cutrona, 1990; House, Kahn, McLeod, & Williams, 1985; Klemm, Reppert, & Visich, 1998; White & Dorman, 2000).

Informational Exchange. A comment was categorized as an informational exchange if it included answers to a question. Some were clearly placed within the question and answer format:

> *Question*: Erika — where does the EFCA claim: 'if a union collects signed cards from more than 50 percent of workers, there can be a forced unionization without

a secret ballot?' *Answer:* From the full text of the Employee Free Choice Act of 2009, SEC. 2. Streamlining Union Certification ["pro-union active positive," 2009].

Informational exchanges also included the questioning of the accuracy of a commenting user, the news media, or the article writer. Typical of such exchanges: "As usual, the *Star-Tribune* editorial board is off base" ("BLM should follow," 2009) and "Sadly, like most media outlets, the DR has chosen to attack those who do not buy into Obama Mania" ("Tax day," 2009). Other types of informational exchanges included hyperlinks to another source or the posting of information related to the article.

Uncivil Exchange. This research looked to literature on flaming in computer-mediated communication to define uncivil comments. Flaming consists of textual attacks intended to offend either people or organizations. They are often in the form of profanity and personal attacks (Reinig, Briggs, Nunmaker, 1998; Reinig & Megias, 2004). A comment was uncivil if it included one or more of the following: a negative character attack toward the writer (e.g., "This editorial is written by a complete idiot"), a negative character attack toward the media (e.g., "The *Free Press* does not know what it is talking about, as usual"), a negative character attack toward another commenter, profanity, or racial slurs (e.g., "This comment shows you are dumb and clueless"). In addition, if the comment included all caps, or an exclamation point with a conflict statement, it also was coded as uncivil (e.g., "I will be glad when this MORON shuts up!!!").

Coder reliability. To establish intercoder reliability, two graduate student coders coded 10 percent (n = 200) of the comments. Scott's Pi computation was selected for the nominal-level variables. Intercoder reliability ranged from .89 to 1.0.[1]

Results

Posters commented more often on traditionalist (27.9 percent) issues rather than rights (19.8 percent) issues. Overall, of the 2,103 comments examined, posts adjacent to the opinion articles varied in comment focus with 30.5 percent containing uncivil information and 43.6 percent containing informational exchanges. The primary goal of this research was to determine whether there was a relationship between the presence of morality within an article and the presence of informational and uncivil exchanges. The results are essentially descriptive due to the inability of researchers to collect a representative sample of all comments on all U.S. daily newspapers.

H1: predicted that comments adjacent to opinion articles that focus on morally-laden concerns would be significantly more uncivil than nonmoral articles. A difference in proportions test supported this hypothesis (p < .01). Commenting users were more likely to share uncivil exchanges on morally-laden articles (34.9 percent) than on nonmoral articles (26.5 percent).

H2: predicted that comments adjacent to opinion articles that focus on morally-laden concerns would contain less information than comments adjacent to nonmoral articles. A difference in proportions test showed no significant difference. Commenting users who commented on morally-laden articles (44.3 percent) were slightly more likely to share information in comment posts than on nonmoral articles (43.0 percent).

Table 1: Presence of Uncivil and Informational Comments Adjacent to Moral Articles.

Comment Type	*Morally-laden* n = 1003	*Nonmoral* n = 1100
Uncivil*	34.9%	26.5%
Informational	44.3%	43.0%

*difference in proportions test, p < .01

Discussion and Conclusion

It was expected that issues of morality would motivate commenting users of newspaper websites to contribute more uncivil comments. And it was significantly found that commenting users did post more uncivil comments adjacent to morally-laden than nonmoral articles. However there was no significant difference between morally-laden and nonmoral articles and the presence of adjacent informational comment posts.

Comments reflect public outspokenness or the willingness to express oneself. To comment online requires motivation; the sample reflects people who are willing to comment on opinion articles. It is unclear what precisely motivates people to participate online (Scheufele, 1999). However, slightly more than 40 percent of comments were in the form of information. For instance, *Des Moines Register* reader *sanityindesmoines* contributed to a discussion by pointing out to another forum user (*aprico*) that a specific court ruling had a 7–2 decision, rather than a 5–4 decision, as initially was claimed by another participant. Furthermore, *aprico* also explained what the ruling has meant for restrictions on abortion in Iowa ("Don't allow tyranny," 2009). The finding from this sample regarding the proportion of information present in the comment section is promising for newspapers because they have been concerned over the perceived negativity present in comment forums. Perhaps, the negative information distracts newspaper editors from recognizing the value of the comment section (Austin, Bolls, Pinkleton, & Goehner, 2005). People in comment forums may function as a community and/or they may function as information disseminators helping others to better understand issues. Additional data analysis of this sample reveals that citizens use the space to engage in discussion with others, with more than 53 percent of comments responding to other posters. Historically, there has been an expectation that the news media create forums to expand public deliberation on important societal issues (Commission on Freedom of the Press, 1947). Our study shows that there is great potential to engage people in issues on news forums. If news organizations choose to interact with participants, they may be able to fulfill this function of encouraging public dialogue.

For the most part, people's everyday interactions tend not to be oppositional in nature (Mutz, 2006). Newspapers have historically sought to engage readers by publishing issues that will encourage the rise of emotions within individuals (Hynds, 1984; Wahl-Jorgensen, 2004). The presence of moral principles within articles suggests that writers are likely either encouraging social change or, conversely, urging the maintenance of the status quo. The idea that opinion articles seek to encourage social control or social change needs to be further explored. Do variations in publication type, writer, or community structure relate to the morals emphasized by the news media? Our research is a start toward raising these kinds of questions as regards using morality within opinion articles. We find that people do respond to issues of morality. Should the media acknowledge their inclusion of moral principles and encourage conversations that center on citizens' values? If journalists, or posters hosted by the news site, present calls to action or inaction, will citizens attack the press for fostering such views or perceive them as less credible? This research shows that citizens react — and some do respond uncivilly — when morals are present. However, despite this potential for reader incivility and the likelihood for related damage to journalism's credibility, a conscious attempt by journalists to address morals inherent in some news frames may inspire people to participate in civic life.

Furthermore, although this sample shows that the presence of morality in opinion articles can provoke negative responses from the online public, it does not automatically suggest that newspapers should prevent and/or sanitize comments near morally-laden articles. In fact, Hurrell (2005) argued against measures to encourage civil/polite conversation because it is a form of censorship that inhibits the potential benefit of discussing controversial issues. The hope is that the online environment will transform into a town hall, (Bentivegna, 2002), where people gather online to discuss how to create change in the physical world (Rheingold, 1991, 2002). News media publications can serve as a microphone for the public through online comment forums. This is because people are likely more able to voice their opinion without suffering attacks on the credibility of their contributions or fear of being cast out from their community when venting about such issues. It may be more difficult for journalists to create dialogue around morally-laden topics, but not impossible. For example, news organizations could strategically place local journalists in community forums around issues of local concern and ask experts to contribute their analysis of such topics to encourage more reflective discussions and discourage the exchange of misinformation or incivility.

Schudson (1978) argued that humans — journalists included — socially filter their interpretations of facts. Just because technological changes can allow journalism to facilitate human interaction online does not mean such a development would be seamless for today's news media. Mindich (1998) explained:

> With so many storytellers trying to tell stories (the Internet alone has millions of sources of news), and with so many departing from the "information model" of "objective" news, journalists once again must attempt to define their craft [p. 5].

By providing online discussion forums, the press calls into question its traditional notions of gatekeeping and objectivity. The traditional news media have attempted to be objective observers who disseminate or interpret facts for the public (Bleyer, 1918; Johnstone, Slawski, & Bowman, 1976). Prior to electronic discussion forums, reporters and editors were responsible for what was published in their newspaper. Even though newspapers have traditionally published public opinion, the editors still possessed the privilege of selecting the content that was printed and placed online. Editorial controls can still be placed upon online discussion forums (and some newspapers delete certain messages that they regard as impolite and offensive), but the existence of the forum implies that everyone with an Internet connection can have their viewpoints presented in debates. The existence of the forums moves journalism away from an overreliance on an objectivity orientation that presents facts as clearly separated from values.

Perhaps the change from gatekeeper to soapbox may not be so radical. After all, in the name of objectivity, "the cornerstone of the professional ideology of journalism," reporters often present competing truth claims without taking a particular side (Lichtenberg, 2000, p. i). Yet, by selecting some sides, but not others (which is often necessary because of space constraints and other priorities) reporters certainly take sides. Some sides are considered more legitimate to report than others, with some other viewpoints consigned to a journalistic black hole.

In contrast, opening the discussions to anyone to participate — and loosening the news media's gatekeeping authority — provides the opportunity for more diverse discussions of public affairs. Indeed, the involved news-consuming public, which this study measures as commenting users, appears to relate, and react, to material presented by the news media. They turn to journalism — through the comments section — as a conduit for social interaction concerning issues they find meaningful. And this points to a valuable lesson for a post-objective press: journalists must realize that the public wants to connect to news content. And news workers can start addressing this by responding to commenters and integrating their contributions into the wider news frame so as to encourage news consumer loyalty and issue involvement.

Chapter Notes

1. Morality (.90); Commenter Transparency (.92); Uncivil (.86–1.0); Informational (.99–1.0).

References

Austin, E., Bolls, P., Pinkleton, B., & Goehner, D. (2005, May). *Processing political advertising: The roles of audio and visual information.* Paper presented at the annual meeting of the International Communication Association, New York, NY. Retrieved May 15, 2010, from http://www.allacademic.com/meta/p14724_index.html

Bandura, A. (1977). *Social learning theory.* New York: General Learning Press.

_____. (2002). Selective moral disengagement in the exercise of moral agency. *Journal of Moral Education, 31*(2), 101–119.

Barger, W. (2003). Moral language in newspaper commentary: A Kohlbergian analysis. *Journal of Mass Media Ethics, 18*(1), 29–43.

Bellah, R. N., Madsen, R., Sullivan, W. M., Swidler, A., & Tipton, S. M. (1985). *Habits of the heart: Individualism and commitment in American life.* New York: Harper & Row.

Bentivegna, S. (2002). Politics and new media. In L. A. Lievrouw & S. Livingstone (Eds.), *Handbook of new media: Social shaping and consequences of ICTs* (pp. 50–61). Thousand Oaks, CA: Sage.

Blanks Hindman, E. (1998). Spectacles of the poor: Conventions of alternative news. *Journalism & Mass Communication Quarterly, 75*(1), 177–193.

Bleyer, W. G. (1918). Introduction. In W. G. Bleyer (Ed.), *The profession of journalism: A collection of articles on newspaper editing and publishing, taken from the Atlantic Monthly.* (pp. ix–xxiii). Boston: The Atlantic Monthly Press.

BLM should follow state's lead on grouse. (2009, April 30). *Casper Star-Tribune.* Retrieved April 30, 2009, from http://trib.com

Brauer, D. (2009, July 22). Newspapers take renewed aim at the comment cesspool. *MinnPost.com.* Retrieved May 9, 2011, from: http://www.minnpost.com/braublog/2009/07/22/10410/newspapers_take_renewed_aim_at_the_comment_cesspool/

Buis, L. R. (2007). Online social support and cancer: Understanding the impact of survival rate, gender and different community characteristics (Doctoral dissertation). Retrieved from ProQuest Dissertations and Theses. (Publication No. 3264147).

_____. (2008). Emotional and informational support messages in an online hospice support community. *Computers, Informatics, Nursing, 26*(6), 358–367.

Cashman, K. (2009, April 17). Access to plan b will tempt teens. *Des Moines Register.* Retrieved April 17, 2009, from http://www.desmoinesregister.com

Coleman, R., & Wilkins, L. (2002). Searching for the ethical journalist: An exploratory study of the moral development of news workers. *Journal of Mass Media Ethics, 17*(3), 209–225.

Commission on Freedom of the Press. (1947). *A free and responsible press.* Chicago: University of Chicago Press.

Connolly, T., Jessup, L. M., & Valacich, J. S. (1990). Effects of anonymity and evaluative tone on idea generation in computer-mediated groups. *Management Science, 36*(6), 689–703.

Cutrona, C. E. (1990). Stress and social support: In search of optimal matching. *Journal of Social and Clinical Psychology, 9*(1), 3–14.

Cutrona, C. E., Shaffer, P. A., Wesner, K. A., & Gardner, K. A. (2007). Optimal matching support and perceived spousal sensitivity. *Journal of Family Psychology, 21*(4), 754–758.

de Vreese, C. (2005). News framing: Theory and typology. *Information Design Journal + Document Design, 13*(1), 51–62.

Dhavan, S.V., McLeod, J. M., & Lee, N. (2009). Communication competence as a foundation for civic competence: Process of socialization into citizenship. *Political Communication, 26*(1), 102–117.

Domingo, D., Quandt, T., Heinonen, A., Paulussen, A., Singer, J. B., & Vujnovic, M. (2008). Participatory journalism practices in the media and beyond: An international comparative study of initiatives in online newspapers. *Journalism Practice, 2*(3), 326–342.

Don't allow tyranny; let the people vote. (2009, April 17). *Des Moines Register.* Retrieved April 17, 2009, from http://www.desmoinesregister.com

Etzioni, A. (1993). *The spirit of community: The reinvention of American society.* New York: Touchstone.

Galley-Stromer, J. (2003). Diversity of political conversation on the Internet: Users' perspectives. *Journal of Computer-Mediated Communication, 8*(3). Retrieved May 9, 2011, from http://jcmc.indiana.edu/vol8/issue3/stromergalley.html/

Gert, B. (2011). The definition of morality. In E.N. Zalta (Ed.), *The Stanford encyclopedia of philosophy (Summer 2011 Edition).* Retrieved May 9, 2011 from, http://plato.stanford.edu/archives/sum2011/entries/morality-definition/

Glover, R. J., Garmon, L. C., & Hull, D. M. (2011). Media's moral messages: Assessing perceptions of moral content in television programming. *The Journal of Moral Education, 40*(1), 89–104.

Gonzenbach, W. J. (1994). Children with AIDS attending public school: An analysis of the spiral of silence. *Political Communication, 11*(1), 3–18.

Haidt, J. (2001). The emotional dog and its rational tail: A social intuitionist approach to moral judgment. *Psychological Review, 108*(4), 814–834.

_____. (2008). Morality. *Perspectives on Psychological Science, 3*(1), 65–72.

Haidt, J., & Graham, J. (2007). When morality opposes justice: Conservatives have moral intuitions that liberals may not recognize. *Social Justice Research, 20*(1), 98–116.

_____. (2009). Planet of the Durkheimians, where community, authority, and sacredness are foundation of morality. In J. Jost, A.C. Kay, & H. Thorisdottir (Eds.), *Social and psychological bases of ideology and system justification* (pp. 371–401). New York: Oxford.

Hartman, T., & Vorderer, P. (2010). It's okay to shoot a character: Moral disengagement in violent video games. *Journal of Communication, 60*(1) 94–119.

Hermida, A., & Thurman, N. (2008). A clash of cultures. The integration of user-generated content within professional journalistic frameworks at British newspaper websites. *New Media & Society, 2*(3), 343–356.

Ho, S. S., & McLeod, D. M. (2008). Social-psychological influences on opinion expression in face-to-face and computer-mediated communication. *Communication Research, 35*(2), 190–207.

House, J. S., Kahn, R. L., McLeod, J. D., & Williams, D. (1985). Measures and concepts of social support. In S. Cohen & L. S. Syme (Eds.), *Social support and health* (pp. 83–108). San Diego: Academic Press.

Hurrell, A. C. (2005). Civility in online discussion: The case of the foreign policy dialogue. *Canadian Journal of Communication, 30*(4), 633–648.

Hynds, E. C. (1976). Editorial pages are taking stands, providing forums. *Journalism Quarterly, 53*(3), 532–537.

_____. (1984). Editorials, opinion pages still have vital roles at most newspapers. *Journalism Quarterly, 61*(3), 634–639.

_____. (1990). Changes in editorials: A study of three newspapers, 1955–1985. *Journalism Quarterly, 67*(2), 302–312.

Janoff-Bulman, R., Sheikh, S., & Baldacci, K. G. (2008). Mapping moral motives: Approach, avoidance, and political orientation. *Journal of Experimental Social Psychology, 44*(4), 1091–1099.

Janoff-Bulman, R., Sheikh, S., & Hepp, S. (2009). Proscriptive and prescriptive morality: Two faces of moral regulation. *Journal of Personality and Social Psychology, 96*(3), 5231–5237.

Janowitz, M. (1967). *The community press in an urban setting: The social elements of urbanism* (2nd ed.). Chicago: University of Chicago Press.

Jeffres, L. W., Neuendorf, K. A., & Atkin, D. (1999). Spirals of silence: Expressing opinions when the climate of opinion is unambiguous. *Political Communication, 16*(2), 115–131.

Johnstone, J. W. C., Slawski, E. J., & Bowman, W. W. (1976). *The news people: A sociological portrait of American journalists and their work.* Urbana: University of Illinois Press.

Kessler, L. (1984). *The dissident press: Alternative journalism in American history* (Vol. 13). Newbury Park, NJ: Sage.

Kiesow, D. (2010). Portland Press Herald drops reader comments in response to "vicious postings." *Poynter.org*. Retrieved August 9, 2010, from http://www.poynter.org/latest news/top-stories/106403/portland-press-herald-drops-reader-comments-in-response-to-vicious-postings/

Kim, R. (2009, May 4). Comments on news stories, a double-edged sword. *SFGate.com*. Retrieved July 15, 2009, from http://articles.sfgate.com/2009–05–04/news/17200 715_1_comments-zodiac-killer-stories/

Klemm, P., Reppert, K., & Visich, L. (1998). A nontraditional cancer support group: The Internet. *Computers in Nursing, 16*(1), 31–36.

Koop, R., & Jansen, H. J. (2009). Political blogs and blogrolls in Canada: Forums for democratic deliberation? *Social Science Computer Review, 27*(2), 155–173.

Krcmar, M., & Viera, T., Jr. (2005). Imitating life, imitating television: The effects of family and television models on children's moral reasoning. *Communication Research, 32*(3), 267–294.

Le Bon, G. (1895/2002). *The crowd: A study of the popular mind.* Mineola, NY: Dover.

Lichtenberg, J. (2000). In defense of objectivity revisited. In J. Curran & M. Gurevitch (Eds.), *Mass media & society* (3rd ed.), (pp. 238–254). London: Arnold.

Lowrey, W., & Woo, C. W. (2010). The news organization in uncertain times: Business or institution? *Journalism & Mass Communication Quarterly, 87*(1) 41–61.

McDevitt, M., Kiousis, S., & Wahl-Jorgensen, K. (2003). Spiral of moderation: Opinion expression in computer-mediated discussion. *International Journal of Public Opinion Research, 15*(4), 454–470.

McDonald, D. G., Glynn, C. J., Kim, S., & Ostman, R. E. (2001). The spiral of silence in the 1948 presidential election. *Communication Research, 28*(2), 139–155.

McKenna, M. Y. A., & Bargh, J. A. (1998). Coming out in the age of the Internet: Identity "demarginalization" through virtual group participation. *Journal of Personality and Social Psychology, 75*(3), 681–694.

Memmott, M. (2011, February 16). Why have many comments about the attack on Lara

Logan been removed? *NPR.org*. Retrieved March 30, 2011, from http://www.npr.org/blogs/thetwo-way/2011/02/16/133804167 /why-have-many-comments-about-the-attack-on-lara-logan-been-removed/

Memos show the brutality of CIA interrogations. (2009, April 21). *Rochester Democrat and Chronicle*. Retrieved April 11, 2009, from http://www.democratandchronicle.com

Meyers, B. (2009, April 9). Culver's word apparently means nothing. *Des Moines Register*. Retrieved April 9, 2009, from http://www.desmoinesregister.com

Mindich, D. T. Z. (1998). *Just the facts: How "objectivity" came to define American journalism*. New York: New York University Press.

Mutz, D. C. (2006). *Hearing the other side: Deliberative versus participatory democracy*. New York: Cambridge University Press.

Napier, K. (2009, April 11). What's the big deal? *Vallejo Times Herald*. Retrieved April 11, 2009, from http://www.timesheraldonline.com

Neuman, W. R., Just, M. R., & Crigler, A. N. (1992). *Common knowledge: News and the construction of political meaning*. Chicago: University of Chicago Press.

Neuwirth, K., & Frederick, E. (2004). Peer and social influence on opinion expression: Combining the theories of planned behavior and the spiral of silence. *Communication Research, 31*(6), 669–703.

Nienaber, D. (2008, November 13). Forum shut down after users go too far. *MankatoFreePress.com*. Retrieved May 9, 2010 from http://mankatofreepress.com/local/x519294062/Forum-shut-down-after-users-go-too-far/

Noelle-Neumann, E. (1984/1993). *The spiral of silence: Public opinion — Our social skin*. Chicago: University of Chicago Press.

_____. (1985). The spiral of silence: A response. In K. Sanders, L. L. Kaid, & D. Nimmo (Eds.), *Political communication yearbook 1984* (pp. 66–94). Carbondale, IL: Southern Illinois University Press.

O'Sullivan, P. B., & Flanagin, A. J. (2003). Reconceptualizing "flaming" and other problematic messages. *New Media & Society, 5*(1), 69–94.

Papacharissi, Z. (2004). Democracy online: Civility, politeness, and the democratic potential of online political discussion groups. *New Media & Society, 6*(2), 259–283.

Perrin, A. J., & Vaisey, S. (2008). Parallel public spheres: Distance and discourse in letters to the editor. *American Journal of Sociology, 114*(3), 781–810.

Pitkin, H. F., & Shumer, S. M. (1982). On participation. *Democracy, 2,* 43–54.

Pro-union act positive, but flawed. (2009, April 9). *Camera*. Retrieved April 9, 2009, from http://www.dailycamera.com

Putnam, R. D. (2000). *Bowling alone: The collapse and revival of American community*. New York: Simon & Schuster.

Reinig, B. A., Briggs, R. O., & Nunmaker, J. F. Jr. (1998). Flaming in the electronic classroom. *Journal of Management Information Systems, 14*(3), 45–59.

Reinig, B. A., & Megias, R. J. (2004). The effects of national culture and anonymity on flaming and criticalness in GSS-supported discussions. *Small Group Research, 35*(6), 698–723.

Rest, J. R. (1979). *Development in judging moral issues*. Minneapolis: University of Minnesota.

Rheingold, H. (1991, Summer). Electronic democracy: The great equalizer. *Whole Earth Review,* 5–11.

_____. (2002). *Smart mobs: The next social revolution*. Cambridge, MA: Perseus.

Rosenberry, J. (2010). Virtual community support for offline communities through online newspaper message forums. *Journalism & Mass Communication Quarterly, 87*(1), 154–169.

St. Cyr, C., Carpenter, S., & Lacy, S. (2010). Internet competition and U.S. newspaper city government coverage: Testing the Lowrey and Mackay model of occupational competition. *Journalism Practice, 4*(4), 507–522.

Salmon, C. T., & Neuwirth, K. (1990). Perceptions of opinion "climates" and willingness to discuss the issue of abortion. *Journalism Quarterly, 67*(3) 567–577.

Scheufele, D. A. (1999). Deliberation or dispute? An exploratory study of public opinion expression. *International Journal of Public Opinion Research, 11*(1), 25–58.

Scheufele, D. A., Shanahan, J., & Lee, E. (2001). Real talk: Manipulating the dependent variable in spiral of silence research. *Communication Research, 28*(3), 304–324.

Schudson, M. (1978). *Discovering the news: A social history of American newspapers*. New York: Basic Books.

_____, (1999). What public journalism knows about journalism but doesn't know about "public." In T. L. Glasser (Ed.), *The idea of public journalism* (pp. 118–133). New York: The Guilford Press.

Shoemaker, P. J. & Cohen, A. A. (2006). *News around the world*. New York: Taylor & Francis.

Shweder, R. A., & Haidt, J. (1993). The future of moral psychology: Truth, intuition, the pluralist way. *Psychological Science, 4*(6), 360–365.

Singer, J. B. (2009). Separate spaces: Discourse about the 2007 Scottish elections on a national newspaper website. *The International Journal of Press/Politics, 14*(4), 477–486.

Skitka, L. J., & Mullen, E. (2002). Understanding judgments of fairness in a real-world context: A test of the value protection model of justice reasoning. *Personality and Social Psychology Bulletin, 28*(10), 1419–1429.

Skitka, L. J., Bauman, C. W., & Sargis, E. G. (2005). Moral conviction: Another contributor to attitude strength or something more? *Journal of Personality and Social Psychology, 88*(6), 895–917.

Sloan, W. D., Wray, C. S., & Sloan, C. J. (1997). *Great editorials: Masterpieces of opinion writing* (2nd ed.). Northport, AL: Vision Press.

Tarrant, W.D. (1957). Who writes letters to the editor? *Journalism Quarterly, 34*, 501–502.

Tax day — Discontent comes on filing deadline. (2009, April 15). *The Daily Reflector*. Retrieved April 15, 2009, from www.reflector.com

Thornton, B. (1998). The disappearing media ethics debate in letters to the editor. *Journal of Mass Media Ethics, 13*(1), 40–55.

Turiel, E. (2002). *The culture of morality. Social development, context, and conflict*. New York: Cambridge University Press.

U.S. Census Bureau. Geography Division. (n.d.). U.S. Department of Commerce. Economics and Statistics Administration. [Map of *Census Regions and Divisions of the United States*]. Retrieved April 15, 2009, from http://www.census.gov/geo/www/us_regdiv.pdf/

Wahl-Jorgensen, K. (2004). A "legitimate beef" or "raw meat"? Civility, multiculturalism, and letters to the editor. *Communication Review, 7*(2), 89–105.

White, M. H., & Dorman, S. M. (2000). Online support for caregivers: Analysis of an Internet Alzheimer mailgroup. *Computers in Nursing, 18*(4), 168–179.

_____. (2001). Receiving social support online: Implications for health education. *Health Education Research, 16*(6), 693–707.

Wilcox, B. L., & Vernberg, E. M. (1985). Conceptual and theoretical dilemmas facing social support research. In I. G. Sarason & B. R. Sarason (Eds.), *Social support: Theory, research, and applications* (pp. 3–20). The Hague, Netherlands: Martinus Nijhoff.

PART III

Global Considerations

8

Post-Objectivity and Regional Russian Journalism

WILSON LOWREY *and* ELINA ERZIKOVA

In the mid-1980s, the policy of perestroika, or re-structuring, triggered an avalanche of political, economic, and social change in Russia (Levashov, 2006). The country's leader, Mikhail Gorbachev, rolled the first stone, pushing for accountability from elites and generating enthusiasm for Western journalism (McNair, 1999). But years later it appears Western-style objectivity as a way of making journalistic truth claims never fully took hold in Russia at national or local levels. As journalism scholar and journalist Valentina Mansurova (2002) has argued, traditional Russian journalists are grounded in a different ethic: They can truly know their world only by mixing "imaginative and logical principles, common sense, intuition and rigorous reasoning." From this viewpoint, a mere fact is "biased and thus subjective" (p. 87).

Subjectivity as professional ideology has also been a consequence of centuries of state-controlled news media and the tendency within the culture to view media as a wing of the state. More recently, at local levels, economic problems and the emergence of political-economic oligarchs have narrowed the critical space necessary for taking a detached position. Rejection of objectivity also reflects age-old tendencies by Russian journalists toward the personal, literary, and philosophical (Sagal, 1978).

Traditional Western forms of journalistic objectivity rely on the existence of a number of factors that are not fully evident in Russian provinces: (1) a public with enough autonomy to act with effectiveness in its own interest; (2) a news system backed by at least a semi-autonomous ownership structure; and (3) a public, a journalistic field, and an institutional field that embrace; impassive, detached reason as an arbiter of society's complexities. Within this traditional western framework, it is assumed journalism has some ability to reveal fact-based "truths" about the world that, in turn, inform citizens' behaviors. That is, journalists can portray phenomena with reasoned balance, thoroughness, and accuracy. It is further assumed that a public exists that is capable of processing and acting on the phenomena relayed through news accounts. Finally, in such a paradigm, the power structure is assumed to be relatively benign and unlikely to squelch journalism's ability to inform and motivate the public toward action.

During perestroika in the 1990s, journalists had a considerable degree of autonomy, as they practiced within a field that was relatively detached from powerful institutions. However, since then, political and economic powers at local levels have squeezed journalists and publics, narrowing public space, and crowding out the logic for a professional autonomy. Consequently, journalists and their organizations are more likely to avoid socio-political news and to reject dispassionate objectivity as a normative touchstone for the occupation.

Yet the constraining political-economic climate is not the only explanation for this move away from objectivity: Russian news workers embrace the subjective and the personal in their craft. Journalists perceive themselves as responsible to citizens by acting as moral teachers, and also view their work as literary philosophy, grounding the legitimacy of their craft in the arts and humanities (Lowrey & Erzikova, 2010). In both cases, Russian journalists show their commitment to seeking and claiming truth — an enduring journalistic value found across a wide range of media systems (Deuze, 2005; Laitila, 1995; Weaver, 1998). Often, Russian journalism is more than reporting verifiable facts; the profession is interested in plumbing deep, personal truths.

Russian journalism is grounded in this emphasis on the personal. Journalists connect intimately with the lives and welfare of readers in a fine-grained way, offering advice on daily questions of individual ethics and virtue, responding to mundane problems such as car repair and soil preparation, and when possible, championing causes of everyday citizens to officials (Lowrey & Erzikova, 2010). Additionally, journalists have personal relationships with official sources that exemplify a clientelist system, where officials reward journalists directly for services (Hallin & Mancini, 2004). Scholars describe Russian journalism as at least partly clientelist as it is a system characterized by dependency on political and commercial resources. Journalists — often on an individual basis — do the bidding of sparring elites in return for financial support (Robinson, 2007; Roudakova, 2008).

This emphasis on personal connections is a significant characteristic of Russian journalism's post-objectivity. Journalists tend to think in terms of personal acquaintance rather than an abstract public, their ethos is often emotive rather than rational, and relationships with officials are often personal as well. The news stories themselves tend to be personal and anecdotal rather than systemic, representing a safe approach in a landscape dominated by powerful institutional interests.

Through case studies of four provincial newspapers conducted over the last four years, we explore shifting positions of local Russian journalists as regards objectivity and subjectivity, and what these shifts mean for these journalists' perceptions of truth. We explore the extent to which these journalists make truth claims on behalf of readers and their communities, and how they make them. Explanations for Russian journalists' positions toward objectivity and subjectivity — grounded in the political-economic context and their journalistic tradition — are explored.

To address these questions, we adopt a field theory framework, which depicts occupational groups as inhabiting fields with varying degrees of autonomy. Occupational groups seek resources and autonomy, and they negotiate their way across the fields of other occupations that exhibit stronger or weaker autonomy. Field theory also suggests occupational members travel an historical arc, shaped by their traditional journalistic values and norms.

From Perestroika to the Rise of Local Oligarchies

The late 1980s and 1990s brought waves of reform-minded proponents of Western journalism to Russia. NGO-supported workshops, conferences and consultants championed the journalism of the West (Miller, 2009). Models of Western-style journalism were readily available in print and on the airwaves. Journalism reformists worked to spread the gospel of a commercially-funded news media that was detached from government and able to "watchdog" the powerful. In the U.S., the ethos of objectivity, born of Enlightenment-era rationalism and nurtured during the Progressive era of the early 20th century (Kaplan, 2002; Schudson, 1978), was perceived as a natural next step for a post-totalitarian Russia.

But results of these efforts were mixed at best, as would-be reformers often failed to account for the cultural countercurrents of a centuries-old, state-sponsored media tradition (Miller, 2011). The populace was relatively comfortable with the idea of media as a natural appendage to a strong central state, a legacy of the preceding 300 years of a clientelist Russian journalism (Arutunyan, 2009). The first Russian newspaper, *Vedomosti*, established by the reform-minded Peter the Great, was unlike many European publications of the 18th century, in that it was launched from the top, and as a product of a feudal society it lacked a market rationale. It seemed predestined to be an organ for state propaganda, and its legacy shapes newspaper missions in Russia today (Arutunyan, 2009).

A generation of journalists who came of age during the heady but brief period of perestroika eventually confronted painful disappointment. The new politicians who were swept into power, many of whom these journalists' news outlets had supported, introduced new informational and financial constraints on the media. The clientelist system reemerged, as those journalists who supported the new politicians received informational and economic subsidies. As economic conditions worsened, editorial teams searched for financial support from government and businesses. Regional governors subsidized media from their regional budgets or through local corporations that financed loyal newspapers (de Smaele, 1999). Today, loyal media receive information unavailable to subversive media, and they rely on unofficial gubernatorial protection in court, curtailing journalistic autonomy. To many Russian journalists, Western-style watchdog approaches appear to have exacerbated the harshness of state reprisals and constraints. Disillusionment set in, reviving a pre-perestroika anti-Western sentiment (de Smaele, 1999; Erzikova & Lowrey, 2010).

Yet, the story is not quite this simple. As a number of studies have shown, power structures at the local level are pluralistic and not absolute: cross-institutional power arrangements are in flux and influential elites are diverse and shifting, sometimes opening cracks for journalistic autonomy (Erzikova & Lowrey, 2010; Koltsova, 2006). Over the last five years, journalists have had some limited success asserting independence, often through repositioning their journalistic focus.

Rediscovery of Personal Journalism

One such repositioning involves news workers calling attention to the problems of everyday citizens, grounding their stories in personal observation and opinion. In this way, Russian journalists emphasize their role as moral leaders for the Russian people. Traditionally, the Russian journalist is an *author* — a *creator* of a public discourse, as opposed to a *reporter*, or fact deliverer. "The author's view, despite its subjectivity, performs an essential function of the media: communication," said Arkhangelsky (2008, para. 40). "It makes the reader ponder the problem regardless of whether he agrees or disagrees with the author."

Russian journalism has differed from the Anglo journalistic tradition, which has generally distinguished journalism from creative literature (Erzikova, 2008). Throughout Russian history, "artistic texts were traditionally seen by the government as a highly effective way of influencing people" (Parthe, 2004, p. 44). *Publitsistika*, or creative newspaper writing, has been "the most prestigious form of intellectual journalism in Russia since the early 19th century"

(Wolfe, 2005, p. 97). Soviet journalists perceived their writings as both art and civil service, and saw themselves as inheritors of such radical Russian writers and thinkers of the 19th century as Herzen, Belinsky, Chernyshevsky, and Pisarev (Sagal, 1978).

In this traditional view of Russian journalism, the myth of objectivity fuels a second myth — that facts are a measure of journalistic truth. Within this view, facts are easily manipulated by elites, especially in a top-down society. Therefore, it is not the facts themselves but their interpretation by an honest, trusted journalist that should matter for Russian society (Arkhangelsky, 2008). Similarly, Lazutina (2001) argued that *pereosmyslenie*— rethinking, or the author's interpretation of well-known phenomena — is the best method for presentation of facts. And so, while in the West, "The objectivity norm prescribes neutrality and the transmission of facts only and not personal opinions" (Broersma, 2010, p. 28), Russian journalism seems to reward partisanship — but a reflective partisanship.

The pursuit of truth is viewed as important, but it is viewed as creative and interactive (Sagal, 1978; Wu, Weaver, Owen, & Johnstone, 1996), infused by stories of the daily struggles of individual readers and journalists' responses to these struggles. Such an approach is consistent with traditional efforts by the state to educate everyday people via media (Koltsova, 2006; Pasti, 2005). Russian journalists

> historically ... have rejected a detached, neutral position and have instead nurtured a personal, emotive side of their work, believing they hone a literary skill capable of providing the people with moral instruction (Pasti, 2005; Sagal, 1978) — a "people" who are not necessarily an autonomous, democratic "public" [Erzikova & Lowrey, 2010, p. 344].

This personal side is evident in journalists' relationships with officials as well. Low salaries may encourage journalists to enter into personal agreements with particular officials, providing favorable coverage or withholding stories for payment. Editors turn a blind eye, as these financial supplements take the pressure off the news outlet to pay livable wages. Journalists may become more loyal to the patron official than to their own news outlet (Lowrey & Erzikova, 2010).

From the rule of the czars, to Soviet government, to today's quasi-authoritarianism under Putin and Medvedev, Russian journalists have become expert at finding small, often personal ways to assert their agency. Today we see evidence that Russian journalists alter the subjective qualities of their work as the objective context of their environment has become more constraining. For example, some who avoid socio-political reporting and its clientelist constraints have refashioned their role as a sort of counselor to readers. They say it is important that they connect with readers morally, spiritually, and practically—a uniquely personal view of the public (Lowrey & Erzikova, 2010).

Relevant here is the Russian word *istina*, often translated to English as *truth*, but differing from its English analogue. *Istina* is not truth as fact; rather, it is a revelation, a result of philosophical meditation about the self, others, and the world. Yet both truth and *istina* have troubled the powerful. While a journalistic search for factual truth in the West can cost officials their careers by revealing verifiable misdeeds, the search for *istina* challenged the philosophical essence of the Soviet regime and its policies (Erzikova, 2008; Turpin, 1995).

Research Questions

The remainder of this chapter explores journalism in the central city of a typical Russian province. We examine the orientation of journalists in this region toward objectivity and subjectivity, and the political, economic and cultural factors that shape these orientations. The analysis is based on a number of research questions:

RQ1: In this Russian region, what are journalists' perceptions of the applicability of Western-style objectivity? Have these perceptions changed over the last four years, and if so, how?

RQ2: How do these perceptions of objectivity correlate with institutional and economic conditions in the region? How has this changed over the last four years?

RQ3: How do these perceptions of objectivity reflect deeper traditional norms within Russian journalism?

RQ4: In what ways do these local Russian journalists make truth claims, and why?

Field Theory

Field theory is a helpful framework for assessing journalistic autonomy within higher-order constraints, and so we adopt this analytical approach. The framework acknowledges that occupational fields involve both structure and mutability through agency, as occupations and occupational members seek control via cultural and economic capital within these fields. This theory offers a way to conceptualize the current dynamics in local Russian journalism. Journalists and their outlets, facing external financial and state constraints, reposition themselves to gain some occupational autonomy. At the same time, Russian journalists are shaped by the past trajectory of events and the historical arc of Russian journalism's subjective, personal, philosophical, and literary traditions.

Bourdieu (2005) has defined journalism as a weak field, susceptible to economic, political, and cultural pressures and constraints (Benson & Neveu, 2005; Shoemaker & Vos, 2009). No doubt this is the case within this Russian region. However, although journalism is a constrained microcosm within a social macrocosm, it is still "obeying its own laws, its own nomos" (Bourdieu 2005, p. 32).[1] Accordingly, the field does have some degree of autonomy as well as its own historical trajectory, which has been determined partly by how the field has, over time, staked out its path.

Method

This study is a longitudinal investigation of four regional newspapers in a Russian province, conducted annually during June-August from 2007 to 2010. The current report is based on a series of in-depth interviews and focus groups with editors and rank-and-file journalists, as well as observations within newsrooms. Informal close readings of newspaper content were also conducted in 2010–2011.

More than 50 dailies and weeklies operate in the region under investigation. The total circulation, including free publications, is more than 800,000 copies a week. The four papers studied here were selected purposively by the following criteria: (1) they were each a regional (not city or rural) paper with a circulation not less than 10,000 copies a week; (2) they have published regularly for no less than 10 years; and (3) they each have a distinct ownership model. Pseudonyms for the papers are used in reporting results.

The Traditional was conceived as a city newspaper 20 years ago. In its first 10 years, the paper grew to the level of a regional outlet. This newspaper has two owners — the city administration and a group of staff members, who worked in the newspaper in the 1990s (the privatization period during perestroika). The former city mayor subsidized the paper from the city budget. A new mayor cut off the subsidies, and staffers have been uncertain of the paper's sustainability from year to year.

The Government, the region's oldest newspaper, has published for nearly 90 years. Formerly the Communist Party's regional newspaper, this outlet is now funded from the regional government's regular operating budget. Its reporters carry IDs with the title "The government of *NN* region," signifying that they work at a newspaper that is an organ of the state. Regional officials offer *Government* reporters preferential treatment, often giving them information first.

The Private, almost 80 years old, was the organ of the regional *Komsomol* organization in the Soviet era. In the 1990s, the paper went bankrupt and was closed down. In the late 1990s, a local businessman resurrected the paper and turned the former propagandistic tool into a sensational yellow outlet. In the mid-2000s, the businessman toned down the paper by redefining its mission. The current paper's mission is reporting on mundane issues (e.g., prices, pensions) and providing readers with advice — like how to estimate taxes or grow vegetables on a balcony.

The Regional Branch is a local branch of a Moscow-based mainstream medium. The parent company was one of the leading news organizations in the Soviet era. Today the newspaper is an entertainment-oriented outlet, and its local branches in various Russian cities mimic the Moscow model while covering local topics and events with a sensational tone.

Over a four-year period, about 60 rank and file journalists, editors, and government officials participated in interview sessions and focus groups. Every participant was interviewed at least twice during data collection. Interviews took place in formal and informal settings and averaged 1.5 hours. Printed newspaper stories were used to prompt and facilitate discussion during interviews. Data were also collected via direct observation of everyday activities and participation in newspaper meetings.

Case Study Findings

RQ1: In this Russian region, what are journalists' perceptions of the applicability of Western-style objectivity? Have these perceptions changed over the last four years, and if so, how?

The 2008 economic crisis increased anxiety among the Russian people. But rather than encouraging political change, the public's concerns have strengthened the influence of the regime. Partly this is because, during crises in Russia, paternalistic expectations and reliance on the state tend to increase (Gudkov, Dubin, & Levinson, 2009). Contemporary Russia is an *adaptive society,* in which everyday people tend to adjust to unfair, unlawful situations rather than try to change them (Gudkov et al., 2009). The society is characterized by a persistent anti-Western attitude and acceptance of the Soviet past. In general, Russians value order, stability, and personal protection over liberty (Gudkov et al., 2009).

Following the Kremlin's nationwide propaganda campaign during the 2000s (Horvath, 2011), the government in the region under study has attempted to reduce social tension and frame harsh living conditions as temporary. While government-supported media are required to exhibit a positive attitude, private papers do so voluntarily because, as *Private* reporters said, bad news doesn't sell the paper. Thus, the journalists' critical space seems very narrow. The *Private's* own unscientific research showed that front-page stories that offered human interest accounts and personal advice on everyday problems (e.g., pensions, utility rates) guaranteed paper sales; recently the *Private* offered a best-selling special section with a list of Russian saints readers could pray to during crises. In this way, the paper emphasized its role as personal and moral counselor rather than acting as a vehicle for galvanizing the citizenry into collective action. The *Private's* journalists say their readers want guidance during tough economic times through explanation of government regulations and through tips to live by rather than through investigation of government directives or motives.

Participants in this study said they believed objectivity in the Western sense is impossible in Russia. As one *Traditional* reporter said, objectivity requires that journalists inhabit an autonomous space. "Objectivity is the ability to critique the authorities; yet, in this province, there are no reporters who were not bought or threatened by the powerful," said this reporter. "The journalistic community is demoralized" (personal communication, August 2, 2010). Also, an airtight, unified power structure has restricted access to information sources. Reporters participated in staged news conferences and media tours, and officials provided limited PR-style information. Participants said authorities disregard requests for additional information. According to one investigative reporter, this limiting environment erodes Western-style watchdog skills and motivation. "Professionalism of Russian journalists is so low that the majority of us would not know what kind of documents to request [from the authorities]," said the reporter (personal communication, July 21, 2009).

Although these journalists said dependency on the government undermines journalistic credibility and autonomy, most see their subordinate status as benefitting ordinary citizens who had enough of the information wars of the 1990s. While the *perestroika* generation of journalists took pride in being confrontational and detached from the power structure — traditional aspects of Western-style political journalism — participants said the more recent generation sees alliance with the government as encouraging order and helping everyday people. As a *Government* reporter said, "Nobody wants to be the last straw" (personal communication, July 21, 2009). In other words, journalists avoided watchdog reporting, which they thought could stir up unrest among an already unhappy populace. These regional journalists called it "professional responsibility." A vice editor of the *Traditional* said, "We don't attack the government and don't push people to erect barricades; instead, we create a conversation with the power." He added, "Why do we need to fight our own state? Maybe it is time to start building it?" (personal communication, June

23, 2010). Journalists see the state as collaborative; bureaucrats want to be perceived as strategic partners, said study participants. As a reporter for the *Traditional* said, "We were overpowered by the bureaucrats [in the 1990s] because we lost our professional unity and our focus — the 'small person' and his everyday concerns — in that fight" (personal communication, July 18, 2007). A senior reporter for the *Government* said that, unlike in the 1990s, the government reaches out to ordinary people and "explains how to improve lives" (personal communication, July 21, 2009). Through these comments, news workers indicated that detached reporting is not a strong news value; in fact, such a pose is antithetical to Russian news writing, which is seen as a personal, interpretive process. The *Traditional* editor discouraged his staff writers from "hiding behind facts": "Whatever you do — support or undermine the government — you cannot be cold-minded like Westerners" (personal communication, June 10, 2008).

RQ2: How do perceptions of objectivity correlate with institutional and economic conditions in the region? How has this changed over the last four years?

Political authorities are the main advertising clients of local media organizations in Russia, and in fact some scholars doubt if commercial media markets exist (Lozovsky, 2009). The regional government subsidizes the entire *Government*'s operations, while the *Private* and *Regional Branch* obtain long-term contracts to cover public officials' activities. Even the *Traditional*'s editor, a critic of the regional government, admitted he would sign a contract to produce PR material for authorities. Not surprisingly, reporters received government awards — in one case a reporter accepted a public relations award for coverage of a city jubilee.

Officials instructed editors at the *Government* newspaper to avoid reporting on problems the government could not solve. For example, the *Government* did not publish a story about rural teachers who lost their jobs after the school was closed. Reporters lived off of the state budget, and they avoided tackling such pressing issues and angering officials who made decisions about financial support for media. According to field theory, this financial dependence reflects pursuit of economic capital for maintenance of the journalistic field, but in such situations, very little cultural capital accrues to journalists. The source of legitimacy comes from journalists' associations with government officials, reflecting the weakness of journalism's own field.

However, journalists do not have unlimited tolerance for dependency on government. As the *Government* editor said, "If the government tells me to attack Ivanov, I will ask what he has done wrong. I will [only] attack him if arguments are convincing" (personal communication, July 1, 2010). At a regional journalists' meeting, the managing editor publicly addressed her outrage concerning a mandatory list of topics the government wanted covered. In response, the *Traditional* editor said, "If you refuse to receive a million rubles a month from the regional budget, the government would not give you a list of topics" (personal communication, July 12, 2010). Eventually, journalists from the *Government* newspaper claimed a small victory about the weekly list of topics — the government decreased the frequency of the list from weekly to every three months. The *Government* continued its fight for marginal autonomy by complaining to Russia's Union of Journalists about the authoritative style of an official in charge of local media. The Union head appealed to the governor, and the governor, wanting to avoid a nationwide scandal, fired the media official. Reporters then ascribed this success to their own power.

After president Medvedev made governors take direct responsibility for the socio-political situation in their regions (Moses, 2010), local newspapers became even more cautious about the consequences of critical coverage. Reporters and editors across the papers said the Kremlin's favorable perception of the region was largely based on how local media portrayed the regional government. If national-level officials are disappointed by news stories, such accounts can adversely affect their decisions to use federal monies to subsidize this economically-depressed province, they said. For example, the *Traditional* drafted a critical piece on officials that was designed to force them to help a World War II veteran fix his house. Yet, the paper withdrew the story because it would "hurt the region if the story gets into the Internet," the vice-editor said (personal communication, July 15, 2010). Although the *Traditional* is not subsidized by the regional government, its editors said they were concerned that publishing the story could adversely affect Kremlin support for the people in the region.

However, portraying the region as too good to be true could damage the credibility of these papers in the eyes of both news consumers and bureaucrats. The media must appear somewhat autonomous and aggressive to have legitimacy in the eyes of the populace and Moscow officials. And so, at times, the region's governor encouraged local media to go after public officials. Reporters were not enthusiastic about such a task, fearing they might accidently criticize a sacred cow. One reporter admitted the fear had a "paralyzing effect" on reporters, especially after it was rumored that the editor of the *Government* was fired because of a "political mistake" (personal communication, July 2, 2010).

The *Private* seems to have found a way to balance economic and ideological interests while appearing relatively autonomous. Instead of open confrontation with the regional or city administration, *Private* reporters asked local authorities to comment on stories that criticized them. As one reporter said, "We critique the city administration on an agreed-upon issue, and then the administration uses it as a public relations strategy, [saying]: 'The *Private* slammed us officials, and we respond to criticism by improving the situation'" (personal communication, June 14, 2010). As a result, the *Private* was able to continue receiving financial support from the budget while also producing a kind of watchdog reporting and regaining a small measure of autonomy. At the same time, the *Private* acquired the reputation of being the people's defender. A senior reporter said she received three to four daily phone calls from readers having trouble and facing injustice. She voiced their concerns to the authorities, and the bureaucrats listened to her to avoid bad publicity, she said.

RQ3: How do these perceptions of objectivity reflect deeper traditional norms within Russian journalism?

Field theory accounts for the constraints that institutions and rival occupations can place on a field's resources, but it also allows for journalistic agency. Journalism has its own nomos, its own historical norms and values. And so we see that these local journalists' rejection of objectivity as a norm is partly a consequence of institutional and socio-political constraints, and partly a consequence of the historical trajectory of their occupation's tradition.

During a focus group discussion, regional reporters revealed a theoretical adherence to the historic messianic principle of Russian journalism — to provide moral and philosophical leadership for the masses. Participants said journalists should have some autonomy from the political and economic power structure because journalists serve an *idea*, not entities.

However, in modern Russia, professed high principles run up against the realities of a powerful state. So, many local journalists tend to seek occupational legitimacy by allying with the government. This collusion is unlikely to bring systemic change, and it leaves journalists subject to censorship and aggressive government PR. But reporters said their collaboration with government officials is better suited for helping readers with daily, ongoing problems, and therefore dovetails with their historic mission to help the masses. Adherence to facts, on the other hand, was seen as less helpful toward this end. A reporter for the *Private* said, "People are tired from 'just facts.' They want to read analytical stories that make them think" (personal communication, June 10, 2008). Russian journalists maintained that a focus on facts is useful during social turbulence, but such a single-mindedness could be potentially destructive during placid times. As a vice editor of the *Government* explained:

> In the 1990s, people were highly interested in facts that were hidden from us for 70 years. After we knew everything about the Soviet past, a "salt water solution"

became oversaturated. These days, readers don't want facts to overshadow a discourse [personal communication, June 11, 2008].

The editor of the *Traditional* said, "There is a growing understanding among journalists that the reader wants us to run information through us" (personal communication, August 1, 2007). That is, the journalist should take information and interpret it from a personal standpoint. Overall, local journalists said there has been a resurrection of a conversational style of writing that reveals the passion of an author's position. Since 2007, this rise of an authentic and unique Russian journalism has become a more prominent topic within newsrooms. And, increasingly, journalists use anti–Western sentiments to articulate a "new old" identity. Said one reporter:

> We have always been unique, and thank God, now we want to resemble or mimic the West less and less. We have always had a special mentality and journalism, and [there's] nothing wrong with it. Let us be us [personal communication, July 14, 2010].

It appears even the *Regional Branch,* which was perceived as a yellow pro–Western paper by local journalists, believes in subjectivity with a human face. Its reporters said they strive to evoke warm feelings in readers via feature stories about good people. While still informing about current events, the *Regional Branch* frequently provides readers with survival tips — for example, a map indicating locations for mushroom foraging in local forests. However, the *Regional Branch* manifests a "mass compassion," distancing itself from readers' individual needs. Observation of newsrooms revealed that the *Regional Branch* was the only paper that neither received reader phone calls nor discussed reader letters during meetings.

RQ4: In what ways do these local Russian journalists now make truth claims, and why?

Journalists who claim objectivity or facticity, or even claim these as guiding lights, can make powerful assertions about what is true. They can claim to hold a mirror up to society and show the world as it is. To the extent that this claim is held as publicly legitimate, the journalistic field is considered by officials and the populace to be relatively autonomous, even encroaching into the field of officialdom. In the language of field theory, such claims bring cultural capital to the occupation. But what happens when objectivity is rejected, as is the case with these Russian journalists? Can they find other ways to gain autonomy and cultural capital, and make truth claims?

From a field theory perspective, these journalists now occupy a weak, tenuous field, and so they must traverse and work within other groups' fields, while tolerating encroachment by other occupations. They work within the field of officials and bureaucrats, writing articles that serve as newsletters for officials, and regurgitating official PR. Or they may traverse fields that are non-political — performing the librarian-like work of answering reader questions about mundane daily tasks (gardening, mushroom foraging or car repair). They may simply pursue the field of entertainment, avoiding political stories and focusing on sensationalized crime and scandal. Or they may continue along the traditional Russian journalistic trajectory, doing the work of providing spiritual and moral inspiration, a harkening back to traditional Russian journalistic values. The problem with these approaches is that they hamper journalistic autonomy because they bring little cultural and economic capital to local Russian journalism (Benson & Neveu, 2005). Writing sensationalized, non-political stories does little to increase public legitimacy. Attempting moral leadership is unlikely to bring in much revenue. And advising individual readers about mundane tasks tends to trivialize a profession that needs a deeper, rooted approach to its own field.

Yet, the recent move by the Kremlin to make provinces accountable for maintaining their own social control holds some slight promise for journalistic autonomy. The negotiated arrangement between the *Private* and local government, while choreographed, does carve out a bit of autonomous space for journalists. It appears the fissure in the political power structure between the local and national government is allowing some journalistic independence to seep through. Obviously the appearance of an autonomous journalism that stands detached from government and protects the populace still garners legitimacy in the eyes of the powerful and the populace — this choreographed arrangement depends on it.

Of course the local government is co-opting this legitimacy for its own purposes and constraining, for example, the *Private* to narrow and relatively tame accounts of official abuse. The truth claims must be targeted and episodic rather than verging into extensive examinations of systemic problems. The journalists' willingness to abide by this arrangement demonstrates the continued vulnerability of their field's autonomy. They remain dependent on the government for economic capital. Still, episodic exposés allow some renewed measure of respect, of cultural capital, for the journalists of the *Private*, who are once again allowed to challenge the powerful and champion the everyday citizen, if only within a scripted arrangement.

Conclusions

The new millennium has brought evidence of a resurrection of Russian journalism's "cultural heritage and mental code" originated in the Russian classical literature of the 18th and 19th centuries: a discovery and fascination with the everyday life (Frolova, 2009, p. 112). News with a human face, a search for moral guidance, and attention to previously abandoned voices of society (e.g., readers' letters) are indicators of a "new old" stage of Russian journalism. However, political realities have dampened the enthusiasm about revitalization of a "true Russian journalism." In this light, one can see that journalists' commitment to human interest stories reflects a search for safe ground through avoidance of political reporting (Erzikova & Lowrey, 2010).

Accordingly, objectivity has never been a good fit with the ethic of Russian journalism, and it seems inappropriate to journalism in this province because of the absence of the notion of an autonomous public. In the West, the myth of journalistic objectivity suggests a public exists that can act and shape the socio-political environment and machinery. For such an entity to work correctly (rationally), the public must believe it has an accurate view of the world from which to act. In the Russian province we examined, there is no such idea or myth to sustain this ethic for journalism in the province.

Journalism in this province has other ethics on which it bases its rationale for work, occupational identity, and jurisdictional claims. Throughout our research on this region, we have observed the identities of journalism as a partner to government (though often more an appendage), journalism as sensationalized entertainment, and journalism as moral helper for individual readers (Erzikova & Lowrey, 2010; Lowrey & Erzikova, 2010). These identities are consistent with types of Russian journalism observed by other scholars as well (e.g., Dzyaloshinsky, as cited in Strovsky, 2004).

This research suggests that some journalism in the region is starting to weave these threads together once again to create a small measure of autonomy. Truth claims about what is going on in everyday people's real lives are beginning to have a stronger and more relevant place in the province's journalism, and this is seen most clearly at *The Private*. This is not because journalists claim to be a mirror on society, but rather because they are again beginning to link the populace to the government. Journalists have more reason to highlight local hardships because there is more hope that local officials will address at least some of these problems, if only to keep up appearances to Moscow, on which the provincial government depends for revenue. To be sure, journalists' autonomy is marginal; they accommodate the government by highlighting problems that are the least inconvenient for officials. But in the process, journalists are better able to connect with citizens on a personal level. And these journalists' rediscovery of an age-old subjective, moral, and literary/artistic journalism has provided a voice through which journalists may assert themselves in this new environment.

We must not make too much of these changes, which are not clearly evident across all the newspaper outlets we studied. Journalists continue to play an institutional role, collaborating with officials behind the scenes, and clientelism is alive and well. Yet these small shifts and repositionings demonstrate the dynamic nature of occupational fields, as well as the important roles of both journalistic agency and the historical trajectories journalists travel within their occupation.

The model of post-objectivity emerging from our study, while nurtured by Russian tradition, is in some ways applicable to other media environments — especially those lacking a tradition of journalistic autonomy, and those conducive to a personal style of journalism. Many developing nations with weak traditions of institutional journalism have age-old clientelist systems, with instrumental relationships between officials and journalists. Often ancestral and tribal connections in these nations trump bureaucratic or legal-rational authority (Hallin & Mancini, 2004). We see similar dynamics in small communities across media systems, which are likely structured around familial and personal ties, fostering both instrumental forms of control as well as a tendency by journalists to focus on the fine-grained, daily needs of citizens (Janowitz, 1967).

The clientelist/personal counselor model described in our study may also have relevance for emerging online media. Online networks ease interaction at the personal level, encouraging journalists' to respond to individual-level needs (e.g., "news you can use" stories). And the online world often displays direct relationships between writers and institutions. For example, bloggers commonly write postings for products or politicians in return for payment or other benefits (Rettberg, 2008).

Will such an orientation toward the personal and instrumental erode emphasis on the public good, which has to date been a critical concept for maintenance of an autonomous journalistic field? We see these dynamics in Russian local journalism, but we must keep its unique context in mind. That is, for centuries Russian journalists have valued both moral education for individuals and a close relationship with the state. It remains to be seen if journalism around the world — buffeted in different venues by the imperatives of culture, political economy, and emerging technologies — will tend to nurture these same tendencies.

Chapter Notes

1. Bourdieu adopts the term "nomos," a Greek term referring to social convention. In ancient Greece, laws were generally thought to derive either from nomos, a social agreement, or from nature.

References

Arkhangelsky, A. (2008). Andrey Arkhangelsky: Dva mifa o zhurnalistike [Andrey Arkhangelsky: Two myths about journalism]. *Vzglyad*. Retrieved January 8, 2011, from http://vz.ru/columns/2008/4/7/157655.html

Arutunyan, A. (2009). *The media in Russia.* Berkshire, England: Open University Press.

Benson, R., & Neveu, E. (2005). Introduction: Field theory as a work in progress. In R. Benson & E. Neveu (Eds.), *Bourdieu and the journalistic field* (pp. 1–25). Malden, MA: Polity Press.

Bourdieu, P. (2005). The political field, the social science field, and the journalistic field. In R. Benson & E. Neveu (Eds.), *Bourdieu and the journalistic field* (pp. 29–47). Malden, MA: Polity Press.

Broersma, M. (2010). The unbearable limitations of journalism. *The International Communication Gazette, 72*(1), 21–33.

de Smaele, H. (1999). The applicability of Western media models on the Russian media system. *European Journal of Communication, 14*(2),173–189.

Deuze, M. (2005). What is journalism? Professional identity and ideology of journalists reconsidered. *Journalism, 6*(4), 442–464.

Erzikova, E. (2008, May). Subversion of censorship in Soviet journalism: *Komsomolskaya Pravda*'s contribution to preparation for Gorbachev's perestroika and its implications for the contemporary Russian media. Paper presented at the annual meeting of the International Communication Association, Montreal, Canada.

Erzikova, E., & Lowrey, W. (2010). Seeking safe ground: Russian regional journalists' withdrawal from civic service journalism. *Journalism Studies, 11*(3), 343–358.

Frolova, T. I. (2009). Dinamika strategii v sotsial'nom mediadiskurse [Dynamics of strategies in media's social discourse]. *Vestnik Moskovskogo Universiteta, seriya 10, Zhurnalistika [Bulletin of the Moscow State University, series 10, Journalism], 5,* 94–116.

Gudkov, L. D., Dubin, B. V., & Levinson, A. G. (2009). Fotorobot rossiiskogo obuvatelya [A sketch of the Russian everyman]. *Mir Rossii, 2,* 22–33.

Hallin, D., & Mancini, P. (2004). *Comparing media systems: Three models of media and politics.* New York: Cambridge University Press.

Horvath, R. (2011). Putin's "Preventive counter-revolution": Post-Soviet authoritarianism and the specter of velvet revolution. *Europe-Asia Studies, 63*(1), 1–25.

Janowitz, M. (1967). *The community press in an urban setting* (2nd ed.). Chicago: University of Chicago Press.

Kaplan, R. (2002). *Politics and the American press: The rise of objectivity, 1865–1920.* New York: Cambridge University Press.

Koltsova, O. (2006). *News media and power in Russia.* New York: Routledge.

Laitila, T. (1995). Journalistic codes of ethics in Europe. *European Journal of Communication, 10*(4), 513–526.

Lazutina, G. V. (2001). *Osnovu tvorcheskoi deyatel'nosti zhurnalista* [The foundation of creative activity of the journalist]. Moscow: Aspekt Press.

Levashov, V. K. (2006). Grazhdanskoe obshestvo i demokraticheskoe gosudarstvo v Rossii. [Civic society and democratic state in Russia]. *Sotsiologicheskie Issledovaniya, 1,* 6–20.

Lowrey, W. & Erzikova, E. (2010). Institutional legitimacy and Russian news: Case studies of four regional newspapers. *Political Communication, 27*(3), 275–288.

Lozovsky, B.N. (2009). Ekonomika manipulirovaniya [Economics of manipulation]. *Vestnik Moskovskogo Universiteta, seriya 10, Zhurnalistika [Bulletin of the Moscow State University, series 10, Journalism], 5,* 50–67.

Mansurova, V. D. (2002). Zhurnalistskaya kartina mira kak factor sotsial'noi determinacii [Journalism's picture of the world as a factor of social determination]. Barnaul: Izdatel'stvo Altaiskogo Universita.

McNair, B. (1999). *An introduction to political communication* (2nd ed.). New York: Routledge.

Miller, J. (2009). NGOs and "modernization" and "democratization" of media: Situating media assistance. *Global Media and Communication, 5*(1), 9–33.

_____, (2011). Questioning the Western approach to training. *Nieman Reports.* Retrieved April

20, 2011, from http://www.nieman.harvard.edu/reports/article/102592/Questioning-the-Western-Approach-to-Training.aspx

Moses, J.C. (2010). Russian local politics in the Putin-Medvedev era. *Europe-Asia Studies, 62*(9), 1427–1452.

Parthe, K. F. (2004). *Russia's dangerous texts: Politics between the lines.* New Haven: Yale University Press.

Pasti, S. (2005). Two generations of contemporary Russian journalists. *European Journal of Communication, 20*(1), 89–115.

Rettberg, J. W. (2008). *Blogging.* Cambridge, England: Polity Press.

Robinson, N. (2007). The political is personal: Corruption, clientelism, patronage, informal practices and the dynamics of post-Communism [review article]. *Europe-Asia Studies, 59*(7), 1217–1224.

Roudakova, N. (2008). Media-political clientelism: Lessons from anthropology. *Media, Culture & Society, 30*(1), 41–59.

Sagal, G. (1978). *Dvadcat pyat' intervyu [Twenty-five interviews].* Moskva: Izdatelstvo Politicheskoi Literatury.

Schudson, M. (1978). *Discovering the news.* New York: Basic Books.

Shoemaker, P.J., & Vos, T.P. (2009). *Gatekeeping theory.* New York: Routledge.

Strovsky, D. (2004, August). Ob'ektivnost' informatsii kak neobkhodimoe uslovie zhurnalistskogo poznaniyu [Objectivity of information as the necessary condition of the journalistic inquiry]. *RELGA, 8.* Retrieved January 8, 2011, from http://www.relga.ru/Environ/WebObjects/tgu-www.woa/wa/Main?textid=237&level1=main&level2=articles

Turpin, J. (1995). *Reinventing the Soviet self: Media and social change in the former Soviet Union.* Westport, CT: Praeger.

Weaver, D. (1998). *The global journalist: News people around the world.* Cresskill, NJ: Hampton Press.

Wolfe, T. C. (2005). *Governing Soviet journalism: The press and the socialist person after Stalin.* Bloomington: Indiana University Press.

Wu, W., Weaver, D., & Johnson, O. (1996). Professional roles of Russian and U.S. journalists: A comparative study. *Journalism and Mass Communication Quarterly, 73*(3), 534–548.

9

Journalism from the Perspective of "We"

How Group Membership Shapes the Role of the Community Journalist

JOHN A. HATCHER

Community journalism, which can trace its roots back to Tocqueville (1835/2004) in the United States, has functioned in a subjective position since before objectivity was even considered an institutional norm. What appears to be changing is not journalism itself but the acceptance of subjectivity as an acceptable — even desirable way — for journalism to operate (Altschull, 1996; Merrill, 2004). Community journalism has a point of view. And, while traditional community journalists may wince at the suggestion that they are *not* objective, seeing them with this context provides an understanding of the community-media dynamic and helps to diffuse the longstanding tension between community media and other mainstream news forms.

The concept of *community media* (which I see as synonymous with *community journalism*) represents a broad array of media. They are any kind of media channel (newspapers, websites, radio stations, etc.) that profess to serve a group that is normally defined by geographic proximity, shared interest, cause, or faith (Jankowski, 2002). The focus of this chapter is media oriented toward geographically-defined communities.

Community media's point of view — "we" — is what English professors call *first-person plural*. The community media journalist is a member of the group to whom they are writing. Community media cannot be defined based on a particular circulation size if it is a newspaper, or a targeted audience if it is an online-only publication. Nor can it be measured based on the types of stories. Instead, it is best understood by measuring the strength of the connection the journalist shares with the audience (Reader, 2011).

In a meta-analysis of data examining community media organizations in the United States and South Africa, a common theme emerges: those who work in community media (at least those who *enjoy* doing so) see themselves as vocal members of the communities in which they are embedded (Hatcher, 2003a, 2003b, 2005, 2007, 2010). They are advocates for issues of shared concern. They are often unapologetic leaders, seeking to join the community in taking on a challenge. They refuse to stand on the sidelines, acting as disinterested observers who gather facts. Instead, in the post-objective community media landscape, this dynamic emerges: community journalists, less constrained by the objectivity imperative, embrace their role as community members. The growing awareness of what it means to practice journalism from this perspective is reconstructing our understanding of community media without the faulty assumption that it should be evaluated using the norms of objective journalism. In that spirit, this chapter has three goals:

• Explore what previous research says about the position of the community journalist as an active community participant.

• Present the findings of a meta-analysis that describes the perspective of community journalists with different cultural and socio-economic situations.

• Make suggestions about what the validation of a post-objective framework means for our understanding of community-focused media and what it portends for the future of media operating from a post-objective position.

Debating the Merits of Membership

The disconnect between community journalism and mainstream media is articulated by longtime *Washington Post* editor Ben Bagdikian, who wrote a scathing critique of his cousins in the community press. "The fact is that most small dailies and weeklies are the backyard of the trade, repositories for any piece of journalistic junk tossed over the fence, run as often by print-shop proprietors as by editors," he said (Bagdikian, 1964, p. 102). That critique was not a new one even then and it shows the misunderstanding that exists between Journalism (with a capital "J") and journalism that is of a more intimate nature. Champions of community media (Byerly, 1961; Lauterer, 2006) have long felt the need to defend their way of doing journalism against a standard that expects — even demands — that the journalist operate from an autonomous position outside of the story (Merrill, 1990; White, 1996). The prevailing wisdom about objectivity was long apparent in the Society of Professional Journalists' (SPJ) code of ethics. Journalists must, said the SPJ, "remain free of associations and activities that may compromise integrity or damage credibility" (Society of Professional Journalists, 1996). Champions of the community press, in contrast, urge journalists to remain unapologetically accountable to a community of readers (usually a geographically-defined one) of which they were a part (Lauterer, 2006). For the community journalist, to operate with objectivity as a guiding principle is to risk becoming out of touch and irrelevant.

This connection with the community was precisely what others saw as a weakness — the timidity of the community journalist as regards conflict-oriented stories within their community (Donohue, Tichenor, & Olien, 1995). The apprehension often voiced in journalism trade magazines was that community journalists would shy away from reporting on contentious issues that involved community members because of a fear of retribution and, more specifically, concerns about losing advertising revenue (Hatcher, 2003b, 2004).

Media ethicists offer another perspective, using the communitarian philosophy to redefine the role of the media. From a political philosophy perspective, Macintyre (1981/2007) saw a community as a group of individuals who, like passengers on a ship, are on a journey toward a common destination. This shared goal, or *telos*, ensures that the community is always on course toward a mutual end. Christians, Ferre and Fackler (1993) asserted that media, too, are passengers on this ship and cannot ignore their responsibility toward the community. Altschull (1996) resisted some of the tenets of communitarian philosophies but believed journalism has to evolve to overcome a crisis of conscience. Journalism practices are suffering, he argued, because media cling to the notion that it is possible to be objective and detached from the community. "Journalistic objectivity and detachment may have been fine once upon a time, but that doesn't bring communities together. It may even drive them further apart," Altschull concluded (1996, p. 172). He used the term *community journalism* to describe a media form that puts public service above profit and that serves as a community mediator where anyone can come to voice their concerns.

Communities can be powerful tools for uniting groups toward a shared goal. They are often a source of what Putnam called bonding capital (1995) — attributes that join and reinforce a group's actions like a fire brigade that works as one while passing buckets down the line to extinguish a blaze. But the communitarian ethic faces a strong critique from those who point out that communities, by their nature, inhibit the fuller range of discourse necessary for a democracy to function (Phillips, 1995). In fact, communities can exclude as easily as they can include and may have little tolerance for those who might like to take that proverbial community ship in another direction. Communities can discourage dissent through promoting a strong sense of loyalty and deference to rules (Barney, 1996).

But communities are not uniform in their structure. Tichenor, Donohue and Olien's structural-pluralism model posits that in a homogenous, usually geographically-small community, media shy away from conflict and instead see their role as consensus oriented (1980, 1989). In their later guard dog theory (1995), they observed how community media are even more hesitant to report on conflict if the source of the conflict emanates from within that community's dominant power structure — an example being a factory town where there is controversy involving the community's largest employer. The community journalist, they predicted, will seek to protect those in power because it is in the news organization's own best interest to maintain the existing power structure (Donohue, Tichenor & Olien, 1995).

Lessons from Prize-Winning Work in the United States

In 1990, the journalists from *The Washington Daily News*—an "other Washington" with a population of 12,946, located in the coastal plains of eastern North Carolina — received the Pulitzer Prize for public service, becoming the smallest daily newspaper to have ever received the award ("Our History," n.d.). The judges decided, as they have a handful of times, that a community newspaper had gotten it right. Unbowed by community opposition, this newspaper uncovered a scandal involving the safety of the drinking water in the community and further revealed that the problem had been known about and ignored by city leaders (Coughlin, 1990). In exposing the problem, the *Daily News* also learned that Environmental Protection Agency drinking water regulations did not do enough to protect smaller communities ("Not a drop to drink," 1990). The publicity from their investigation eventually lead to changes in these drinking water regulations. The *Daily News* used anonymous sources to uncover documents and publish a story that revealed government corruption and led to legislative changes. What's more, they did so in spite of the fact that many in the community despised the paper for its actions. "You may think you're a hard-nosed editor in the proudest of journalistic traditions; [the community] may just think you're a jerk" then-editor William Coughlin wrote of the experience (1990, p. 96).

When small papers win the Pulitzers, a similar thing seems to happen: The journalism industry's larger newspapers and trade publications look for ways to explain it as an anomaly (Hatcher, 2003b, 2005, 2007). Editor Coughlin, it would later be noted in most of the follow-up articles about the paper's efforts, was from the big leagues, having worked as a correspondent for *The Los Angeles Times* (Pitt, 1990). Reading a little like a Hollywood script, the stories recounted how Coughlin had retired from his real journalism career and was looking for a place to slow down a bit. Instead, he found himself doggedly leading his small paper on an investigation that, the articles implied, simply could not have happened without a journalist oriented to the profession's objectivity norms.

The implication from such an argument is that community media are capable of producing such work only if they are willing to abandon their foundational ethic and step out of their community-embedded situation. However, there is ample evidence to suggest that such a notion proposes a fallacious "either or" proposition. Media that espouse a "we" perspective produce work that is relevant and meaningful to community members and, on occasion, can still impress the Pulitzer judges.

In 1998, the family-owned newspaper *The Riverdale Press* became one of only a handful of weekly newspapers to win a Pulitzer Prize. A close analysis of the editorials written by the *Press'* co-publisher Bernard Stein that were chosen as the best in the nation that year challenge almost every assumption about what it takes to produce community journalism considered "good enough" to compete with mainstream journalism (Hatcher, 2003b, 2005). The editorials addressed topics one might find in any community newspaper in the nation. They talked of the importance of protecting open space, facing the challenges of school overcrowding, and fighting for the preservation of historic structures in the community. The tone and goal of the editorials in the *Press* could be described as seeking to build consensus on important community issues.

However, consensus-oriented should not be confused with being soft, or cowardly. In 1989, the *Press* wrote an editorial defending the right of a local bookstore to carry copies of the Salman Rushdie novel, *The Satanic Verses*. Later, the *Press'* offices were firebombed (Robertson, 1998). Two things happened after this incident. The first was that community members showed up to help the paper publish its next issue. The second was that the paper published another editorial restating its stand on this issue — a message it repeats every year on the anniversary of the bombing.

Admittedly, editorials are, by their nature, decidedly not objective. Their goal is to persuade and encourage action. Nevertheless, the choice in topic and in what issues the paper is willing to challenge set the agenda for the newspaper and the issues that it reports on. The *Press'* editorials gave a voice to a community that, by bureaucratic standards, is not technically a community at all: Riverdale is a neighborhood that has no official designation as a municipality. Still the *Press* connected with a definable community through the following signposts of post-objectivity:

• *Accountability*: Riverdale citizens knew the small staff of journalists at this paper. And the journalists at the paper knew that there was every likelihood they would know citizens who would be topics in their stories
• *Courageousness*: The newspaper prided itself on not being afraid to ask hard questions or point out problems regardless of the backlash that might incur.
• *Community-building*: The newspaper built consensus and joined with the community to solve problems.
• *Community-bridging*: The newspaper unified disparate parts of the community — those with great wealth, those who lived in poverty, those who traced their families back in the community for generations, and those who were new arrivals to the community and to the country.

Community journalists are inextricably tied to the issues they report. Community journalism operates from a perspective that is informed by communitarian philosophies. Its approach runs counter to the professional norms of journalism that require a journalist to remain outside of the community looking in. Community journalists have long been conflicted by this because to admit to having a different ethic is also to suggest that community journalism is an anomaly and, on some level, should not be taken as seriously as media operating within the objectivity paradigm. However, in a post-objective framework, community media journalists are free — for better and for worse — to bring themselves to the discussion. *Better* because *first-person plural* means that Bernard Stein does not have to deny that he was raised in Riverdale, that he has studied and knows the community's history as well as anyone, has sent children to its schools, and has helped in historic preservation efforts. When he speaks, he does so with a credibility that is respected and recognized by his readers. *Worse* because he is personally and continually accountable for what he has written. He knows the subjects that appear in his stories; he may even see them at the grocery store the day he has criticized them. As a community journalist, he is as much a public figure as the mayor (though Riverdale doesn't have one), and is, essentially, never off duty.[1]

Ubuntu in South Africa

Such an interconnectedness is apparent in post-apartheid South Africa, where the concept of ubuntu has seen a resurgence. This traditional African ideology encourages individuals to define themselves based on their relationships to others in a community (Kamwangamalu, 1999). In exploring the many definitions of ubuntu, Kamwangamalu said they all share a theme of interdependence or communalism, analogous to the relationships in a traditional African village. "These values, like the ubuntu system from which they flow, are not innate but are rather acquired in society and are transmitted from one generation to another by means of oral genres such as fables, proverbs, myths, riddles, and story-telling," he said (1999, p. 27).

It's not hard to see how ubuntu might shape the role of media. Ubuntu asks a community not to *think* a certain way but to *act* in a way that invites all to participate and be heard (Blankenberg, 1999). It strives for a horizontal relationship between all members of a community. It seeks to impart information through storytelling: "Ubuntu can be used in an exploration of a form of journalism, whereby, as in traditional African village structures, the concerns, ideas and opinions of all the people are able to occupy real space in any public discussion" (Blankenberg, 1999, pp. 44–45). Informed by ubuntu, journalists are expected to help a community arrive at a solution through consultation (Blankenberg, 1999).

U.S. media ethicist Clifford Christians draws a parallel between ubuntu and the communitarian ethic. Journalists operating under the precept of ubuntu may eschew the professional norms of detachment from the community (Christians, 2004). Journalists are community members first and media professionals second, he said. Therefore, journalism in an ubuntu culture may be less influenced by elite-driven definitions of news: "Its liberatory journalism empowers citizens to come to agreement about social problems and solutions among themselves rather than depending on the political elite or professional experts," he said (Christians, 2004, p. 235).

Media must be put in historical context in South Africa. During the apartheid era, race and ethnicity were used as ways to regulate and oppress some groups while raising the status of others (Sparks, 1991). Since the election of Nelson Mandela in the 1990s, the country has created a democracy that strives to recognize the voices of all groups; the country has designated 11 official languages (Sparks, 2003). As Kamwangamalu noted (1999), difference was once used to divide and oppress; it is now used to unite diverse communities. Community media have been seen as one way of realizing these goals.

In such a complicated cultural situation, what is the role of community media? To explore how journalism in South Africa may be shaped by ubuntu, a secondary, qualitative analysis was conducted of in-depth interviews with South African community journalists. This chapter expands on previous findings from this data (Hatcher, 2010) by zooming in on two South African community media outlets. The comparison of these news organizations illustrates some striking differences that appear to be brought on by the structure of the local community. However, the findings also suggest that the journalists share a common ethic. Specifically, the news workers at these two outlets seem empowered to take their role well beyond the notion of the journalist as mainly an objective disseminator of information.

One News Organization, Multiple Channels

The Zoutnet newspaper group is located in the northeastern province of Limpopo. Here, there are two distinct and historically separate cultural groups: the black African residents, who primarily are part of the Venda tribe, and the white Afrikaans community (Hatcher, 2010). The newspaper group operating in this region has decided that the best way to serve these disparate communities is by offering separate media channels (Hatcher, 2010). One newspaper, the *Zoutpansberger*, is published in Afrikaans, with some English. Its primary audience is the Afrikaner population that lives primarily in one city in the region. Another newspaper, the *Limpopo Mirror*, serves the Venda community. It is published in English and is distributed across a vast, rural geographic region where the Venda live, mostly in smaller, traditional villages. A third publication, *Makoya*, is a newspaper that also serves the Venda community but is oriented toward young readers.

The journalists who work at *Zoutpansberger* are all members of the Afrikaner community and speak Afrikaans as their first language. However, the local government is now comprised primarily of black Africans. In a day-long discussion of their work, the journalists talked candidly of the challenge of practicing journalism in this multicultural environment. They explained that Afrikaner readers are protective of their culture and will count the number of articles published in English, compared to those written in Afrikaans. "They phone you if there are not more Afrikaans stories than English stories and will complain to [us] if there are more English articles," the editor of the paper said (van Zyl, personal communication, May 28, 2009).

One of the reporters said that if the newspaper reports critically on the local government, they will be accused of racism:

> As a white journalist I can write and say look, it is wrong ... and my white readers will say "yes." The black readers will say, "what is wrong with that? They are in power, they know what is right. You actually jeopardize your credibility as a journalist to do such a thing." That causes a serious dilemma. How do you handle that? [F. van der Merwe, personal communication, May 28, 2009].

Meanwhile, the structures of the news organizations that serve the Venda community are complicated by their own set of dynamics. The most obvious challenge is that these media outlets are owned by members of the white, Afrikaner community. The *Limpopo Mirror* is published in English because the black Africans in the region speak a variety of languages and dialects and English is the one common tongue. The paper's reporters are all part-time correspondents who live across a vast geographic region. The paper is managed by an Afrikaner who works at the central newsroom. The editor said the reporters for the *Mirror* will always be loyal to their local villages first and foremost and would never write anything that would be poorly received in their immediate community. Communication between him and his staff as to how to approach news and how to write in English can be very difficult.

> Our situation here ... we're a multicultural society. For me to be a white guy in command of a fully black African staff.... Their first language is Venda. Their second language may be Tsonga. Their third language may be Sepedi. So, if we're talking about English, it can be their fourth or fifth language [W. Lee, personal communication, May 29, 2009].

Zoutnet has taken a different approach with its Venda region youth publication, *Makoya*. The paper faces the challenges of serving a region where poverty and literacy are huge issues. However, the newspaper group decided years ago that education offered the greatest chance of improving the lives of this region's residents. In fact, in 2004 the newspaper group won the World Young Reader Prize from the World Association of Newspapers for a series of educational supplements that were distributed by Zoutnet directly to schools throughout the area (van Zyl, 2005). These kinds of efforts led to the creation of *Makoya*, which is run by two young men from the Venda community. It is published in Thohoyandou, a city in the heart of the Venda community. The sales manager of Zoutnet, who is Afrikaans, said complete editorial control of the paper is given to these editors, "I don't want to have input because I am too far removed from the young people in this region, you know ... their world and my world are two different, different worlds.," he said (P. Jooste, personal communication, May 27, 2009). The editors at *Makoya* said their mission is to offer young readers hope. "We try to motivate people to realize what is possible," one of the editors said (N. Gabara, personal communication, May 27, 2009). "You can dream big ... if he's doing it, you can do it as well. The more we do these kinds of stories, the more people can relate."

Bridging Diverse Communities

More than 1,800 kilometers to the southwest of the Limpopo Province, the front door to Cape Town's world-famous *Bush Radio* has a brick façade with the sign "Building democracy brick by brick."[2] Behind that wall is a community journalism experiment that offers a starkly different vision of how best to reach its particular community. *Bush Radio* was born out of the struggle to end apartheid. Originally, the station did not have a license to broadcast; operating as CASET (Cassette Education Trust) it put its "broadcasts" on audiocassettes and distributed them throughout the community (Bush Radio, n.d.). Today, the radio station's primary audience is the residents of the Cape Flats township, an impoverished area where black residents were forced to live during the apartheid era. However, the station's mission is more expansive — it attempts to build a community that connects the many groups that comprise the complex fabric of this international city, which includes staggering wealth and stark poverty (Bosch, 2005).

The station's program director said the rule at *Bush Radio* is that if you are there you are a student. No one has a permanent job; everyone is there to learn. And they come from around the world to do it.

> Our mission is to facilitate ... young people having access to the station ... to build bridges between those communities. It all links to our mission — that people can see that humans are humans and that we all share, we all hopefully share, a common humanity. And yes that's all glorified terms and we try to steer clear of using them. We try to do this practically [A. Louw, personal communication, June 4, 2009].

Bush Radio attempts to address a complex world through its content. Tune in at any time and something different will be on. There is a kids' radio show that is run completely by children. There is an afternoon, drive-time talk show where, on one afternoon, the hosts had an irreverent discussion about a waiter at a restaurant who insisted — in English — that he only spoke Afrikaans. "We've got a long way to go South Africa. If we're a new democracy, we're only a teenager," one of the drive-time deejays said.[3]

The station devotes a considerable amount of time to public affairs programming that addresses the tough issues of racism, poverty, crime and, of course, HIV. One of the hosts said she is from the townships and her listeners know that she is speaking from experience. The focus of her program, she said, is to talk about problems in a way that will help listeners think about how to make their lives better.

> We don't really want to throw things out there that there is [sic] scandal and bad things. You know, most people in communities know that next door, there is a drug dealer there — they have been knowing that for the past 20 years — so they do know that crime happens every week. They know all these things, but what they don't know is that there are alternatives to their life [D. Adams, personal communication, June 4, 2009].

Different Visions; Shared Goals

Limpopo's Zoutnet and Cape Town's *Bush Radio* present very different journalistic conceptions of the audience and how to reach it. In Limpopo, there are two cultural groups that are completely separate in language and culture. In Cape Town, there is a dizzying array of languages and cultural groups.

The decision by Zoutnet to create separate media channels for different community groups is not without its critics. Other South African journalists interviewed during a 2009 visit strongly opposed this approach, saying that if each group is not exposed to the news or stories of the other, there is no chance for the groups to learn about one another and to see that, ultimately, they share similar hopes and concerns for their geographic region (Hatcher, 2010). Separate media channels may reinforce stereotypes and do little to work toward developing the bridging capital that could foster a stronger sense of shared community (Hatcher, 2011).

The Zoutnet publisher takes a more pragmatic approach, asserting that he is structuring his news organization based on the demands of his different audiences. And his approach may well be an effective route to presenting a wider array of news that is particularly relevant to a community. There is scholarly support for the publisher's segmented approach. The assumption that a one-size-fits-all media is favorable ignores the possibility of a hegemonic situation in which the dominant or privileged group makes the decisions about what is news and how that news is framed (Heider, 2000).

Could (or should) Zoutnet change its approach? What would happen in Limpopo, for example, if the publisher suddenly announced that there was going to be one paper that would be distributed to all the groups in the region? Would this new publication be embraced by both the Venda people and the Afrikaners who would, in turn, begin to bridge their differences? It may be a bit idealistic to think that any one media organization has the power to change a community. Rather, it is more likely that media are a reaction to the communities in which they exist and to fight against that is akin to trying to swim up a waterfall (Donohue, Olien, & Tichenor, 1989).

This is not to say that media cannot effect change. In spite of differences in structure, the news organizations in this analysis share a good many common ideals. In these situations, journalists express a passionate vision of being more than just members of their communities; they are activists, speaking — and acting — on behalf of their fellow citizens. There is no attempt to be distant or removed from this relationship. In Limpopo, the publisher of the newspaper believes that his media organization can be instrumental in making life better for all of the residents of the region. He uses the power of his media to not just report on issues but to champion important causes and, beyond that, to actually get involved in solving those problems through the investment of publicity, money and sweat. Furthermore, in Cape Town, the radio station does not produce content for the community; the community produces content for itself. It is run by citizens who come to *Bush Radio* to learn how to be citizen journalists. The listeners know that the people at the station are not outsiders. *Bush Radio* journalists are community members who speak about issues that directly affect their own lives.

These themes were not only found when examining Zoutnet and *Bush Radio*—they were echoed in discussions with journalists across the country. In all, more than 62 individuals from 11 newspapers, five radio stations, and universities and programs dedicated to journalism education in South Africa were interviewed on-site in 2009. The data suggest that community journalists are not only aware of their community membership, they embrace it, operating in a manner that defies the objectivity norm. In South African community media, ubuntu empowers journalists to envision themselves as stakeholders and activists in their communities, a finding supported by previous research (Milne, Rau, Du Toit, & Mdlongwa, 2006). As Blankenberg noted, "The media is there to ensure first and foremost, the well-being of the collective, rather than the protection of individual rights" (1999, p. 47).

Even so, South African community journalism should not be idealized. There are plenty of criticisms of the media and its relationships with both government officials and with advertisers who may have great sway over media content (Milne, Rau, Du Toit, & Mdlongwa, 2006). Inequalities based on race and class remain profound in South Africa and many of the communities that need media the most do not have it.

Conclusion

The goal of this chapter is not to suggest that journalism practiced from the point of view of "we" is either good or bad. It is to say that it simply "is," and has been a way that community media have operated since long before the notion of an objective press, at least in the U.S., was considered the norm. Understanding community media in this context is useful for seeing how it operates now, and for how it may evolve in a post-objective media environment. The comparison between community media in two cultural settings suggests a number of key findings important to this understanding.

This analysis hopefully underscores how powerful a force culture is in shaping the role of the journalist. It is a reminder that the rules of journalism are not universal. Culture shapes our notions of community. In turn, community defines the boundaries within which a journalist can operate. Seeing journalism as embedded within the community can be an empowering vision. Like the recent trend to buy local food and support local agriculture, the message might say, "Consume locally produced content; it tastes like your community made it." The challenge for the community journalist is to understand the preferences of the community setting and, at times, be willing to test the boundaries of that community, sometimes at great risk.

The post-objective media landscape encourages community media to embrace their "we," and to explore — in a transparent fashion — who they are, as journalists, in a community. Just as each individual in a group has a personality, so, too, does the news worker. It is up to journalists to decide what kind of personality they will have in that community. Community media owe it to their citizens to be transparent and scrutinize how their allegiances, biases and backgrounds may shape their vision of what is news.

Accordingly, this community-focused style of journalism, and its communitarian philosophy, should be closely critiqued. Just as it is foolhardy to be naïve about the impact of an objective approach to journalism, it is equally dangerous not to be aware of the threats that may come from a community-focused media ethic. Barney's (1996) words about how communities can work to suppress dissension should be seen as a caution. Communities are built on rules and may create a shared vision, but they are also rigid and resistant to change and growth. Community media face a great challenge in trying to discuss and even question the rules of a community, especially if such rules exclude certain groups.

Still, even press outlets that are increasingly in tune with post-objective news practices must ask what the rise of community-connected journalism portends for news workers in an era of globalism. For example, Castells (2004) predicted that globalization is fostering *resistance identities*, which forego community relationships based on geographic proximity and encourage the bonding of groups that share common ideologies, ethnicities, and faiths. It is not hard to see how such associations might cultivate some of the aspects of community that are less than desirable. Encouraging likeminded people to band together has never been a difficult task. The true challenge for the community journalist is to build relationships that bridge disparate groups.

The professional journalist drawing on objective notions of what is and is not news is fast becoming obsolete. In the community press, news workers should see themselves as part of a community: writing from a perspective of "we" — a stakeholder in the community. This perspective has a profound impact on news work. Objective journalists profess to ask only one question in making news decisions: Did it happen? Using this criteria, they disseminate stories as detached observers. Like the referee at a sporting event, they have no choice but to call it the way they see it.

But holding strictly to objectivity as a foundational ethic is ignorant at worst, naive at best. Yes, perhaps "it" did happen (insert your own "it" here). But plenty of other events also transpired that went unnoticed for different reasons. Some of those events may have been overlooked because they were things that happened to people in privileged groups who have the resources and power to ensure that the bad news about them does not face the same level of public scrutiny. Other events that happened simply may not have been considered "news" from the vantage point of the professionally defined objective journalist. Is it news that a local woman overcame the obstacles associated with living in an impoverished region to go on to become a quality engineer for a car company? It is for readers of the youth publication *Makoya* in the South African city of Thohoyandou (Tshisevhe, 2011). Is it news that a biology teacher in Riverdale, New York, got his students to help him count the number of warblers that migrate through that community every year? It was for the readers of *The Riverdale Press*, who learned that the students observed how small patches of green space — sometimes just seemingly scruffy lots — were crucial habitats for the birds in the community ("Learning from the 'Fieldston warblers,'" 1997).

These are often the types of stories that contain information relevant to the lives of individuals; they are accounts that give a community a sense of progress and cohesion. Even in the most beleaguered community — or, perhaps, especially in the most beleaguered community — there are people doing inspiring things to solve problems and make a difference. Using traditional U.S. news values, for example, these stories often cannot be told. Instead, news accounts too often focus on individuals who embody spectacle, like the church secretary brought up on charges of embezzlement or child abuse.

There is a false dichotomy in this debate, which goes like this: Those who bemoan the communitarian view say media writing from a perspective of "we" will shy away from tough stories and only publish cozy news that creates a distorted view of a community. Eventually these news outlets' credibility erodes and the community begins to see the content offered by these news organizations as little more than propaganda. To guard against such loss of credibility, this argument proceeds, a news outlet must remain removed from the community, providing stories based solely on the "what are the facts" criteria. If the community does not like what it reads, views or hears, that is really not something that the news outlet can be concerned about.

This is not the only option. In the post-objective journalism environment, the community journalist is encouraged to have a personality and to let the readers know what that personality is and what they can expect. A news organization has a personality. Yes, that may mean conveying a sense of friendliness, compassion, and hope. But the personality can have more dimensions. It might also be courageous, fair and honest — even feisty. Of course, the personality of the journalist (and the journalist's news outlet) is not conceptualized and conveyed in a vacuum. Journalists are hopelessly embedded in the context of their culture, which in turn shapes the rules of a community. To thrive, a journalist's personality has to exhibit more than moving beyond the facts — it must be connected to the tastes and interests of its community.

Chapter Notes

1. Richard and Bernard Stein have since sold the *Riverdale Press*, but remain connected to the newspaper holding the titles of emeritus co-publishers.

2. In South Africa, it's important to expand the study of community media beyond print to include radio, which has historically been the principle media source due to challenges in literacy, language differences and geography (Bosch, 2005).

3. The author heard these comments on an unidentified radio program while driving around Cape Town; unfortunately the date and broadcast time was not noted.

References

Altschull, J.R. (1996). A crisis of conscience: Is community journalism the answer? *Journal of Mass Media Ethics, 11* (3), 166–172.

Bagdikian, B. (1964, December). Behold the grass-roots press, alas! *Harper's Magazine,* 102–110.

Barney, R.D. (1996). Community journalism: Good intentions, questionable practice. *Journal of Mass Media Ethics, 11*(3), 140–151.

Blankenberg, N. (1999). In search of a real freedom: Ubuntu and the media. *Critical Arts: South-North Cultural and Media Studies, 13*(2), 42–66.

Bosch, T. (2005, February). Community radio in post-apartheid South Africa: The case of Bush Radio in Cape Town. *Transformations, 10.* Retrieved August 31, 2011, from http://www.transformationsjournal.org/journal/issue_10/article_05.shtml

Byerly, Kenneth R. (1961). *Community journalism.* Philadelphia: Chilton.

Bush Radio: A modern day success story. (n.d.). *Bush radio.* Retrieved May 18, 2011, from http://www.bushradio.co.za/history/frameset.htm

Castells, M. (2004). *The power of identity.* Malden, MA: Blackwell.

Christians, C. (2004). *Ubuntu* and communitarianism in media ethics. *Ecquid Novi: African Journalism Studies, 25*(2), 235–256.

Christians, C., Ferre, J., & Fackler, P. (1993). *Good news: Social ethics and the press.* New York: Oxford University Press.

Coughlin, W. J. (1990). Think locally, act locally. *Gannett Center Journal: Covering the Environment, 4*(3), 95–103.

Donohue, G.A., Olien, C.N., & Tichenor, P.J. (1989). Structure and constraints on community newspaper gatekeepers. *Journalism Quarterly, 66*(4), 243–253.

Donohue, G.A., Tichenor, P.J., & Olien, C.N. (1995). A guard dog perspective on the role of media. *Journal of Communication, 45*(2), 115–132.

Hatcher, J.A. (2003a). Passion for the minor leagues: Nurturing devotion in an increasingly corporate community press. *Columbia Journalism Review, 42*(1), 66.

_____. (2003b). *Small papers, big stories: How community journalists won the Pulitzer Prize.* Unpublished master's thesis, Syracuse University, Syracuse, NY.

_____. (2004). Community journalism: Nowhere to hide. *Poynter.org.* Retrieved August 31, 2011, from http://www.poynter.org/content/content_view.asp?id=61526.

_____. (2005). Small papers, big stories: A case study comparison of community newspapers that have won the Pulitzer Prize. *Grassroots Editor, 6*(1), 1–10.

_____. (2007). Were those the days? Revisiting the Pulitzer-winning efforts of community newspapers in the 1970s. *American Journalism, 24*(1), 89–118.

_____. (2010, August). *Journalism in a complicated place: The role of community journalism in South Africa.* Paper presented at the Association for Education in Journalism and Mass Communication Conference, International Communications Division, Denver, CO.

_____. (2011). A view from the outside: What other social science disciplines can teach us about community journalism. In B. Reader & J. A. Hatcher (Eds.), *Foundations of community journalism* (pp. 129–149). Thousand Oaks, CA: Sage.

Heider, D. (2000). *White news: Why local news programs don't cover people of color.* Mahwah, NJ: Lawrence Erlbaum.

Jankowski, N. W. (2002). The conceptual contours of community media. In N.W. Jankowski & O. Prehn (Eds.), *Community media in the information age: Perspectives and prospects* (pp. 3–16). Cresskill, NJ: Hampton.

Kamwangamalu, N. M. (1999). Ubuntu in South Africa: A sociolinguistic perspective to a Pan-African concept. *Critical Arts: South-North Cultural and Media Studies, 13*(2), 24–42.

Lauterer, J. (2006). *Community journalism: Relentlessly local.* Chapel Hill: University of North Carolina Press.

Learning from the "Fieldston warblers." (1997, Jan. 2). *The Riverdale Press.* Retrieved September 19, 2011, from http://www.pulitzer.org/archives/6119.

Macintyre, A. (1981/2007). *After virtue.* South Bend, IN: University of Notre Dame Press.

Merrill, J. (1990). *The imperative of freedom: A philosophy of journalistic autonomy.* New York: Freedom House.

_____. (2004). Going, going, coming: Ephemeral media ethics. *Ecquid Novi: African Journalism Studies, 25*(2), 336–338.

Milne, C., Rau, A., Du Toit, P., & Mdlongwa, F. (2006). *Key editorial and business strategies: A case study of six independent community newspapers.* Cape Town, South Africa: Media Digital.

Not a drop to drink. (1990). In K.J. Wills (Ed.), *The Pulitzer prizes: Our history in the making, 1990* (pp. 3–6). New York: Simon & Schuster.

Our History. *Washington Daily News.* Retrieved July 27, 2011, from http://www.wdnweb.com/our-history/

Phillips, D. (1995). *Looking backward: A critical appraisal of communitarian thought.* Princeton, NJ: Princeton University Press.

Pitt, D. E. (1990, April 16). Town gets clean water as paper gets a Pulitzer. *The New York Times,* p. A10.

Putnam, R. D. (1995). Bowling alone: America's declining social capital. *Journal of Democracy, 6*(1), 65–78.

The Pulitzer Prizes: Public Service. *Pulitzer.org.* Retrieved May 12, 2011, from http://www.pulitzer.org/bycat/Public-Service

Reader, B. (2011). Community journalism: A concept of connectedness. In B. Reader & J. A. Hatcher (Eds.), *Foundations of community journalism* (pp. 3–19). Thousand Oaks, CA: Sage.

Robertson, L. (1998). Score one for the little guys of Riverdale. *American Journalism Review.* Retrieved May 13, 2011, from http://www.ajr.org/article.asp?id=2336

Society of Professional Journalists: SPJ Code of Ethics. (1996). *Society of Professional Journalists.* Retrieved October 11, 2010, from http://www.spj.org/ethicscode.asp

Sparks, A. (1991). *The mind of South Africa.* New York: Ballantine.

_____. (2003). *Beyond the miracle.* Jeppestown, South Africa: Jonathan Ball.

Tichenor, P.J., Donohue, G.A., & Olien, C.N. (1980). *Community conflict and the press.* Beverly Hills, CA: Sage.

Tocqueville, A. (1835/2004). *Democracy in America.* A. Goldhammer (trans.). New York: Penguin.

Tshisevhe, N. (2011, August 26). Meet quality engineer — Kate Mushi. *Makoya*. Retrieved August 31, 2011, from http://www.makoyazone.co.za/.

van Zyl, A. (2005, August 26). Limpopo Mirror wins world young reader prize. *Zoutnet*. Retrieved August 29, 2011, from http://www.zoutnet.co.za/details.asp?StoNum=3526.

White, H.A. (1996). The salience and pertinence of ethics: When journalists do and don't think for themselves. *Journalism and Mass Communication Quarterly, 73*(1), 17–28.

10

Engagement as an Emerging Norm in International News Agency Work

JOHN JIRIK

Nowhere is objectivity in journalism more prominent than in the work of global news agencies the Associated Press (AP) and Reuters.[1] Because their client base is not restricted to a particular geographical region, or cultural or ideological space, agency journalists and their editors are extremely sensitive to the possibility of bias in their reports, since almost any event, situation or state of affairs invites a range of interpretations (Hampton, 2008; Paterson, 2007). In an increasingly inter-connected world, news coverage inevitably invites scrutiny from their subscribers who have different viewpoints and from audiences who are at odds with one another. No agency journalist or editor wants to deal with an irate client outlet or audience member — whether it be an individual reader or a national government. But even strict impartiality is no guarantee that these news agencies will avoid being criticized for taking sides. Audiences invested in how they are portrayed in the news rarely see themselves portrayed in the imagined middle-ground that balance and objectivity claims to provide.

After the September 11, 2001, attacks on the United States, Reuters was criticized for an internal memo where global editor Stephen Jukes wrote, "We all know that one man's terrorist is another man's freedom fighter, and that Reuters upholds the principle that we do not use the word terrorist" (Kurtz, 2001, p. 1). Reuters later apologized for the insensitivity of the memo, but the policy remained in place:

> Reuters mission is to provide accurate and impartial accounts of events so that individuals, organizations and governments can make their own decisions based on the facts.... Our policy is to avoid the use of emotional terms and not make

value judgments concerning the facts we attempt to report accurately and fairly [Reuters, 2001, para. 5].

The Al-Qaeda attacks were the most reported event in news history. International coverage of 9/11 showed multiple audiences and multiple broadcasters in play — Al Jazeera, BBC, CNN — each claiming impartiality, each shaping the story for their particular audience, and each of them relying on the AP or Reuters for some if not much of the raw material of that story.

Satellite television and the Internet are changing the way the agencies are seen, leading to a transnational mediascape where the reality of multiple audience subjectivities has replaced the myth of a single objectivity. "Reuters, like the BBC, the CBC in Canada, and ABC in Australia, have all emphasized that digital media and satellite television have turned formerly local viewers into global ones," argued Moeller (2008, p. 14). "Word choices are now scrutinized by a larger and more diverse audience," she noted (p. 14).

Given the challenges facing the news agencies in this increasingly contested news environment, this chapter examines how objectivity and impartiality are handled and whether post-objectivity is a relevant concept for agency narratives. In this chapter, I focus on the two global news agencies: the AP, with its long roots in U.S. press history; and Reuters with an equally long association with British news culture. I look at the concept of objectivity and its relevance for these news agencies. I then examine how pertinent business imperatives, coupled with the rise of the Internet, have led to differences between the AP and Reuters. Finally, I look at both the AP's and Reuters' emerging online news models and their implications for the evolution of a form of post-objectivity in agency news.

The Concept of Objectivity

Allan's (2004) summary of the literature indicates that, in the United States and Britain, objectivity has been shaping elements of the newspaper industry and journalistic practice since the early 19th century. The penny and popular press replaced the partisan and elite press. The telegraph fostered preference for a strong lead, brevity and facts. Commercial pressure to maximize readership produced the human interest story that avoided politics and focused on everyday life. A paid (hence the term "professional") press corps developed as a mass reading public expanded under conditions of industrialization and democratization. Proprietors and journalists embraced norms of fact-based and impartial reporting to justify the term "professional" and address public disillusion with the yellow press and, subsequently, the press's publishing of WWI propaganda.

After World War I, objectivity came of age as an editorial and reporting norm. In the United States, Walter Lippmann (1920/2007, 1922/1998) challenged the press to limit itself to reporting the facts and "fight for the extension of reportable truth" (1922/1998, p. 361). In 1923, the American Society of Newspaper Editors (ASNE) announced their canons of journalism. The fifth canon read: "Impartiality — Sound practice makes clear distinction between news reports and expressions of opinion. News reports should be free from opinion or bias of any kind" (quoted in Allan, 2004, p. 22). In Britain, objectivity was not canonized within a set of standards. Hampton (2008) drew attention to differences between the two news cultures, despite similarities between the two press systems, especially the commitment to a fact-based journalism. In Britain, "Rather than objectivity, notions of truth, independence and 'fair play' held greater appeal," he said (2008, p. 478). Partisanship was accepted. British journalists saw no "contradiction between truthfulness and commitment to specific political principles," said Hampton (2008, p. 483).

The different discourses on objectivity in the U.S. and British press indicate that, by itself, the concept of objectivity cannot be used to adequately describe journalism. The ideal typical press implied by ASNE's codification of objectivity norms has never existed. Rather, what the British experience teaches is that objectivity has a history and, that under different historical circumstances, diverging discourses will produce different practices. Objectivity has been an important guideline that helps journalists to make decisions. But it has never been more than a guideline. What matters is what journalists do and why they do it.

Objectivity in News Agency Work

The AP and Reuters were founded in the mid-19th century, decades before the discourse on objectivity was formalized. Five New York newspapers in 1846 launched the forerunner of the AP to cut costs by sharing news, including accounts from the 1846–1848 Mexican war (Associated Press, 2011a). In London, by 1851 Reuters was using the recently-invented telegraph to relay stock market information between the British capital and the European bourses. From the outset the agencies had a vested interest in objectivity as a news value, although neither wire service characterized the evolution of fact-based reporting in this way. From its inception, the AP appealed to newspapers that served different audiences. Its copy had to appear free of bias. For its part, Reuters wanted to provide its business-oriented constituency with equal access to market-impacting news and bourse prices.

The AP and Reuters emerged as capitalism and industrialization were changing what Wallerstein (2004) has called the world system. Boyd-Barrett (1997) described the news agencies as "agents of globalization" (p. 142) in an era of incipient modernity. As Bayart (2007) noted, local, national, and global forms of consciousness were constituted co-extensively with the spread of Europe and U.S.–centered capitalism, imperialism, and colonization. The mutually-constituted discourses of the national and international were mediated by these news agencies, which traded information as commodities. The globalization they mediated was not inclusive. It was the deliberate crafting of a world functional to the demands of its principals — the expanding European empires, and the emerging United States (Boyd-Barrett, 1998). From the beginning the news agencies made no attempt to provide a balanced and inclusive picture of the world. Rather, they generated and channeled much of the flow of information that was crucial to the extension and maintenance of the nascent capitalist world system. As Boyd-Barrett (1997) noted, "Study of news agencies confirm that globalisation is Westernisation. Agencies themselves inflected globalisation as Westernisation when taking Western-interests-as-norm" (p. 143).

In the 1970s and 1980s proponents of the New World Information and Communication Order (NWICO) were right to point out the imbalance in news flow between the North — the United States and former colonial powers in Europe — and the South, which consisted of poorer regions in Africa, Asia, and Latin America. Their argument rested on a normative premise that information was a public interest that should not be traded as a commodity. This was nonsensical to the agencies, which equated fair flow of news with the free flow of news within the marketplace of information. This market treated information as a commodity, as part of a natural order. The agencies understood the public interest not as an interest of all people treated equally, but as an interest defined by commercial demand for news and the ability to pay. As Gerald Long, Reuters Managing Director in 1980, made clear in outlining his company's opposition to the NWICO-inspired and UNESCO-backed attempt to replace the "free flow" of information with a "free and fair flow": "We are being asked to put up the money and provide the technical, human and operational resources to spread throughout the world that very view of information that is most repugnant to us" (Kleinwachter, 1993, p. 16; Nordenstreng, 1995, p. 431).[2]

Contextual Objectivity and Media Construction of Reality

Historically domiciled in emergent modern states, from the outset the AP and Reuters saw the world in similar ways. They developed a comparable range of services for news clients operating first in text, then in radio, pictures, and television. Editorial and journalistic practice eventually normalized around an ethos of public service, defined as service to the paying public, and professionalism, codified in journalism handbooks and institutionalized in newsrooms. As businesses, the agencies competed and cooperated to supply news retailers with a modular product that any subscriber could plug into their content. The agencies developed and used technologies to foster a competitive edge. But any margin of advantage was quickly eroded, returning the field to an equilibrium that did not threaten the survival of agency news even in the face of mergers, acquisitions, and innovations.

Today, the AP deploys some 2,500 journalists in 300 locations. Reuters employs some 3,000 journalists in almost 200 bureaus. Between them, according to their own estimates, the AP and Reuters on any given day generate news seen by over half the world's population (Associated Press, 2011b; Thomson Reuters, 2011). For most of their history, there was little variation in their news products. Analysis of the kinds of information, events, and sources they produced provide a picture of organizations that consistently emphasized powerful nations, institutions and people as stories and story sources without in any way questioning the ideological assumptions that would privilege such a world (Boyd-Barrett, 1980, 1997, 1998; Paterson, 1996, 2007, 2011; Rantanen, 1997). From the agencies' point of view, their pieces reflected reality. However, critical analysis of news agency material has consistently shown that the particular picture of the world they produced privileges one media construction of reality over other social constructions of reality.

Attempting to account for the different stories that equally professional organizations such as Al Jazeera, the BBC and CNN tell about the same event, situation, person or facts, El-Nawawy and Iskandar (2002) described the process of the social construction of multiple realities in the news as contextual objectivity. They defined contextual objectivity as news which reflected "all sides of any story while retaining the values, beliefs, and sentiments of the target audience" (p. 27). Within the confines of the supplier-client relationship that characterizes news agency work, contextual objectivity confirms one of the claims agencies have traditionally made — their job is to provide the raw material for stories, which clients then tell as they like (Hampton, 2008; Paterson, 2011). However, contextual objectivity does not address the much stronger claim that critics level against agencies: they are not so much reporting as creating reality. Allan (2004) summed up the critical position:

> "News" exhibits certain evolving yet characteristic features which are shaped in accordance with cultural rules or conventions about what constitutes "the world out there" ... while journalists typically present a news account as an "objective," "impartial" translation of reality, it may instead be understood to be providing an

ideological construction of contending truth-claims about reality.... The news account, far from simply "reflecting" the reality of an event, is effectively providing a codified definition of what should count as the reality of the event [p. 4].

In 1998, Boyd-Barrett made an analogous point with reference to the work of the AP and Reuters. He saw their product as "spot news" and a

> journalism of information which privileges "facts" together with the routines in which this style of journalism engages to convince readers of the authenticity of such "facts." The "facts" thus privileged overwhelmingly favour certain categories of information and events over others, certain sources over others, and certain locations over others [p. 20].

Applied to the AP and Reuters, contextual objectivity establishes that objectivity is not a canard. Rather, objectivity needs to be understood as part of a reality-making approach that cannot be isolated from the desire of news makers to adequately serve different audiences.

Divergence and Engagement in Agency News

Two key breaks in the evolution of the business models that have guided the development of the AP and Reuters have led to subtle but increasingly visible changes in the way the two agencies present themselves and report the news. The first break was Reuters' diversification away from news into financial services. The second is the two agencies' approaches to the Internet.

The divergence in the two agencies' business models reflects their different histories. The AP was founded as a cooperative and exists today as a not-for-profit corporation. In 2010, it had 1,400 U.S. daily newspapers as its core members, with broadcasters and non-daily newspapers as associate members (Associated Press, 2011c). The scope of the AP's business is determined by the needs of its members. Reuters is a for-profit company that has latitude to change its business model. From 1925 until 1984, Reuters' majority owners were the British press (Mooney & Simpson, 2003). Despite superficial similarities with the AP in this period, Reuters lacked the AP's institutional base and only several dozen British newspapers subscribed to its service (Mooney & Simpson, 2003). After World War II, with television expanding rapidly and taking readers away from newspapers, Reuters struggled financially and, in the words of a senior manager, "could easily have disappeared in the 1960s."[3] Instead, looking to its history of servicing business, Reuters diversified in 1964 and launched the first of a series of products for financial institutions that would eventually turn Reuters into a multi-billion dollar conglomerate within which media would provide an increasing small proportion of revenue (Mooney & Simpson, 2003; Read, 1992).

However, despite its size, as a financial services and information provider Reuters remained captive to fluctuations in global business cycles and to competition in fields it pioneered (e.g., the arrival of Bloomberg L.P. in 1981). In the midst of the global financial meltdown in the late 2000s, Reuters' board determined that the company was vulnerable as a stand-alone entity and in April 2008 sold it to Canada-based transnational Thomson (Edgecliffe-Johnson, 2007). In 2007, its last year as an independent company, just over six percent of Reuters' revenue was from news media (Reuters, 2007). In 2010, reflecting the relative diminution of media revenue in the enlarged company, only 2.5 percent (324 million USD) of revenue was from media (Thomson Reuters, 2011).

Unlike Reuters, the AP is a one-product business — news. As a non-profit corporation, it exists to serve its members, not deliver its shareholders a dividend. It cannot diversify, unless its institutional structure is changed. While the relevance of news for Thomson Reuters' bottom line is shrinking, the AP's commitment to news directly reflects its members' appetite for news. Despite the financial weaknesses of newspapers — the AP's traditional source of greatest revenue — AP revenue in 2010 was 631 million USD, almost double Reuters' media revenue for the period (Associated Press, 2011c). However, the future of the AP remains directly dependent on its members' continued willingness to pay for the AP's service. Meanwhile, Reuters is free to innovate, but does so at the risk of failure. Some of that risk is mitigated, however, because news media provides an increasingly small contribution to the company's bottom line.[4]

News and the Internet: The AP and Reuters Respond

Research to date indicates that utopian hopes that the interactive capacity of the Internet would challenge established media by fostering greater public participation in news making have proven either to be unfounded or still too faintly realized to be exerting any significant impact on mainstream institutions' control of news (Paterson, 2007; Van der Wurff, 2005; Van der Wurff et al., 2008). Traditional media are remaking themselves to meet the challenges of the Internet, while shaping the medium to meet their needs. As the Internet siphons off advertising as a source of revenue for text, radio and television, traditional media are moving online, using the Internet to deliver much the same product available offline. For newspapers, changes include opening up articles and opinion pages to reader feedback, delimiting story length, providing links to other stories (including those on other websites), and providing in-depth sourcing and investigative materials that traditionally were not visible to the reader. Perhaps most importantly, traditional media outlets are increasingly providing an easily accessible archive, and, on major stories, embedding a minute or so of video, often from the AP or Reuters.

The net effect: the continued predominance of institutionalized news sources and their ongoing reliance on the AP and Reuters for material they are unwilling or unable to generate themselves. As Van der Wurff noted, despite the potential for the Internet to impact news, online versions of newspapers were "subordinate and subservient" to the print version (2005, p. 107). A related study indicated that print and online versions of newspapers complement one another and "report on similar topics in similar ways" (Van Der Wurff et. al, 2008, p. 403). Much the same case could be made for mainstream radio and television news online. One difference is that websites provide textual features and give listeners and viewers much greater control over where, when and how they listen and watch, albeit in the case of television almost always with a loss of quality.

Carey's (1989) assessment of the ritual character of communication, its ability to situate one in the wider world and provide the comfort of shared relationships through media, is key to understanding the behavior of the online news audience. Not surprisingly, it behaves in much the same way as the offline news audience. As Paterson (2007, p. 59) observed, it chooses "a few favorite channels of information, and develops a loyalty to these that is extraordinary in view of the potential for taking in a wider view of the world" that the Internet offers. The "top news sites correspond almost precisely to the top media companies worldwide," he said (2007, p. 60).

Given the revenue problem the Internet created for traditional news, the AP and Reuters have developed strong presences online in a bid to capture some of the advertising and subscriber revenue now flowing there. But reflecting their different business models, they have adopted divergent approaches to the problem. Said Paterson:

> While Reuters and the Associated Press are equally ubiquitous in cyberspace, they have pursued different online strategies. Reuters aggressively moved away from its roots [in] terms of distribution, while the AP has mostly remained tied to the subscription model it has relied on for 150 years [2007, p. 61].

Paterson's (2007) observation was correct. Chris Ahearn, president of Reuters Media, said ahead of the company's launch of its online portal in early July 2005, "We increasingly don't want to be the company that's always in the background.... This is an opportunity to show the world what makes Reuters unique" (Seelye, 2005, para. 4). The AP's senior vice president for media marketing, Tom Brettingen, said, "Reuters' strategy is a destination-site strategy.... Our strategy is not to be the destination. Our member newspapers and broadcasters are the destination, and our content is available through them" (Seelye, 2005, para. 9).

The AP's content is directly available online to non-subscribers through its clients' online outlets via a hosting service *Custom News*, which can be accessed from the AP homepage (www.ap.org) or found at hosted.ap.org. Subscribers can customize the modular service to suit their sites, but the AP editors decide the content of the feed, which is constantly updated. It consists of the AP's selection of the top ten news stories in twelve news categories, providing some 400 stories a day that are designed to look an feel "like content produced locally" (Associated Press, 2009, p. 3). The AP's approach is to make it attractive for subscribing Web outlets to fill their pages with third-party content that is designed to blend into subscriber's websites. *Custom News* takes the hard work out of news making, removing the cost of original reporting that has always been one of the agencies' key selling points. However, clicking through from the AP homepage to different member newspapers across the United States that host *Custom News,* and finding the same ten stories in every category on every site, disconcertingly brings home how dependent these news outlets are on the agencies. *Custom News* is a good indicator of the further homogenization of news that Paterson (2007) contended the Internet would foster.

In contrast to AP's commitment to continue as a news wholesaler, Reuters (www.reuters.com, hereafter Reuters.com) has moved into the retail business, putting its general news file online, while continuing to sell the same stories to its retail subscribers. Paterson (2007) argued that Reuters has "gone into competition with its subscribers" (p. 61). How this will affect Reuters' bottom line in the long run is unclear. Despite the breadth of Reuters' material online, its offerings rarely touch upon local news; that niche could be the difference that continues to make outlets like the *New York Times* or the BBC a preferred alternative to Reuters. Therefore, Reuters' strength — its comprehensiveness — can sometimes be a weakness. By offering so much from so many places, in effect attempting to be a placeless source of news, Reuters can leave its readers unsure of where it is coming from. It risks appearing to be no more than a news aggregator, when one of the company's traditional strengths has been its ability as a news wholesaler to set the retail news agenda. As a British TV news editor noted in 1986, "The role of the agencies is the crucial thing ... the major force deciding what ends up on television screens from abroad" (Harrison, 1986, p. 73).

Meanwhile, if Reuters' subscribers are unhappy with the competition they now face from their news supplier, they have the option of dropping the service. But there is little advantage to that when the only real alternative is the AP. Moreover, as the news industry seeks to further cut production costs, the opposite seems to be the case with the agencies as they expand their client bases. As Paterson noted (2007), non-traditional online portals and aggregators like Yahoo rely heavily on the agencies to provide news, while traditional news retailers are placing more news online, cutting back on original news production, in effect deepening their dependence on the agencies to fill their news holes.

Irony best describes this dependency. The journalism business — which deals in facts, objectivity, and the truth — has historically thrived on the illusion that news retailers (newspapers and broadcasters) were producing the news, when they actually were buying it from news wholesalers. In 2008, senior AP executive Eric Braun noted that television audiences do not understand that "most of the most dangerous pictures are taken by the agency photographers, not by the people who work for the branded networks" (Paterson, 2011, p. 134). Until Reuters opened its online portal, the agencies had remained the unseen bulwark of the news business. That has now changed. Visitors to hosted.ap.org and Reuters.com can see the work of the two companies that provide much of the world's non-local news.

Engagement Replaces Objectivity

In keeping with the character of the Internet as an interactive medium, the AP and Reuters are increasingly embracing social media and making themselves visible to readers and audiences. Both companies have Facebook and Twitter feeds. As of early September 2011, Reuters had just over one million Twitter followers and the AP just under half a million. Both companies followed their own reporters who had Twitter feeds, and tracked feeds from non-agency sources that their social media editors had deemed newsworthy. A reporter's feed served various functions, most of them news-related, from advertising their own or a colleague's articles, to soliciting story material and checking facts and sources on a story in development. Both companies have superficially similar Facebook pages, which function as news sites, replete with space for reader comments. Clicking through a story on the AP's Facebook wall takes a reader to a site, hosted by ap.org, that provides the same ten stories in twelve categories that the AP made available as plug-in modules to its traditional subscribers. The Reuters' Facebook wall directed readers to Reuters.com, unless Reuters was sourcing its own story from a third party, in which case a click through on a story took a reader to the third party site. Neither company's Facebook feed offered more than an illusion of interactivity. Each company had harnessed the site to its existing product, directing visitors to their traditional content, without openly engaging with their audiences beyond providing a space for comment, an online function that has lacked the seriousness of the opinion pages in an offline newspaper.

Nevertheless, because of their diverging business models, as of late 2011, Reuters had gone much further than the AP in establishing an interactive online presence. From Reuters.com a click through on a journalist's byline took a reader to his or her feed, hosted at blogs.reuters.com. There, one had the choice of up to three channels: article, post and Twitter, depending on how available a reporter had made their work and themselves. Articles are news stories, by-lined reports that constitute the traditional Reuters file. Posts ranged from articles, through personal observations to re-posts of third-party content. Posts that were not simply repeats of articles tended to provide greater insight into a story than the version submitted as an article. For example, a photographer might write about why a particular picture was taken in a certain way. A journalist might provide the back story to an article he or she had published.

Typical of this kind of post was Fabrizio Bensch's (2011) account of his coverage on of the July 22, 2011, Norwegian massacre:

> Aug 1, 2011. The way to the island of horror
> It was a typical Friday afternoon in Berlin — traffic in the streets and people looking forward to their weekend ... I was at home and not aware of the latest news when I got a phone call from the Berlin office: "It's an emergency. There was a bomb explosion in Oslo. Can you book a flight to Oslo and immediately fly there?" At first I did not know what exactly had happened. My wife searched for information online and the first breaking news images from Oslo had flooded the media. People were wandering amid the rubble in the governmental area of the Norwegian capital ... [Bensch, 2011, para. 1].

The account was intensely personal and packed with detail about how Bensch rushed to pack up, flew to Oslo, rented a car, and drove to the massacre site, where he and colleagues rented a boat for Utoeya Island:

> With the help of that lens I could see legs and feet under the white blankets. Everywhere on the shore were corpses.... It was an eerie, gruesome and frightening moment.... This image has been engraved in my memory.... One nightmarish moment [Bensch, 2011, para. 6].

Woven through the account were Bensch's images of the massacre and related bombing in Oslo. From the point of view of an objective, fact-based news account, most of the written material in Bensch's account was superfluous. We learned little about the massacre that was not already obvious from the pictures. What Bensch's account did was contextualize the event, not within a broader historical or socio-cultural horizon, but through the reduction of the event to the journalist's experience of his work. The account was a compelling piece of first-person reportage. We were transported to the scene of the crime and allowed to see through the photographer's lens. In contrast to watching from the outside, the reader adopted Bensch's point of view. Subjectivity was substituted for objectivity. This was not agency journalism as it is traditionally understood. It recalled a much earlier era, the first person and narrative-based accounts that were the precursor of literary journalism. As Habermas (1989) noted, modern journalism originated in these accounts that reported on the disputes inside the 17th-century coffee house and salons of the early public sphere, long before the canons of facticity, balance and objectivity replaced the narrated story as journalistic norms.

Bensch is a photographer. Traditionally, photographers and videographers have had low profiles in journalism, providing color for a journalist's story and pictures to illustrate the story a reporter was telling for television. But just as television taught media owners about the importance of star power for audience loyalty, so Reuters put its reporters into the picture and branded them in a bid to use their visibility to improve its revenue stream. For an institution whose marketability was historically its invisibility, attempting to follow the lead of television by making the reporter integral to the story is a radical innovation.

In keeping with the increasing visibility of the reporters, perhaps an even more radical innovation at Reuters has been the collapse of the firewall that traditionally isolated the company's editorial operation from outside influence. The trail from any story on the Reuters.com front page via the reporter's byline leads to blogs.reuters.com, where one finds a link to "all journalists." That link goes to http://blogs.reuters.com/journalists/, where hundreds of journalists are listed in alphabetical order. But not all of these people are Reuters' journalists. For example, Philip Baum is the "editor of Aviation Security International and the managing director of Green Light Limited, an aviation security training and consultancy company based in London" (Baum, 2009, para. 1). His piece, "Why we must profile airline passengers," published as part of Reuters' *The Great Debate* series is not journalism as traditionally understood. It is opinion. Moreover, as a security consultant, Baum would be in conflict of interest if he were writing as a journalist about the need for passenger profiling. But apparently he is neither writing as a journalist in the traditional sense nor as a Reuters' journalist because "the opinions expressed are his own" (Baum, 2009, para. 1).

Baum's (2009) piece was not unique. On the contrary, Reuters is increasingly marketing third-party content and opinion at Reuters.com. One can find such material under the front page drop down header, "Opinion," which links to pieces such as Bensch's and Baum's, and countless other opinion pieces from dozens of journalists and contributors. The problem is that, despite the disclaimers, Reuters.com bears the Reuters logo, implying an association between the content of the website and the Reuters' brand, a brand which has built up customer loyalty over decades because of the perceived accuracy, impartiality, and facticity of its news product. As the *Reuters Handbook of Journalism* states:

> Reuters journalists do not express their opinions in news stories, voiced video or scripts, or on blogs or chat rooms they may contribute to in the course of their work. This fundamental principle has generated huge trust in Reuters among customers and the public over many years [Reuters, 2009, p. 8].

But at Reuters.com, the Reuters' brand clearly provides an umbrella endorsement for news and opinion, regardless of the source. Reuters is obviously aware of the problem, but rather than address it head on, it apparently wants to sidestep the challenges the online and interactive news environments pose for traditional journalism by shifting to a post-objective news model. In 2010, then Reuters Editor-in-Chief David Schlesinger attempted to explain the blurring of journalism and opinion that characterizes this emerging paradigm. Not surprisingly, given Reuters' traditional definition of news as a commodity, Schlesinger (2010) began with a market metaphor by defining the value of news in terms of scarcity. He then argued that the Internet undermines value by providing facts free of charge that the agencies once charged for. He suggested that a new understanding of value was required, one anchored in the abundance dynamics of the Internet. "Technology has created a completely new concept of community," he said, noting that it gives communities "new powers to inform and connect" through social media such as Facebook, blogging and Twitter (Schlesinger, 2010, para. 7). Technology, he said, has "upended the power equation to give control to the end consumer" (Schlesinger, 2010, para. 14). In order for Reuters to survive, Schlesinger (2010) said he believed the company must abandon the paternalism of editorial authority (which this author reads as impartiality and objectivity), and embrace a push pull publishing model that "embraces both the professionalism of the journalist and the power of the community" (para. 19). What matters today is "context, connectedness and community," he said (para. 39). He pointed to the global financial crisis of 2007–2008 as a major trigger for these changes. What Reuters learned from its reporting of the crisis was that

> pure facts are not enough. Pure facts don't tell enough of the story; pure facts won't earn their way.... The facts were there. But they weren't put together in a way that was compelling enough or powerful enough to change the course of events [2010, para. 34–36].

In calling for a journalism that will "change the course of events," Schlesinger abandoned the bedrock assumption of objectivity, that the "images and stories must reflect reality" (Reuters, 2009, p. 4). Wanting to shape the news to affect events was a radical shift for a company that has considered impartiality the holy grail of journalism. Clearly Reuters actually intends to have it both ways. The company wants to combine the traditional model of journalism, anchored in the ethos of a report as an accurate reflection of reality, while simultaneously recognizing that they have a role in helping to construct the reality on which they report. Schlesinger (2010) admitted as much, arguing that his job is "to ensure that the journalistic tradition of yesterday melds with the social media ethos" (para. 30). So, what the new journalism at Reuters.com does is embed the reporter (and the reporter's connection to community) deep inside the story.

Schlesinger asked of this emerging paradigm, "Is it journalism?" He answered, "Sometimes it is pure journalism. Sometimes it's commentary. Sometimes it's just a sharing of ideas.... But whatever you call it, it is an intelligent service between the journalist and the customer and that's something we should be aiming for" (para. 46–48). Foregrounding engagement as the norm, he said "the old one-way relationship between editor and audience has no place in the world any more" (para. 53).

Conclusion

In closing, what should be remembered is that technology did not force Reuters to embrace the Internet. Changing business conditions triggered the sale of the company to Thomson. The Internet enabled, but did not compel the embrace of social media and a more engaged journalism. The relative diminution of the contribution of news to the bottom line at Thomson Reuters opened up space for a relatively risk-free experiment in harvesting revenue from the developing online news environment. If technology was a driver for change in the manner that Schlesinger assumed, then the AP should have been forced to abandon its allegiance to the traditional news model. But the AP operates in a protected business environment that prevents it from diversifying in a manner inconsistent with the demands of its members. The AP has moved online without attempting to change its core product, and its move has been no less successful than Reuters.

There is nothing new in Reuters' recognition that facts are not enough. When Lippmann in the 1920s outlined the argument for a fact-based journalism devoid of opinion, he encountered the opposition of John Dewey, who argued for news that would serve the public by mediating the latter's relationship with power (Carey, 1989; Schudson, 2008). Dewey believed the public interest was best served by an engaged press. Reuters' turn to engagement is in some ways a revival of the Lippmann-Dewey debate and also a return to the pre-agency past when reason and opinion clashed in the coffee houses and salons of Europe in an era that launched modern news but pre-dated the canons of objectivity (Bybee, 1997; Schudson, 2008).

But just as the coffee houses and salons of the late 17th and early 18th centuries served an elite clientele that excluded many segments of the population, Reuters' turn toward engagement tends to privilege the voices of the clients the company already serves — finance and business communities and elite segments of the world's most powerful nations. From the evidence on Reuters.com, it seems unlikely that Reuters will broaden its engagement to give voice to a wider range of global public interests.

In sum, when the AP and Reuters were founded in the mid-19th century, the United States was beginning to assert its independence in a world still dominated by Britain. Contextual objectivity helps explain the different ways in which the two companies operationalized objectivity as a shared journalistic norm. The 9/11 events clarified that different realities are now the norm in the news. The changing business and technological environments in which news makers operate have further separated the types of work that the AP and Reuters do. Where the AP currently remains committed to a traditional definition of reporting, Reuters has embraced engagement in the online reporting environment. Different business models and approaches to the Internet are beginning to pull two of the world's most powerful news sources in different directions. Reuters' attempts to foreground the work of journalists — as limited as it may be — acknowledges that a more engaged style of reporting is not at odds with fact-based reporting. In effect, Reuters' actions are a long-overdue recognition that reporters are central to the stories that they tell. What's emerging at Reuters.com — the embrace of opinion and broader engagement with the audience — further undermines the old objectivity tenet that news reflects, rather than creates, reality.

Chapter Notes

1. This chapter focuses on the AP and Reuters. The author worked at Reuters from 1992 to 1999, which, despite every attempt to be even-handed in his treatment of both agencies, has undoubtedly influenced his understanding of the issues discussed. The third global news agency is Agence France-Presse (AFP). But AFP does not have the reach of its Anglophone competitors, and should be considered a strong second-tier agency.

2. To be fair to Long, his anger primarily was directed at Cold War state control of media and propaganda. However, in so doing he conveniently ignored the important role state-controlled media could play in nation building in the de-colonized South and Reuters' long historical association with the British government as a servant of colonial, imperial, and official policy (Kleinwachter, 1993; Nordenstreng, 1995; Thussu, 2006, p. 22)

3. Michael Nelson, Reuters' Manager of Economic Services (1962–1974) and Reuters' General Manager (1976–1989), cited in Mooney & Simpson (2003, p. 9).

4. Against its marginal relevance in monetary terms, the symbolic value of news and the Reuters' brand to Reuters Thomson should not be underestimated. For an excellent discussion of the symbolic capital of being in a marginally profit-generating business like news, see Bielsa (2008).

References

Allan, S. (2004). *News culture* (2nd ed.). Maidenhead, England: Open University Press.

Associated Press. (2009, October). AP: Kentucky reports. Retrieved September 2, 2011, from http://www.ap.org/kentucky/documents/multipagekynewsletter1009 — revised.pdf

_____. (2011a). AP history. Retrieved June 5, 2011, from http://www.ap.org/pages/about/history/history_first.html

_____. (2011b, March). AP: facts & figures. Retrieved June 13, 2011, from http://www.ap.org/pages/about/about.html

_____. (2011c). Associated press consolidated financial statements 2010. Retrieved June 12, 2011, from http://www.ap.org/annual11/

Baum, P. (2009, December 28). Why we must profile airline passengers. *Reuters.com*. Retrieved September 7, 2011, from http://blogs.reuters.com/great-debate/2009/12/28/why-we-must-profile-airline-passengers/

Bayart, J.-F. (2007). *Global subjects: A political critique of globalization.* Cambridge, England: Polity.

Bensch, F. (2011, August 1). The way to the island of horror. *Blogs.reuters.com*. Retrieved September 6, 2011, from http://blogs.reuters.com/fabrizio-bensch/

Bielsa, E. (2008). The pivotal role of news agencies in the context of globalization: A historical approach. *Global Networks, 8*(3), 347–366.

Boyd-Barrett, O. (1980). *The international news agencies.* Beverly Hills, CA: Sage.

_____. (1997). Global news wholesalers as agents of globalization. In A. Sreberny-Mohammadi, D. Winseck, J. McKenna, & O. Boyd-Barrett (Eds.), *Media in global context: A reader* (pp. 131–144). London: Arnold.

_____. (1998). "Global" news agencies. In O. Boyd-Barrett & T. Rantanen (Eds.), *The globalization of news* (pp. 19–34). London: Sage.

Bybee, C. R. (1997). Media, public opinion and governance: Burning down the barn to roast the pig. Retrieved August 28, 2011, from http://www.infoamerica.org/teoria_articulos/lippmann_dewey.htm

Carey, J. W. (1989). *Communication as culture: Essays on media and society.* Boston: Unwin Hyman.

Edgecliffe-Johnson, A. (2007, May 16). Thomson accepts Reuters voting code. *The Financial Times.* Retrieved June 3, 2011, from http://www.ft.com/cms/s/0/6460287a-03e4-11dc-a931-000b5df10621.html#axzz1OFhAV5Qi

El-Nawawy, M., & Iskandar, A. (2002). *Al-Jazeera: How the free Arab news network scooped the world and changed the Middle East.* Cambridge, MA: Westview.

Habermas, J. (1989). *The structural transformation of the public sphere.* Cambridge, England: Polity Press.

Hampton, M. (2008). The "objectivity" ideal and its limitations in 20th-century British journalism. *Journalism Studies, 9*(4), 477–493.

Harrison, P., & Palmer, R. (1986). *News out of Africa: Biafra to band aid.* London: Hilary Shipman.

Interbrand. (2010). Best global brands 2010. Retrieved September 7, 2011, from http://www.interbrand.com/en/best-global-brands/Best-Global-Brands-2010.aspx

Kleinwachter, W. (1993). Three waves of the debate. In G. Gerbner, H. Mowlana, & K.

Nordenstreng (Eds.), *The global media debate: Its rise, fall and renewal* (pp. 13–20). Norwood, NJ: Ablex.

Kurtz, H. (2001, September 24). Peter Jennings, in the news for what he didn't say. *The Washington Post*, p. 1.

Lippmann, W. (1920/2007). *Liberty and the news.* Princeton, NJ: Princeton University Press.

_____. (1922/1998). *Public opinion.* New Brunswick, NJ: Transaction Publishers.

Moeller, S. (2008). *Packaging terrorism: Co-opting the news for politics and profit.* Oxford: Wiley-Blackwell.

Mooney, B., & Simpson, B. (2003). *Breaking news: How the wheels came off at Reuters.* Chichester, England: Capstone.

Nordenstreng, K. (1995). *The NWICO debate.* Leicester, England: Leicester University Centre for Mass Communication Research (CMCR).

Paterson, C. (1996). Global television news services. In A. Sreberny-Mohammadi, D. Winseck, J. McKenna, & O. Boyd-Barrett (Eds.), *Media in global context: A reader* (pp. 145–161). London: Arnold, 1997.

_____. (2007). International news on the Internet: Why more is less. *Ethical Space: The International Journal of Communication Ethics, 4*(1/2), 57–66.

_____. (2011). *The international television news agencies: The world from London.* New York: Peter Lang.

Rantanen, T. (1997). The globalization of electronic news in the 19th century. *Media, Culture & Society, 19*(4), 605–620.

Read, D. (1992). *The power of news: The history of Reuters.* Oxford: Oxford University Press.

Reuters. (2001, October 2). Media statement. *Reuters.* Retrieved June 2, 2011, from http://web.archive.org/web/20011002123400/http://about.reuters.com/statement3.asp

_____. (2007). Reuters annual report 2007. *Reuters.* Retrieved June 12, 2011, from http://ir.thomsonreuters.com/phoenix.zhtml?c=76540&p=irol-reportsOther

_____. (2009, November 24). Handbook of journalism. *Reuters.* Retrieved June 5, 2011, from http://handbook.reuters.com/

Schlesinger, D. (2010, October 15). Changing journalism; changing Reuters. *Reuters.* Retrieved June 17, 2011, from http://blogs.reuters.com/reuters-editors/2010/10/15/changing-journalism-changing-reuters/

Schudson, M. (2008). The "Lippmann-Dewey debate" and the invention of Walter Lippmann as an anti-democrat 1986–1996. *International Journal of Communication, 2,* 1031–1042.

Seelye, K. (2005, June 27). Reuters, seeking brand awareness, to offer G-8 news online and direct. *The New York Times.* Retrieved September 7, 2011, from http://www.nytimes.com/2005/06/27/business/media/27reuters.html

Thomson Reuters. (2011). Thomson Reuters annual report 2010. Retrieved June 12, 2011 from, http://ir.thomsonreuters.com/phoenix.zhtml?c=76540&p=irol-reportsOther

Thussu, D. K. (2000). *International communication: Continuity and change.* London: Hodder Arnold.

_____. (2006). *International communication: Continuity and change* (3rd ed.). London: Hodder Arnold.

Van der Wurff, R. (2005, February 1). Impacts of the Internet of newspapers in Europe: Conclusions. *Gazette, 67,* 107–120.

Van der Wurff, R., Lauf, E., Balcytiene, A., Fortunati, L., Holmberg, S., Paulussen, S., & Salaverria, R. (2008). Online and print newspapers in Europe in 2003. Evolving towards complementarity. *European Journal of Communication, 33*(4), 403–430.

Wallerstein, I. (2004). *World-systems analysis: An introduction.* Durham: Duke University Press.

PART IV

Objectivity and Theory

11

Why Objectivity Is Impossible in Networked Journalism and What This Means for the Future of News[1]

David Michael Ryfe

Objectivity has been a cardinal principle of American journalism since the 1920s. Some version of it appears in the mission statements of most every news organization, professional association, and journalism school across the country. But its time may well be passing. As historians and sociologists have argued for decades (Cook, 1998; Mindich, 1998; Schiller, 1981; Schudson, 1978, 2001; Sparrow, 1999; Tuchman, 1972), objectivity arose and persisted in the 20th century because it met particular needs. Put more precisely, it met the needs of news organizations and journalists working in an increasingly mass-mediated environment.

The future of objectivity is in doubt, in large part because the Internet is not a mass medium; rather, it is a networked medium. More specifically, online interaction typically takes on a small-worlds, networked structure of dense clusters of nodes organized around hubs. These hubs are then linked to other dense clusters through bridges. As news is increasingly produced, distributed, and consumed in this small-worlds setting, journalism is changing. Objectivity is proving to be an ineffective response to these developments. For example, online journalists must attract the attention of dense clusters of passionate, committed, like-minded people. How are they to do so? Objectivity, with its insistence that journalists remain detached and independent, does not seem especially helpful for answering this question. To the extent that objectivity fails to resonate with the news preferences of online news consumers, we may expect objectivity in online news to wane.

This raises a question about the future of news. What will happen when objectivity is no longer central either to the self-definition of journalists or the practice of journalism? Borrowing from the field theory of Pierre Bourdieu (1971, also see Benson & Neveu, 2005), I argue that journalism is a social field. The disconnect between objectivity and the needs of online news producers and consumers has had the effect of weakening the relations of force, as Bourdieu calls them, that hold journalism together. With this deterioration, journalists and news organizations have begun to move in different directions, much as our solar system's planets would spin away from one another in the absence of the gravitational force provided by the sun. In short, journalism has begun to unravel.

In this piece, I sketch this argument through several steps. I begin by defining objectivity. I then review several of the ways that objectivity has met the needs of journalists, and place this relationship in the context of a mass-mediated environment. Next, I describe the small-worlds, networked structure of online interaction. I show how this networked environment poses a new set of dilemmas for journalism, problems that objectivity may be ill suited to address. I conclude by outlining what these factors mean for journalism's future.

Defining and Situating Objectivity

What is objectivity within journalism? Even journalists find this question difficult to answer. John Boyer (1981) once asked fifty wire service editors to define the term — and got 26 different definitions. Similarly, the academy has struggled to define objectivity. Hackett and Zhao (1998) describe it as a "discourse" of the profession. Kovach and Rosenstiel (2001) prefer to call it a "method," and Richards (2005) refers to it as a "perspective." Schudson (2001) argues that, although a precise definition may elude us, objectivity is indirectly observable in journalistic values, practices, and patterns of news writing. Mindich (1998) offers perhaps the most concrete definition of the term. Drawing on a review of 19th-century textbooks and press criticism, he suggests that objectivity is principally defined by five traits: detachment, nonpartisanship, the inverted-pyramid style of writing, facticity, and balance. To Mindich, journalistic objectivity clearly lays out press values and practices. Reporters should be independent. They ought to be unemotional, uninvolved, and detached from the events they cover and the sources they turn to. They should stick to the facts and strive for accuracy in all things. They ought to balance one point of view with another. They should never insert their own views into stories, but attribute every perspective to a source. They ought to give the reader the five Ws (who, what, when, where, why) in dry, factual prose.

They must never embellish, or say more than they know or can verify. This list is not exhaustive, but it is enough to give the reader a sense that objectivity provides both a moral standard and a set of practices that serve as a guide for daily newsgathering.

These values and practices made their appearance in American journalism at different moments in time. The notion that journalism ought to be neutral regarding events it covers dates back in the United States to at least Benjamin Franklin's newspaper piece "Apology for Printers" (1731/1987). It was in 1835 that James Gordon Bennett introduced the idea that journalism ought to stick to facts "stripped of verbiage and coloring" (Bennett, 1835, p. 2). In the 1850s, liberal reformers within the Republican Party, many of them editors, celebrated an educational (or fact-centered) model of journalism (McGerr, 1986). And by the mid-19th century — during the heyday of the party press — many newspapers trumpeted their nonpartisanship (Rutenbeck, 1990). But the specific term objectivity was not applied to journalism until the early 20th century (Dicken-Garcia, 1989; Schudson, 1978), an indication that, by then, these ideals and practices began to congeal into a coherent model of journalism.

From the outset, the term proved contentious. Already in the 1920s H.L. Mencken (1927) complained that journalists were too ignorant of the subjects they covered — and too beholden to their news organizations — to live up to the label. More famously, Walter Lippmann (1922) argued that the news was too fleeting and sensationalistic to provide an accurate picture of reality. The term has suffered continuous abuse ever since, from both inside and outside the profession. Cunningham (2003), for instance, traces much of the passivity displayed by journalists during the George W. Bush administration to their mindless devotion to objectivity; he argues such dedication to objectivity turned news workers into "passive recipients of news" (p. 26). And Gillmor (2005), questioning its relevance, asserts that objectivity has more to do with the economic needs of large corporate news organizations than with the needs of journalists.

Despite such criticisms, objectivity remains a core element of modern journalism, so much so that journalists often treat it as a natural way of approaching their craft. But objectivity is not inevitable; it has a particular history. It emerged at the turn-of-the-20th century just as news organizations were freed from political parties, became bigger and more profitable (especially in urban areas), and as journalistic professionalism took shape. Why did objectivity arise at this time, and why did it come to play such a central role in 20th-century journalism? Traditionally, historians have answered the first of these questions with an appeal to economics and technology (Ryfe & Kemmelmeier, 2011). In part, the argument goes, objectivity arose for marketplace reasons (Emery & Emery, 1996; Schiller, 1981). At the end of the 19th century, owners of commercial newspapers saw great profits to be made in selling news to mass (rather than partisan) audiences. To the extent that objectivity allowed reporters to produce news for no one in particular (that is, for everyone), it helped owners work toward the goal of increased circulations. Objectivity also has its roots in technological breakthroughs, especially the introduction of the telegraph in the 1840s (Carey, 1989; Shaw, 1967). The telegraph opened the way for newspapers to share stories with each other, but they could not do so easily without some consistency in style, form, and practice. Objectivity served as a set of standard reporting and writing practices that ensured uniformity in news reporting. Thus, the availability of new technologies coupled with the growth of a mass market produced the conditions for objectivity to take hold.

Until about the 1970s, this answer was received wisdom among those who studied objectivity in the news. Since then, however, researchers have agreed that the appeal to economics and technology is not sufficient for explaining objectivity's rise and persistence. They argue that additional forces, for example the synergies and tensions between journalism and PR, have also been at work (St. John, 2009, 2010). And there are many intra-field factors that have sustained objectivity. For example, Schudson, reflecting how objectivity has evolved over time (2001), notes four different functions served by objectivity:

• Objectivity serves as a method of social control within the newsroom. Since the newsgathering process involves many individuals, editors cannot directly monitor the daily activities of everyone in the newsroom. Via objectivity, however, they can ensure consistent standards and practices.

• Objectivity allows journalists to distinguish themselves from contiguous occupations, especially public relations. We are journalists, reporters can insist, and not advertising agents, public relations specialists, public information officers, or any of a host of other communication specialists, because we are independent, factual, and impartial.

• Objectivity is a principal means for recognizing distinction within the field of journalism. A "good" journalist is defined as someone who gathers more facts, is more vigorous about protecting press independence, and remains more detached than other journalists.

• Objectivity functions as a cultural glue linking generations of journalists. Every culture has a need to perpetuate itself. Older journalists ensure this happens in journalism by socializing younger journalists into the canons of objectivity.

Other scholars have identified still other functional purposes of objectivity. Tuchman (1972), for example, views it as a strategic ritual that journalists employ to insulate themselves from political criticism. Cook (1998) argues that it is an institutional response to uncertainty. And, of course, as the *New York Times* suggests with its famous motto — "All the News That's Fit to Print" — objectivity has had a branding function for news organizations. Newspapers compete for audience attention by trumpeting their relative objectivity.

In sum, according to the extant scholarship, objectivity has become and remained central to journalism for the most mundane of reasons: it is useful. It is important to place this conclusion in context. Objectivity arrived, thrived, and persisted within news organizations that operate as traditional mass media. That is, objectivity is practiced within organizations that have the following characteristics: they produce news for a profit; they pay a relatively small cadre of experts (journalists) to produce news; these professionals push the news product out to a mass audience; and, this audience passively and anonymously consumes the information (Ohmann, 1996). Figure 1 offers a simple sketch of these dynamics. News organizations share this basic structure with all mass media, including Hollywood movie studios, advertising agencies, broadcast networks, and music companies. In each of these instances, organizations employ a small number of professionals to produce cultural information (news, songs, movies) for a passive audience numbering in the millions. When we speak of modern mainstream journalism we are referring to a traditional mass medium. And when we speak of objective journalism, we are saying that it emerged within the context of a mass-mediated environment.

Part of what this means is that the mass-mediated structure of modern journalism (profit-oriented organizations, small, expert-oriented professionals, and much larger, passive audiences) went a long way toward shaping the sorts of problems modern news organizations and journalists now face. Take the problem of professionalization. It is only as specialists that journalists develop a need to distinguish themselves from other specialist occupations. If anyone could practice journalism, then there would be no need to make such distinctions. And it is only when journalism becomes a professional occupation that a need arises to transmit its myths and traditions across generations of workers. Objectivity in journalism is useful for similar reasons. As one example, the objective, inverted pyramid style of writing for everyone, and therefore to no one, only makes sense in the context of organizations that are literally trying to reach the masses with their products. Additionally, while being mass-oriented, such news organizations have become large and unwieldy. And it is only because they are large and unwieldy that something like objectivity is necessary to ensure a measure of social control in the newsroom. Objectivity, this is to say, is not useful in the abstract. Rather, it is useful for specific kinds of journalists working for particular kinds of news organizations. This implies that

Figure 1: Journalism as a Mass Medium.

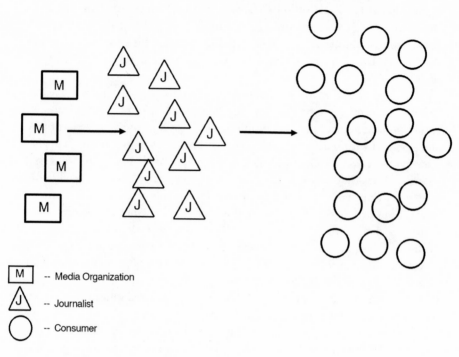

M — Media Organization

J — Journalist

◯ — Consumer

journalism practiced by different sorts of people for different sorts of organizations might have different needs that objectivity does not necessarily meet.

Networked Journalism

The structural arrangements of online cultural production are dramatically different from those of mass media. This "is the core characteristic of mass media," Yochai Benkler (2006) writes: "Content is produced prior to transmission in a relatively small number of centers, and when finished is then transmitted to a mass audience, which consumes it" (p. 209). Online, in contrast, everyone is ostensibly a "user"—a consumer and a producer of information. As users, we "are substantially more engaged participants, both in defining the terms of [our] productive activity and in defining what [we] consume and how [we] consume it" (p. 138). This is a simple but profound point. Compared to mass media, the Internet gives individuals much more control over their information environment, and correspondingly dilutes the control of professional journalists.

Journalists sometimes minimize these factors by arguing that much of the culture produced by amateurs is, in a word, bad. They are right. Most people, including people producing news, have little journalistic talent. But the law of large numbers shows that the question of amateur talent is irrelevant. Today, about one billion people have access to the Internet, and this number will only grow in the future. Suppose that only one percent of these people have any talent for cultural production. They write well, or have a nice visual eye, or know a lot about a particular subject. One percent of one billion is ten million people. Each of these individuals possesses as much talent as the average journalist, and together they surpass the total number of professionals by a large margin. Even if most online content is crud, a large amount — a number far larger in the aggregate than material that is produced by professionals — will be very good.

It turns out that when people are given a choice, they do not choose to interact with others in a random way. Rather, online they tend to congregate in "small worlds" (Barabasi, 2002; Ferguson, 2002; Schnettler, 2009). A small world is a network structure characterized by dense clusters of individuals linked together via bridges or connectors (Figure 2). Within these dense clusters, individuals conduct their virtual lives much as they do their real ones: they interact with people who are familiar, or with whom they share a common interest. In fact, one way of thinking about the Internet is that it amplifies a social tendency to interact with people like us. However, this is not to say that people completely insulate themselves from one another online. Much as in real life, they remain linked to other clusters of people through the activities of bridges — individuals who have links to more than one dense cluster. Together, dense clusters plus these bridges equal small worlds.

Researchers have been studying small world structures for decades. One of the things they have discovered is that the distribution of links within small worlds tends to skew toward highly active, popular individuals. Why this should be the case is easy to explain. Suppose that there are three individuals, whom we will call "A," "B," and "C." Further suppose that "A" and "B" are linked together, and "A" and "C" are linked together. If a new individual "D" were to enter this network, with whom is she most likely to link? The answer is clearly "A," because "A" gives "D" access to both "B" and "C." Now suppose that "E" enters the scene. Given that "A" provides access to every other individual in the network, "E" is even more likely to link to "A." By this logic, "A" is likely to become ever more popular. This phenomenon, called a "power-law," produces a situation where the more popular a node is in a network at time T_0, the more popular it is likely to be at time T_1, the likelier still at time T_2, and so on. It produces, in other words, "hubs" — individuals with far more ties than the average person in a network.

Hubs play a distinctive role in small worlds. In fact, their role is so special

Figure 2: The Structure of Small Worlds.

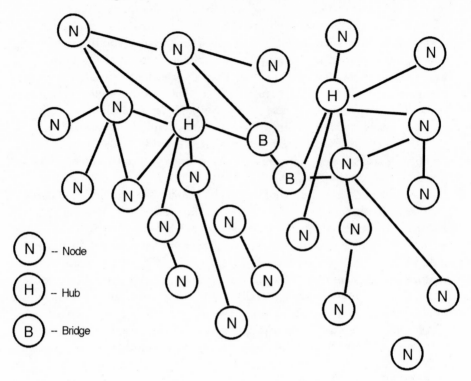

it makes them utterly unlike anyone else in their clusters of intimates. To demonstrate this point, scientists sometimes turn to the example of height. To find the average height of people in a given population, you simply add the height of all individuals and divide by the number of people. The result gives you a bell curve, with roughly half of the people falling on one side, and half on the other. The average height lies in the middle. Because they describe a relationship between individuals (and not individuals themselves), power-law distributions work in a very different way. For example, consider the relationship between academics who write research papers. Suppose that ten academics combined to write 100 papers. If we took a simple average, we might conclude that the average academic writes ten papers. It is perfectly possible, however, for this relationship to vary exponentially as a power of papers-written, which in simple terms means that a small number of academics may write most of the papers, and everyone else may write few papers. When relationships between two variables (in this case, between papers written and academics) vary exponentially, we say that they follow a power law. This is in fact the case for academic research production (Lotka, 1926).

In the case of online hubs, a power-law distribution creates a situation in which a few highly passionate, highly interested, highly knowledgeable individuals do most of the work of online communication. Hubs are most likely to post content, most likely to engage in collaborations, and most likely to link to others and to be linked to. We can be even more precise: about 20 percent of online users (hubs) perform as much as 80 percent of the work. Vilfredo Pareto, an Italian economist, coined the 80/20 rule when he observed that 80 percent of the land in Italy was controlled by 20 percent of the population. This Pareto Principle is very nearly an iron-law of small-world structures, including online interactions. If an online community forms around baseball, most of its members will be moderately interested in baseball, and a very few members will be highly interested. If an online community forms around a neighborhood, most of its members will be somewhat interested in the neighborhood and a few people will be highly passionate. And as much as 80 percent of the interaction that takes place in these online communities will be accomplished by the 20 percent who are most interested, most passionate, and most knowledgeable. This can seem unfair. Why should 20 percent of a community's members be responsible for producing the bulk of its online activity? In fact, however, this division of labor is key to a small world's success. The willingness of highly active people to do most of a cluster's work makes it possible for everyone else to contribute a little bit. Absent this willingness, online clusters quickly dissipate.

This structure of nodes, links, hubs, and bridges poses a new set of challenges to journalism. To see this clearly, imagine for a moment that you are a journalist wishing to reach an audience. In a mass-mediated system, you accomplish this goal in one of two ways. On television, you broadcast a sequence of news stories to everyone (and therefore to no one in particular), hoping to catch the attention of a mass audience. Alternatively, in a newspaper, you might compile a large number of news items, with the hope of aggregating an audience by making each item very interesting to a few people. The small worlds structure of the Internet dramatically alters this situation. Online, individuals have more choice about which information they receive, and more of this information will come from people within their cluster and with whom they have a personal connection or share a common interest.

As a journalist, you stand outside these clusters of activity. How will you get inside? One answer might be to make an appeal to bridges. After all, these individuals will give you access to at least two different dense clusters. But a bridge is an inefficient way of gaining entry into a small world, because it provides access only to a small number of additional nodes. It is much more efficient to appeal to hubs. They are the only individuals with a great number of links to others within the cluster. Recall that in a system privileging personal interest and choice, people become hubs because they show more interest or have more passion than the average member of a cluster. If an online group forms around kayaking, for example, its hub will very likely be someone who is very passionate or has a lot of knowledge about this subject. Others link to this passionate person because she represents a one-stop shop for all things kayaking.

So, to get inside online clusters, you need to attract the attention of a hub. How will you do so? Well, if hubs tend to be very passionate and/or knowledgeable, then they are likely to respond to you only if you are similarly passionate and knowledgeable. In the small-world, power-law distributed structure of the Web, hubs are far more likely to respond to people like themselves, people similarly enthused and knowledgeable about particular subjects. The Web, in other words, rewards passion, familiarity, and expertise. If you are the traditional professional journalist — detached and objective — you face a significant challenge. If you want to survive in the densely clustered world of online interaction, you will have to make personal, even intimate, connections with others. As one scholar has pointed out, you will have to learn to love (read: be passionate about) the issues you cover, and to love the communities of people with whom you interact; in fact, you should love them *more* than you love your professional identity (Shirky, 2008).

When I present this scenario to journalists, they sometimes say that, rather than attract the attention of hubs, they would rather *be* hubs. By this they mean that they would rather form communities around themselves than join other communities. This response has intuitive appeal, but it does not alter the underlying dilemma. As Benkler (2006) argues, part of the great transformation precipitated by the Internet has been to unleash the intrinsic motivations that lead people to produce, distribute, and consume culture. In opposition to the online world, in the mass-mediated setting few people produce culture for any reason other than to make money, and most every instance of cultural consumption is accompanied by an economic transaction. In a mass-mediated setting, extrinsic motivations reign supreme. And the costs of producing, distributing, and consuming culture on the Internet are so low that people become willing to produce material for intrinsic reasons — because they love the subject, for example, or wish to do something fun with their friends, or wish to gain status in their communities. This is not to say that every online community is driven by intrinsic concerns. But it is to say that intrinsic motivation plays a more prominent role online. This fact means that, without intrinsic motivations, journalists will have limited ability to form communities around themselves. Put another way, even when acting as hubs journalists will have to love the communities with which they interact.

At this point, the problem with objectivity is evident. It is not especially helpful to journalists needing to foster affinities between themselves and the communities they serve. Indeed, in many respects objectivity leads journalists precisely in the opposite direction. Where the online context invites journalists to become involved, objectivity requires them to remain uninvolved. Where the online context celebrates passion, objectivity rewards dispassion. Where the online context rewards commitment, objectivity requires detachment.

For a clear illustration of traditional journalism's disconnect from audience passions, consider the case of Tom Bowles. On a night in February 2011, Bowles, a freelance sports writer for *Sports Illustrated* magazine, clapped in the press box for Trevor Bayne, who had just become the youngest driver ever to win a NASCAR event. Within the traditional world of sports journalism, Bowles had committed a cardinal sin: by clapping, he had not maintained detachment. His editors duly reprimanded him. This might have been the end of it, except that Bowles then defended his actions on Twitter and on frontstretch.com, a website devoted to fans of NASCAR racing. He argued that he had been a racing fan all of his life, and that he had begun writing on the subject "as a side job ... [using] gut instincts built from a lifetime of devotion, knowledge, and persistence toward following stock car racing" (Bowles, 2011, para. 5). To him, clapping was a natural response by a person passionate about the sport. To him, the problem lay not with his clapping but with a professional media that did not comprehend the importance of passion. His news bosses, he said, did not understand that in "a changing culture [increasingly] beyond their control" journalists gain credibility not by being detached, but by being committed to the communities they serve (Bowles, 2011, para. 10). Of course, most of the blogosphere, including people who took the time to comment on his defense, applauded Bowles for taking a stand. "Bravo," one fan wrote, "for standing up for what you believe in" (Bowles, 2011, comment 3). His more traditional-minded editors at *Sports Illustrated* were less convinced, and fired him on the spot.

Bowles' defense nicely summarizes my case: online, individuals have more freedom to choose and more options from which to choose, and this has dislodged journalism from its role as a primary filter of public information. Also, when exercising their choice, individuals tend to cluster with like-minded others, much as they do in their daily social interactions. The links within these clusters are skewed toward highly-popular individuals — what scientists call "hubs." These hubs are the most active, knowledgeable, and devoted individuals within online clusters. To have a chance of online success, journalists need to exude the same level of knowledge, passion, and interest as the hubs that stand between them and everyone else within a cluster. Far from being disinterested observers, success online requires that journalists be interested and active participants — precisely the opposite of the objective journalist.

The Future of Journalism

If objectivity, as it appears, is problematic, what would its demise mean for online journalism? In thinking through this question, I have found the work of Pierre Bourdieu helpful (1971, 1985, 1986). Bourdieu argues that much of society is organized as social fields. He borrows the word "field" from science, which uses the term to describe invisible relations of force like a gravity field (Martin, 2003). Bourdieu often refers to social fields in a similar way, as invisible relations of force that cannot be shown except through their influence on actors. The "intellectual field," he said,

> is, like a magnetic field, made up of a system of power lines. In other words, the constituting agents or system of agents may be described as so many forces which, by their existence, opposition or combination, determine its specific structure at a given moment in time [1971, p. 161].

The major power lines within journalism are those of professionalism, commercialism, and politics (Benson, 2006). For example, professionalism would have journalists produce news according to professional values, practices, and identities. In contrast, commercialism requires that journalists produce news for profit, and politics emphasizes that journalists remain close to the official discourse of the state. All of these power lines exercise a gravitational force within the field, pushing and pulling journalists in different directions. As a central property, or form of capital within the field of journalism, objectivity is key to helping journalists manage all of this pushing and pulling — all in a bid to maintain journalism's integrity.

There is more to Bourdieu's theory than what I have just described. For example, he has more to say about the relation of social fields to a broader field of social power. And he has a complicated story to tell about the socialization of individuals within fields. But I have sketched enough to show that if objectivity wanes in online journalism, then the field loses one of the principle ways that journalism is held together. And if this occurs, then we can expect to witness within journalism what happens to any field when its relations of force weaken: the field will begin to lose its integrity. Partly, this means that the boundaries between the inside and the outside of the field will blur and become more porous. It means that it will be easier for new actors to enter the field. And it means that journalists and news organizations within the field will begin to spin away from one another.

However, at this point, early signs of systemic erosion of the journalistic field are difficult to measure. Online journalism is only about 15 years old, so we lack sufficient trend-lines to lend empirical support to claims of a widespread breakdown of the traditional journalistic field. However, there is growing evidence that something like what I have described is happening to the field. For example, we see it in the inability of journalists to convincingly argue that bloggers are not journalists. Consider Mayhill Fowler, a citizen journalist writing for Huffingtonpost.com who broke one of the biggest stories of the 2008 presidential election: then-candidate Obama talking about the bitterness of working-class Pennsylvanians. We see it in the wide diversity of organizations now engaged in journalism — from the Council on Foreign Relations to Circle of Blue, a network of scientists, journalists, and communication design experts. It is evident in communities like Seattle, where dozens of news sites owned by many different sorts of people, most of them non-journalists, have filled the space left by the demise of the *Post-Intelligencer*. It is apparent in the point-of-view reporting style of new-fangled journalists like Ezra Klein (*Washington Post*), Dave Weigel (slate.com), and Josh Marshall (tpm.com), and in the fact that political actors increasingly use social media tools to maneuver around journalists to organize and catalyze their communities. We see it in the activities of Andy Cavin, a social media coordinator for NPR, who has gained a following larger than most medium-sized newspapers for his Twitter feed (acavin) featuring 140-character accounts of events in the Middle East.

Each of these examples is a data-point suggesting that journalism is losing its integrity as a social field. As the field weakens, and its boundaries become porous and permeable, professional journalists are no longer able to keep others out. Journalism becomes something like a natural act, to borrow from scholar Jay Rosen, that anyone can do. And as new players enter the field, it becomes increasingly difficult for journalists to set the terms of what counts as good or credible journalism. This opens the way for journalists like Ezra Klein to credibly claim that offering his point-of-view in news stories is preferable to the detached mode of traditional reporting; for programmers like Adrian Holovaty to argue that database platforms like his Everyblock program are just as much a part of journalism as a fifteen-inch news story; and for aggregators like Google and Huffingtonpost to assert that their curation of information is as important and valuable as original reporting.

Now that I have made the point, let me qualify it. The fact that journalism is unraveling does not mean that it will come completely undone. The Internet makes available a global audience for media companies. As of this writing, according to the website Internet Worldstats, nearly 600 million English-speaking people worldwide use the Internet. As the Internet becomes more widely available, this number is likely to grow. The operation of power laws means that a few very large companies will likely divide up this audience, as has happened in other parts of the media economy (Doctor, 2010). These companies (which might include Reuters, News Corporation, and *The New*

York Times) will have sufficient resources to produce news across the variety of platforms (TV, online, mobile, print) that exist. This should produce a situation in which a few media companies continue to employ professional journalists. It also opens an opportunity for a feeder system to develop composed of smaller professional organizations like Propublica, Globalpost, and Mediastorm which make money by selling high-end, professional content to the dominant media companies.

Still, it is difficult to know how large the space for doing traditional journalism online will become. Part of the answer will be determined by the ability of these companies to re-create an environment of scarcity in the form of paywalls and apps. Will consumers be willing to pay for news put behind a paywall? Will they be willing to buy apps and pay a daily, monthly, or yearly subscription for the information provided by these apps? No one knows. The other part of the answer will be determined by public policy. If government allows tollbooths to be set up along the information superhighway, this will give media companies another path to regain control over news distribution. As of this writing, Congress seems amenable to allowing media companies to do just this. But, as with everything in politics, this may change. How these issues play out will strongly shape the ability of news media companies to operate as mass media in the online world.

Overall, the mechanics of power laws should mean that most news companies, like the regional newspaper, will no longer be able to sustain themselves as mass media within the online environment, at least not at anything like the size they obtained when they operated as monopolies in their communities. In place of these news organizations a great diversity of journalists and journalism will grow. This is already happening in places like San Francisco, Seattle, Austin, and Boston. No longer pulled by the gravitational force of objectivity, we should expect these journalists to be oriented more to the communities they serve than to the profession. We should expect them to adopt whatever practices and values are useful for making themselves valuable nodes in their networks. And, therefore, we should expect them to be as different from one another as there are different sorts of communities. In short, as objectivity wanes, we should expect professional journalism to become much smaller and more concentrated within a small handful of very large companies, and for the rest of journalism to explode into many different values, practices, and identities across the online network. We should expect, this is to say, the end of a widespread, cohesive, integrated, and insulated field of journalism.

Chapter Notes

1. Portions of this chapter are adapted from the book *Will Journalism Survive? An Inside Look into American Newsrooms* (Cambridge, England: Polity Press, 2012).

References

Barabasi, A.L. (2002). *Linked: The new science of networks*. Cambridge, MA: Perseus.

Benkler, Y. (2006). *The wealth of networks: How social production transforms markets and freedom*. New Haven: Yale University Press.

Bennett, J.G. (1835, May 6). Prospectus. *The New York Herald*, p. 2.

Benson, R. (2006). News media as a "journalistic field": What Bourdieu adds to new institutionalism, and vice versa. *Political Communication, 23*(2), 187–2002.

Benson, R., & Neveu, E. (Eds.). (2005). *Bourdieu and the journalistic field*. Cambridge, England: Polity Press.

Bourdieu, P. (1971). Intellectual field and creative project. In M. K. D. Young (Ed.), *Knowledge and control: New directions for the sociology of education* (pp. 161–188). London: Collier-Macmillan.

_____. (1985). Social space and the genesis of groups. *Theory and Society, 14*(6), 723–744.

_____. (1986). From rules to strategies: An interview with Pierre Bourdieu. *Cultural Anthropology, 1*(1), 110–120.

Bowles, T. (2011). Clap, clap goodbye ... How I lost my job with SI. Retrieved September 1, 2011, from http://www.frontstretch.com/tbowles/32940

Boyer, J. (1981). How editors view objectivity. *Journalism Quarterly, 58*(1), 24–28.

Carey, J. (1989). *Communication as culture*. Boston: Unwin Hyman.

Cook, T.E. (1998). *Governing with the news: The news media as a political institution*. Chicago: University of Chicago Press.

Cunningham, B. (2003, July/August). Re-thinking objectivity. *Columbia Journalism Review*. Retrieved September 1, 2011, from http://www.cjr.org/feature/rethinking_objectivity.php

Dicken-Garcia, H. (1989). *Journalistic standards in nineteenth-century America*. Madison: University of Wisconsin Press.

Doctor, K. (2010). *Newsonomics: Twelve trends that will shape the news you get*. New York: St. Martin's Press.

Emery, M., & Emery, E. (1996). *The press and America: An interpretive history of the mass media*. Boston: Allyn & Bacon.

Ferguson, M. (2002). *Nexus: Small worlds and the groundbreaking science of networks*. New York: W.W. Norton.

Franklin, B. (1731/1987). Apology for printers. In J.A. LeMay (Ed.), *Writings*. (pp. 171–177). New York: Library of America.

Gillmor, D. (2005). The end of objectivity. Retrieved September 1, 2011, from http://dangillmor.typepad.com/dan_gillmor_on_grassroots/2005/01/the_end_of_obje.html

Hackett, R., & Zhao, Y. (1998). *Sustaining democracy? Journalism and the politics of objectivity*. Toronto: Garamond Press.

Kovach, B., & Rosenstiel, T. (2001). *The elements of journalism: What newspeople should know and the public should expect*. New York: Crown.

Lippmann, W. (1922). *Public opinion*. New York: Free Press.

Lotka, A.J. (1926). The frequency distribution of scientific productivity. *Journal of the Washington Academy of Sciences, 16*(12), 317–324.

Martin, J.L. (2003). What is field theory? *American Journal of Sociology, 109*, 1–49.

McGerr, M. (1986). *The decline of popular politics: The American north, 1865–1928*. New York: Oxford University Press.

Mencken, H.L. (1927). *Prejudices: Sixth series*. London: J. Cape.

Mindich, D. (1998). *Just the facts: How objectivity came to define American journalism*. New York: New York University Press.

Ohmann, R. (1996). *Selling culture: Magazines, markets, and class at the turn of the century*. New York: Verso.

Richards, I. (2005). *Quagmires and quandaries: Exploring journalism ethics.* Sydney: University of New South Wales Press.

Rutenbeck, J. (1990). Editorial perception of newspaper independence and the presidential campaign of 1872: An ideological turning point for American journalism. *Journalism History, 17,* 13–22.

Ryfe, D., & Kemmelmeier, M. (2011). Quoting practices, path dependency, and the birth of modern journalism. *Journalism Studies, 12*(1), 1–17.

St. John, B. (2009). Claiming journalistic truth: U.S. press guardedness toward Edward L. Bernays' conception of the minority voice and the "corroding acid" of propaganda. *Journalism Studies, 10*(3), 353–367.

_____. (2010). *Press professionalization and propaganda: The rise of journalistic double-mindedness, 1917–1941.* Amherst, NY: Cambria Press.

Schiller, D. (1981). *Objectivity and the news: The public and the rise of commercial journalism.* Philadelphia: University of Pennsylvania Press.

Schnettler, S. (2009). A structured overview of 50 years of small-world research. *Social Networks, 31*(3), 165–178.

Schudson, M. (1978). *Discovering the news: A social history of American newspapers.* New York: Basic Books.

_____. (2001). The objectivity norm in American journalism. *Journalism Studies, 2*(2), 149–170.

Shaw, D.L. (1967). News bias and the telegraph: A study of historical change. *Journalism Quarterly, 44,* 3–12.

Shirky, C. (2008). *Here comes everyone: The power of organization without organizations.* New York: Penguin.

Sparrow, B. (1999). *Uncertain guardians: The news media as a political institution.* Baltimore: Johns Hopkins University Press.

Tuchman, G. (1972). Objectivity as strategic ritual: An examination of newsmen's notion of objectivity. *American Journal of Sociology, 77,* 660–679.

Disrespecting the Doxa

The Daily Show *Critique of CNN's Struggle to Balance Detachment and Connectedness*

BURTON ST. JOHN III

As the oldest 24-hour cable news channel, CNN operates with a deep connection to traditional journalistic values and associated "rules of the game," or doxa. In fact, CNN maintains that its focus is on traditional objective journalism in contrast to the partisan tendencies of both MSNBC and the Fox News Channel (Elliott, 2010). However, in the current climate, news consumers have an increasing number of digital platforms they can turn to, including websites and blogs where news consumers also produce news (McBride, 2010; Robinson, DeShano, Kim, & Friedland, 2010). Still, CNN's particular orientation toward objective journalism, even in an era of more user-created news, persists. Correspondingly, as these various news platforms proliferate, CNN's ratings have dropped precipitously, with some prime-time programs losing half of their viewership (Carter, 2010). Accordingly, CNN attempts to balance the established doxa of the professional press against the pressures brought about by changing news-media technologies, news consumer patterns and news operation business models. Professional press doxa has, for decades, privileged the idea that journalistic objectivity can be realized, in great part, by a detached stance (Merritt, 1998; Rosen, 1999). However, in the face of sagging ratings, CNN also is compelled to show its audience how it can be credible and connected to its viewers. Its efforts at balancing both imperatives are often cumbersome. Accordingly, *The Daily Show with Jon Stewart* (TDS), a news parody program on Comedy Central, points out that CNN's attempts to be both detached and connected are often incoherent. As such, TDS's critiques of the network's tortured balancing act clearly delineate the problems that can come from a dysfunctional press doxa. Furthermore, TDS's critiques point to the need for a more authentic journalism that is tuned into the events and issues that matter to citizens.

Objectivity, Detachment and Journalistic Doxa

David Mindich, in an extensive work on objectivity, said that if journalism was a religion, objectivity would be its "supreme deity" (1998, p. 6). Over the last several years, many scholars have discussed objectivity in a similar manner, calling it a "governing ethos" (Hackett & Zhao, 1998, p. 8), an approach to news that produces "a description that is more accurate than any other process allows" (Ryan, 2001, p. 5) and, therefore, a "guiding principle of newswork" (Allan, 1997, p. 308). However, as others have pointed out (Iggers, 1998; Merritt 1998; Rosen 1999), objectivity is actually a practice, reifying what is a core principle for journalism — the assertion of autonomy. The principle of autonomy allows journalists to claim that they are free of coercive forces (such as economic interests and government interference) that could shape the news. According to Woo (2007, p. 162), objectivity-centered routines allow journalists to "pick and choose among the truths at [their] disposal to create the story." In essence, objectivity routines, by focusing on the "disinterested reporting of verified facts" (Borden, 2007, pp. 101–102) allow journalists to approximate truth, assert their independence, and claim to news consumers that they are providing credible renditions of the day's events.

Objectivity's rituals are, for the professional press, quite clear. Mainstream news media outlets claim to relay truthful news by focusing on facts, turning to experts and attempting to balance sources (Iggers, 1998; Merritt, 1998; Rosen, 1999). All of these routines are designed to further the appearance of journalistic detachment. Such a posture is important to traditional journalism because it signals to the public that the press is not compromising its autonomy by taking sides on issues and events. The detached stance of the news worker, said Merritt, allows mainstream journalists to assert authoritatively that the news they report is believable. "If we maintain the proper separations," he said, in a critique of detachment, "then surely our product is pure and will be perceived as such; its objectivity is insured and we therefore will have credibility" (Merritt, 1998, p. 24).

While many scholars have examined how journalistic routines have been built over time, this paper addresses the self-directing aspects of newsroom actions that help sustain both the objectivity imperative and its practices. Bourdieu's (1977) observations about how a field of practice determines its own routines are particularly informative. Professions, he maintained, feature a habitus — persistent orientations that feature taken-for-granted sensibilities or assumed knowledge suppositions that are normally not questioned or re-evaluated. To be able to act in congruency with a habitus there must be an inexplicit sense of the rules of the game, or doxa. Bourdieu noted that doxa helps workers position themselves so that they have a practical knowledge that

> falls right, in a sense, without knowing how or why, likewise the coincidence between dispositions and position, between the "sense of the game" and the game, explains that the agent does what he or she "has to do" without posing it explicitly as a goal, below the level of calculation and even consciousness, beneath discourse and representation [Bourdieu & Wacquant, 1992, p. 128].

The Daily Show as Media Critic

Scholars have approached *The Daily Show* as an entertainment program that, through a combination of parody and satire, holds politicians, their political handlers, and the traditional mass media accountable (Borden & Tew, 2007; Painter & Hodges, 2010; Young, 2008). Most scholarly analysis of TDS has examined how the program critiques the arena of political communication — particularly the traditional news media's role in communicating and amplifying the messages and wishes of the political elite (Jones, 2010; Warner, 2007). Baym (2010) saw TDS as an example of an emerging neo-modern journalism that uses a comedic prism so that it can provide "information and interrogation" (p. 102). In contrast, Brewer and Marquardt (2007) described TDS as an entertainment program that can be classified within "soft news media," an arena that is "known for [its] entertainment value rather than [its] informative value" (p. 251).

Painter and Hodges (2010) claimed that TDS is effective in holding the news media accountable because its caustic observations and parodies of the press remind the public how journalism falls short of its own standards. Their 12-month study of TDS found that the show faults the news media for (1) failing to point out falsehoods, (2) offering up contradictory messages that betray a news operation's conflict of interest, (3) placing a high priority on inconsequential news, and (4) inordinately focusing on the branding and marketing of continuing news coverage. Borden and Tew (2007) found that TDS's criticism is particularly aimed at cable news channels' propensity for triviality, sensationalism, personality-centered reporting, and its susceptibility to manipulation by power elites.

Different scholars have noted that TDS uses a range of strategies to criticize modern journalism. First, the format of the show as "fake news," allows

TDS to both parody the TV news form and to weave together news actualities with satirical comment (Baym, 2005; McKain 2005; Warner, 2007). The program's news reports feature language choices designed to engage the audience. Baym found that TDS uses "discursive integration," or merging common vernacular into its reports (Jones & Baym, 2010, p. 284). Words like "dude" and "douchebag" allows TDS's criticisms to be more conversational, displaying how TDS is more aligned with the concerns of the news viewer than the news producers. Sotos (2007) noted that TDS, by reporting on apparently dysfunctional news media actions with feigned incredulity, takes a stance of naiveté that non-confrontationally invites viewers to critically think about the choices news producers make. Such feigned naïveté, she said, allows TDS to point out how several news decisions do not appear to make sense, revealing the ignorance that often underlies apparently authoritative presentations and rhetoric. The program, Sotos noted, "often reveals the gap between a reasonable view of things and the quite dangerous assumptions of those in power and pompously claiming to be experts" (2007, p. 33). Finally, the "straight" interview segments also often advance TDS's media criticism. Young (2008) found that the interview segments with political elites and journalists revealed that the program stressed "an alternative in which truth is assessed and neutrality is abandoned in favor of critical analysis" (p. 249).

Methodology

To gauge the quality of TDS's criticism of mainstream news media practices, this study examined how TDS critiqued CNN. Using *The Daily Show*'s archive of programming, this author examined a total of 98 videos tagged "CNN" beginning in September 2004 and continuing through the end of 2010. This period of analysis roughly corresponds with the rise of viewership of TDS (Baym, 2010) and heightened media interest in TDS (Tenenboim-Weinblatt, 2009).[1] Videos analyzed included Jon Stewart-led news reports, accounts from TDS correspondents, and interviews with CNN anchors and reporters. "Moment of Zen" videos, small segments aired at the end of the show that include no commentary from the program, were not included in the analysis. The author transcribed each program segment that involved CNN and also concurrently noted non-verbals (expressions, visual imagery, physical movements) that amplified messages within those segments. A textual analysis approach was used, examining how TDS content concerning CNN pointed to clear relationships and themes among categories (Wimmer & Dominick, 2010). Transcript notes were collapsed into main categories. Using this approach, this work finds that TDS critiqued CNN news practices and choices that revealed CNN's struggle to balance an objective, detached stance against its perceived need to be more connected to its viewers. TDS critiques maintained that CNN stumbled in these areas: (1) simulating a focus on detail, (2) exhibiting an excessive love of technology and, (3) demonstrating an unreflective approach to news. Within all three of these criticisms, TDS points to a larger problem for CNN — its doxa reveals a news network caught in a superficial balancing act rather than moving boldly into the arena of substantive, meaningful news presentations.

Simulating a Focus on Detail

As Tuchman (1978) asserts, the press attempts to demonstrate its credibility by providing trustworthy accounts that are bolstered by a "web of facticity." Data, facts, and descriptions of happenings are all key components of this web. Not surprisingly, TDS found that CNN, as befits a 24-hour cable news operation that needs to fill airtime, tends toward dwelling on details. One of the problems for CNN, however, is that there are only so many new pieces of information in any given day. To compensate, CNN relies on live feeds of happenings, even when the news operation does not have new information or cannot verify what actually is occurring. When these dynamics inevitably present themselves, CNN simulates details by reporting on what is known and then speculating about other details. This is illustrated in an October 19, 2005 TDS episode, when Stewart displayed that CNN could take a series of seemingly bad news events in progress and incessantly dwell on each situation. However, these particular events — a possible bomb threat, a New York City bridge fire, and a potential dam break near Boston — were all shot by CNN from a distance, with reporters telling CNN anchors that they did not know many details. This penchant for visuals as information allows the cable giant to still say it is on top of breaking events, even when there is a dearth of facts. "Seriously," said Stewart, "it seems like CNN is basically the dope standing next to you on the overpass, going 'What do you think's going on down there?'"

On April 10, 2008, TDS found CNN's coverage of the running of the 2008 Olympic Torch in San Francisco to be particularly uninformative, even as Wolf Blitzer's *Situation Room* devoted live coverage to protests derailing the torch from its course. "So, there you have it, the Olympic Torch detoured by protestors into a warehouse," said Stewart. "Now, unless OJ is somehow inside this torch, I guess there's no more need to follow the torch and we can all get on with our lives." TDS then quickly offered a montage of CNN's aerial shots of the warehouse, as Blitzer and reporters speculated about what might happen next to the torch. Stewart, in disgust, noted that the *Situation Room* spent an uninterrupted one hour and 42 minutes on the subject, mostly engaging in conjecture. "And it's not like nothing else was going on," said Stewart as TDS mocked-up a CNN crawl that read "Wolf Blitzer's house on fire."

TDS pointed out that, when CNN had time to fill, its reporters and anchors tend to speculate, and digress into tedious observations of the obvious. When ex-president Bill Clinton was en route to the U.S. with two reporters he helped release from China, CNN stationed a correspondent at the receiving airport. TDS showed a series of clips of this reporter standing in an airplane hanger, biding time by offering routine details about Clinton's arrival like "those [airplane hanger] doors will open, that jet will come in," "the jet's stairs will come out," "the border and custom agents will board that plane," and finally, "they will all go up to that microphone that's right out in the middle of the floor and they will hold a news conference." Immediately at the end of these sound bites, Stewart parodied the reporter's tone, holding up what appears to be notes and declaring:

> They will be inhaling oxygen. They will release carbon dioxide. The oxygen, we are being told, will be absorbed through the alveoli in their lungs. Then, they will go home and, after an estimated life expectancy of approximately 77 years, sources say, they will welcome the sweet embrace of death [August 5, 2009].

The network relies on more than just reporters to provide the image of a relentless focus on details. CNN turns to pundits and experts so that they can ostensibly surface more information. The danger with such an approach, of course, is that journalists will receive only the data and facts that align with these sources' interests. TDS found particularly frustrating a Kyra Phillips interview of both a supporter and opponent of a proposed Texas bill that would ban same-sex couples from adopting foster children:

> Stewart: As one supporter of the bill told CNN, this law is based in science.
> Cathy Adams (of the Texas Eagle Forum): We also have to look at research that does show that children in same-sex coupled homes are eleven times more likely to be abused sexually.... It is a proven fact. And that is a research study that was done in the state of Illinois.
> Stewart: Wow. Hard to argue with that. But Kyra Phillips on CNN gave opponent Randall Ellis a chance to respond.
> Ellis (of Lesbian Gay Rights Lobby): Well, I've certainly never seen that research.... No child healthcare professional that I have ever spoken to — no one who has access to the credible research being done on these issues has ever mentioned anything close to that.
> Stewart: Actually, you know, he's right. The study that [Adams] mentions is based on the work of one knucklehead who did a search on the Internet.... It's a specious claim. And no doubt Kyra Phillips will cut through the spin and point out the facts.

Phillips: It's an interesting debate. A good debate, thank you both very much.

Stewart: (pauses, looking stunned) Really? A good debate? Because it kind of seemed the one lady was lying.... Co-anchor Carole Lin, you going to let [Adams] get away with that?

Lin: I have some opinions about that story. You and I are going to share them during the commercial break.

Phillips: (laughing): We'll be talking about it, that's for sure.

Stewart: (laughing, then yelling): Why don't you call them on their bullshit on the air? You're an anchor, for fuck's sake! [April 26, 2005].

By highlighting this exchange, TDS singled out a significant problem for CNN when it comes to using interviewees — the real details of the story can be obscured. Worse, CNN personnel, who should have a handle on the fuller range of details, allow their sources to monopolize how information is be framed and discussed. CNN anchors are then often relegated to adjudicating the arguments and counterarguments that dominate the news segments and, in the process, allow such seeming debates to appear as though CNN is focusing on details. To demonstrate this dynamic, TDS' October 12, 2009 program showed a series of clips where journalists failed to challenge interviewees with additional facts, observations or context. TDS tracked numerous instances where CNN anchors, in the midst of the healthcare debate, did not interrogate interviewees' assertions. John King failed to challenge Arizona Senator Jon Kyl's claims that most medical savings could come from tort reform. Tony Harris did not address the Family Research Council's Tony Perkins's assertions about how many people are uninsured. Nor did Harris question Utah Senator Orrin Hatch's proclamation that health care reform would lead to socialism. Wolf Blitzer abruptly ended a health care roundtable after an interviewee claimed that drug companies were funding President Obama's health reform effort. In all of these cases, CNN anchors said, "we have to leave it there," allowing the unchallenged assertions to appear as factual news. At the end of a long montage of CNN personnel saying versions of "we have to leave it there," Stewart screamed and ripped up his script, saying, "You have 24 hours in a day! How much more time do you need? Well, I guess that explains CNN's new slogan: 'CNN. Nobody Leaves More Things There.'"

With this line of criticism, TDS exposes one of CNN's rules of the game — simulate the providing of substantive detail. TDS asserts that CNN simply does not do enough homework to provide substantive reporting. Stewart was adamant about this after showing a clip of two CNN news workers finishing their discussion of the different estimates of the cost of the health care bill:

Heidi Collins: Can we check those numbers?

Christine Romans: That's a good question.

Stewart: (long pause): You're not sure whether or not you can check.... Oh, you know who could check those numbers? (Yelling) All those fucking people behind you on the computers! Shouldn't they be checking the numbers? [October 12, 2009].

Love of Technology

News, as Merritt (1998) has pointed out, is customarily about what is "now." Broadcast news, he observed, is particularly prone to covering what is "hot," relaying an audience-grabbing story for a brief moment in time, then quickly moving on. This presentism within journalism, while a strength, can also be a significant liability for a 24-hour news network. Of course, new advances in technology easily fit the "now" orientation of journalism. However, TDS critiques of CNN point to a news operation overly enamoured with the latest in high-tech gadgets and mindlessly reliant on new technologies as determinants for both the form and content of its news. Of course, devoting such air time to what technology can offer has immediate implications for a 24-hour news operation that has time to fill. First, it becomes too easy for journalists to unthinkingly use citizen contributions and pass them off as news. In the spring of 2005, TDS was particularly skeptical of how CNN used such citizen contributions when it profiled CNN's new segment, "Inside the Blog." Stewart called it "a daily re-hash of the Internet so important that their seasoned commentators can't be trusted to do it" and that "only two hot, recent Vassar grads are up to the task." Then, after showing CNN's Abbi Tatton reading a blogger's comments and spelling out his URL, Stewart added, "You know, when I want hard-hitting news, I turn to CNN, who turns to Skippy the Bush Kangaroo." Then, continuing a critique of "Inside the Blog," Stewart turned to *Daily Show* Correspondent Rob Corddry, who sat in front of a laptop:

Stewart: Rob, a good blog can be a valuable news resource, but it doesn't make for very good television. Why the rush ... to put it on the air?

Corddry: Terror, John. Pure undiluted fear of their own extinction. The lumbering TV dinosaurs have spotted a free mammal called "blog" running around, and in this jungle it's evolve or die ...

Stewart: But, I have to say, Rob, I wonder if people fill up air time sitting there reading blogs — it's more of a function of the news channels' laziness rather than analysis.

Corddry: Perhaps, John. In fact, some of the loudest voices of protest are coming from the bloggers. (Starts to read from his laptop). Here's one recent post that says, "It seems the only thing these TV assclowns know how to do is read blogs out loud directly off of a computer screen." Ouch. That's gotta hurt [May 15, 2005].

The Daily Show maintained that CNN's love of technology was endemic within the news operation, particularly apparent in the way that CNN haphazardly used citizen contributions through Twitter and social networking sites like Facebook and My Space. Four years after Corrdry satirized the incautious live reading of blogs, Stewart ran clips on his July 27, 2009 show of CNN's Don Lemon asking viewers to use Twitter to send him positive comments about Sarah Palin's resignation as the governor of Alaska. Lemon used unvetted tweets on the air, stumbling as he read, "You want a positive comment about Sarah Palin? I'm positive she's an idiot." Stewart then mimicked Lemon, saying under his breath that maybe Lemon should start reading Twitter comments before using them on the air. Nevertheless, acting as Lemon, Stewart plugged on: "OK, here's one ... Rand Dog 40 says, 'Yo, Lemon. Go fuck yourself!'" CNN's apparently haphazard reliance on the Internet for live content also fuelled TDS's criticism of the news channel's reporting of Iranian protests following that country's 2009 presidential election:

> David Mattingly: Because western journalists are not allowed to cover these events, we are looking at the social networking sites to see what is posted on there ... we're looking at Facebook, we're looking at Twitter....
>
> Stewart: We're getting news on a possible Iranian revolution and also re-connecting with high school friends ... Of course, CNN wants you to know they don't normally just report whatever they find on the Internet [July 22, 2009].

TDS then showed Kyra Phillips and Mattingly explaining how restrictions on reporting in Iran resulted in CNN relaxing its vetting process and showing unverified information. Stewart then chided, "And this is different from what you normally do, how?" Next appeared several clips of CNN using information from social networking sites, Twitter, blogs, email and citizen material submitted through CNN's iReport website. Then Stewart pointed out that CNN, when using the Iranian reports, placed the disclaimer "unverified material" in the lower right portion of the screen. Stewart said that there were other disclaimer graphics that CNN had available, for example "Something we heard," "Prove us wrong," "You weren't there," and "What is truth, really?"

Clearly, the program's critiques about CNN's use of technology point to concerns about how such an addiction to digital platforms can adversely affect the content of the network's news. TDS asserted that CNN's love of technology often appears as sloppy expediency, calling into question the validity of citizen contributions as news. The program's satirical jabs, however, went further, critiquing CNN's overweening use of technology as actually interfering with the communication of news. TDS showed how CNN's use of digital effects and multi-screen imagery often poorly served the viewing audience. On its January 9, 2008 episode, TDS examined CNN's 2008 presidential primary coverage. Stewart showed a clip of Anderson Cooper fumbling with a device that magnified a moving pie chart across the center of the screen. Stewart quipped, "I'm glad that they had to show [Cooper's] pie chart so that you didn't get confused by the other pie chart" that was already visible near the crawl part of the screen. A few weeks later, on the January 30, 2008 show, Stewart voiced more confusion about *The Situation Room*'s six-screen coverage of John Edwards' withdrawal from the 2008 presidential primaries. TDS showed that, while the five other screens had some visual tie-in to both Edwards and the presidential primaries, the sixth screen, in the upper-right, showed footage of a life-size SpongeBob SquarePants dancing on a street corner. Stewart, exclaiming "What the fuck is that," could not come up with any rational explanation, observing with resignation that the six-screen configuration is "like a modern art installation as news." By its April 30, 2009, airing, TDS elaborated on its criticism of graphics obscuring comprehension when it analyzed CNN's coverage of President Obama's first 100 days. TDS showed clips of Wolf Blitzer encircled by large color-coded grids that indicated what the President did on each of those 100 days. Stewart remarked, "It's no coincidence the graphic there looks like prison bars; CNN has officially become prisoners of their own technology." The program again picked up on CNN's overweening use of technology when it examined the network's analysis of Obama's 2010 state of the union speech. "What about all the people who watched the speech, but found it too straightforward and understandable," Stewart began, "Well, there's always CNN." And, as befits TDS' penchant for letting video clips deliver the satirical message, the program immediately offered an extensive montage of CNN technology-centered segments: magic walls that featured pie charts of Twitter-based opinions, boxes that showed flash poll results and graphics of dial meters that revealed real time reactions to the President's speech.

For TDS, CNN's rules of the game concerning technology appears to be, as Stewart observed on the April 30, 2009, episode, "throw a bunch of shit at a big shiny wall and see what sticks." But the program critiques not just how the uncontemplative use of technology interferes with news consumer comprehension; TDS demonstrates that CNN's "now-centered" technology focus shapes news content. Rather than attempting to engage viewers by disseminating stories that address public concerns, the technology imperative at CNN is such a dominant structuring force within CNN's doxa that the network has, in Stewart's words, "given up." That is, the network too often is desperate to use technology — not the quality of its news coverage — to assert it is connected with its viewers. In a June 30, 2009, TDS "I on News" segment, Stewart referred to CNN's desperation by showing a series of clips where the network asks viewers to interact with it through blogs, Twitter, iReports and Facebook. At the end of the clips, Stewart shook his head and said, "Am I going to have to take a restraining order out against CNN?" With this one sentence, Stewart pointed to a significant problem with CNN's doxa involving technology: a news channel without sufficient news substance cannot simply leverage trendy digital platforms to reinvigorate within its audience the perception that the news operation is relevant.

Unreflective Approach to News

As TDS' critiques show, CNN's problems with the loss of audience share are not well addressed by dysfunctional doxa like simulating a focus on details and fixating on technology. Correspondingly, a significant problem for any journalistic outlet is being able to realize when newsroom practices lead to uninformative journalism. A lack of such awareness within a newsroom is not surprising as the pressures of daily reporting lead to a journalism that lacks "reflexive epistemological examination" (Tuchman, 1972, p. 662). TDS has also seen that this lack of reflexivity appears to be more than just a by-product of the work environment. Rather, it appears to be yet another element of the newsroom doxa, what Stewart, on the April 27, 2005, show, referred to as CNN's "irony-free zone." TDS found that CNN's lack of reflexivity is visible in ham-handed attempts to, yet again, make CNN appear less detached and more connected to its viewers. In early 2007, TDS reviewed how CNN spotlighted the recent passing of celebrity Anna Nicole Smith, particularly the network's interest in what items were left in Smith's refrigerator, what CNN called the "death fridge":

> Stewart: The story got me wondering, how is a "death fridge" news I can use?
> Soledad O'Brien: There certainly has been plenty of talk in recent days about that final, sad image of Anna Nicole Smith's refrigerator — mostly empty, but filled with methadone, diet drinks, and mostly nothing else. Did you know that your own refrigerator can reveal clues about you?
> Stewart: (stunned expression): What? Smooth segue. Soledad O'Brien going from tragedy to fun in the kitchen in about 3.2 seconds. (Assumes announcer voice) Kidnappers say they are going to execute the hostages in under three hours. And did you know that you can keep track of time at home on your very own potato clock? (pause) Yes, apparently CNN was concerned that it was headed for collapse in a Florida hotel room, because it turned the lens on itself.
> Alina Cho: So, let's take a look inside the CNN breakroom fridge, and I say this with hesitation ... (Cho opens refrigerator). We got some condiments, lots of milk for all the coffee we drink.

Stewart: Yes. They drink lots of coffee at CNN. You've got to work pretty long hours to come up with stuff like: "uh, maybe we should look in our fridge" [February 13, 2007].

As Stewart pointed out, there is an undercurrent of expediency within CNN's doxa of irreflexivity. CNN tried to show connectedness with viewers through a "we're on your side" sensibility. In actuality, CNN simply took a trivial aspect of a spectacle and attempted to massage it into a consumer story trope. But that is not the only trite approach that merited TDS' ridicule. One cliché involves putting the reporter on the front lines of a traumatic situation. On March 30, 2009, in the wake of the floods in Fargo, North Dakota, Stewart showed footage of CNN's Susan Roesgen reporting while participating in a sandbag relay line, then driving a forklift and, finally, sitting on a bulldozer. But Stewart was suspicious of the artificiality of these segments and showed the end of one of Roegsen's clips. As Roegsen finished the report, she wiped her hands and put them on her hips. Stewart quipped, "She's done ... Flood over. Excuse me, can a girl get a wet wipe?"

It also comes as no surprise, considering CNN's fascination with technology, that TDS found an especially ill-considered attempt by the network to show how it was connected to today's digitally-literate audiences. First, Stewart commented about CNN's continual drop in ratings and offered:

The bottom line is that CNN's got to get in the game, man. Here's what they can do, they can go partisan, like their brethren at MSNBC or Fox ... They could pursue a network-wide dogmatic newspinion effort. Or, CNN could exercise some editorial authority and integrity. Start breaking apart the entire right-left politico-journalist symbiotic paradigm. Lead a new generation of truth-seekers on an anti-talking point jihad. Or they can just throw random bloggers into an octabox and see what sticks [April 1, 2010].

With that, Stewart then reviewed how CNN had hired right-wing blogger Erick Erickson whose "incendiary political commentary had just won him a job for no apparent reason on CNN." Stewart pointed out that CNN had vetted Erickson, but only after the hire, showing clips from CNN's *Reliable Sources* program, where Howard Kurtz grilled Erickson about ad hominem attacks against public figures in Washington. TDS continued:

Kurtz: When Justice Souter announced his retirement, you ... wrote, "The nation loses the only goat fucking child molester ever to serve on the Supreme Court." Do you regret writing that?
Erickson: It was about the dumbest thing I've done.
Stewart: (with mock enthusiasm) You're hired ... Only CNN could hire a guy whose entire resume is incendiary partisan rhetoric and then act like that's the part of him they don't like. CNN is like the guy at the strip club who says, "I'm gonna hang out, but I'm not getting a lap dance.

I'm here for the buffet." I guess that explains their new slogan: "CNN. We have no idea what the fuck we're doing" [April 1, 2010].

Clearly, TDS saw Erickson's hire as another ill-advised, expedient attempt by CNN to display that it was aware of the subjectivities of what sometimes passes for news on the Internet. While TDS found reprehensible such posturing by the news organization, it was acutely disturbed when CNN's lack of reflexivity led to choices that smacked of juvenile pandering. After pointing out, on its December 15, 2010, program, that CNN was "really about the serious coverage of serious events," Stewart showed that the news channel had transitioned from a story about student riots in England to a clip from the movie *Dumb and Dumber* that showed Jeff Daniels experiencing explosive diarrhea. CNN's Ali Velshi then announced that programming was heading into a "For Your Health" segment that dealt with repetitive bloody bowel movements. Stewart then added, with a disdainful tone, "I understand the principle: use a little comedy to draw people in." Then, Stewart, assuming a reporter voice while running the same Daniels footage, said: "CNN, in a move to battle sagging ratings, promises explosive new programming." TDS also found obnoxious Carol Costello's use of a shrug and the tag line "just saying" after selected news stories. "Wow," said Stewart, on his August 18, 2009, program, "they report the news like I talked — when I was a 12-year-old girl." Then, Stewart backed away slightly from his criticism and allowed that "just saying" could be an effective way to report on lighter topics. But, after next running clips that showed Costello using such an informality at the end of stories on feminism, affirmative action, and the health care town hall dustups, Stewart was no longer so sanguine. "Want to know what I'm thinking?" he said. "I'm thinking you're using the same phrase to discuss important issues that we use in Jersey to determine that someone's mom is a whore."

In sum, TDS critiques CNN's lack of reflexivity as a doxa that informs the news channel's tone-deaf attempts to appear connected to various sensibilities within the real world of their viewers — a we're in tune with you pose. Whether it is straining to find "news you can use" from a celebrity death, asking journalists to act as if they are involved in a relief effort, hiring a blogger who was not vetted, using comedy to appear approachable, or simply appropriating a clichéd catch phrase, CNN's routines are dysfunctional, said TDS. Within the news operation, CNN's doxa would likely, as Bourdieu and Wacquant said, "fall right." But that self-perpetuating doxa is not attuned to the realization that overt attempts to signal connectedness to the viewer can simply degenerate into pedestrian formulas. In a November 18, 2009 interview he conducted with Lou Dobbs, just days after Dobbs left CNN, Stewart said the problem with the news channel was that they were a grey, flavourless environment that refused to assert itself by performing substantive news-gathering and analysis. In journalism today, he said, "you have to take a position ... it has to be for authenticity."

Implications

While scholars have focused on TDS' penchant for criticizing the often-symbiotic relationship between political actors and the mainstream media, this chapter establishes that the program offers another vital line of satirical critique. In illuminating certain routines that CNN follows, TDS highlights how the organization's newsroom doxa often ill-serves the public. The program's criticisms show that CNN's doxa often interferes with citizens' needs for clearly communicated and substantive accounts of daily events and the issues that are often interwoven into those happenings. In a wider sense, TDS' observations point to concerns that CNN's artificial attempts to look detached, yet connected, likely contribute to the public's sense of alienation regarding the mainstream press. As the Pew Research Center's most recent State of the Media Report indicated, CNN, Fox News and MSNBC all recorded noticeable declines in viewership for 2010. It is evident that CNN struggles with market dynamics that are particular to cable broadcast news. However, CNN shares with all mainstream journalism the predicament of increasing public disaffection. One startling example of public alienation regarding the mainstream press appeared in a 2004 Pew Research Center survey. In the period from 1994 through 2004, regular viewership of TV news dropped 10 percent (and regular readership of newspapers dropped 16 percent). By 2009, another Pew survey revealed that the public was troubled by inaccuracies in the news. Slightly above 60 percent of respondents indicated they found mainstream news stories to be incorrect. Considering how newsroom doxa can muddle the delivery of cogent and substantive news, these figures are not surprising.

Accordingly, the current news environment is ripe for TDS' approach to media criticism. The power of TDS' approach is that, through satire, they foreground the network's assumptions about what "rules of the game" can help it regain some pertinence. While the public indicates that they have qualms about the essential soundness of many news stories, CNN's doxa, as TDS has shown, tends to focus inward on its own survival impulses. Objective journalism is CNN's watchword, so it must find ways to show that it holds onto that maxim. Simulating a detached focus on details through endless speculation and use of experts and pundits allows it to seemingly assert that tenet. However, CNN also feels compelled to affirm to its viewers that it really is not so formal, but is actually connected to the sensibilities and concerns of an increasingly wired society. So, it attempts to counterbalance the traditional, detached approach by incessant use of digital flourishes, increasing calls for citizen participation in actual program content and offering irreflexive visual and linguistic gestures that imply a connectivity. In essence, TDS's critiques disrespect a newsroom doxa that operates as a house divided. They provide evidence that CNN's cognitive dissonance — its drive to balance objective detachment with pandering connectivity — bubbles outward for public consumption, signalling an aimlessness that Stewart, on the June 30, 2009, program, described in a faux promo: "CNN. We're all like, I know."

Behind the lack of respect TDS directs toward CNN's journalistic doxa is the message that the network's routines, in a desperate effort to show both detachment and connection, reveal a significant misreading of news audiences. As Stewart offered in his interview of Dobbs, and as the Pew Surveys on accuracy substantiate, news consumers want authenticity. The sense of "real" the public desires from the news is not just about a series of details. Nor is it relentless attempts by a news outlet to appear salient through a hyper-focus on technology, irreflexive attempts to be "on the news consumers' side" and token efforts at common vernacular. Rather, news consumers want to believe that journalism frames credible accounts of events and issues. As Stewart mentioned while interviewing Anderson Cooper for the June 21, 2006, episode of TDS, CNN appears to not understand it needs a "tenacity and relentlessness" that would allow it to provide more sustained, credible accounts of reality. Rather, CNN's desire to be objective, yet subjectively relevant, derails such a sense of dedication. TDS summed up this lack of commitment to substantive news when, on its August 2, 2007, edition, it criticized a promotional ad boasting that CNN's *American Morning* show offered the most stories per hour, or SPH. Stewart mocked the promo by pointing out that, if one watches NBC's *Today Show*, one sees only about 11 SPH. "Then you watch CNN, and you're like [seeing] an SPH of 50 [or] 60," he said. "You can't understand a fucking thing they're saying." Then, with a biting tone, he closed the segment with the observation that, since people are so busy, "they don't want a few stories thoroughly investigated, they want a lot of stories barely mentioned." And, with this observation, TDS offers that their disrespect for CNN's journalistic doxa is only surpassed by CNN's disregard of its viewers. The show maintains that the whole concept of SPH is thoughtless; an indictment of a news operation that treats news stories as ingredients to be thrown together quickly, as if readying the burgers, buns, and cheese slices for delivery to the customer in the fast food line. With the SPH brand, CNN is the detached provider of individual news bites, served up quickly because the news channel is ostensibly in step with the news consumers' need to get their news on the run. For TDS, this kind of expediency orientation within professional journalism is the ultimate disregard. As such, TDS highlights a challenge to CNN and all news operations: In an age when traditional news outlets' "rules of the game" no longer have exclusivity over what is considered news, worrying about old polarities of detachment and connectivity are passé. Instead, modern journalism is called to suss out events and facts, but also dig to surface nuance, expose posturing by various interests and — as Stewart mentioned in his June 21, 2006, Anderson Cooper interview — stand for "emotional right or wrong." TDS makes the case that mainstream journalism needs to move beyond reifying objectivity and make sure to report in the public interest. It is a timely warning that should be given careful heed. Otherwise, CNN and many other mainstream news outlets risk becoming, as Stewart warned on TDS' October 27, 2005, program, "what the news is kind of like."

Chapter Notes

1. Tenenboim-Weinblatt (2009), in a review on how journalists see the program, maintains that, by the 2004 political conventions, TDS began to garner currency as a source of media criticism. She asserted that, by mid-2005, the traditional press saw TDS as a cultural authority concerning both political communication and mainstream journalism.

References

Allan, S. (1997). News and the public sphere: Towards a history of objectivity and impartiality. In M. Bromley & T. O'Malley (Eds.), *A journalism reader* (pp. 296–329). London: Routledge.

Baym, G. (2005). The Daily Show: Discursive integration and the reinvention of political journalism. *Political Communication, 22*(3), 259–276.

_____. (2010). *From Cronkite to Colbert: The evolution of broadcast news.* Boulder: Paradigm.

Borden, S., (2007). *Journalism as practice: MacIntyre, virtue ethics and the press.* Burlington, VT: Ashgate.

Borden S., & Tew, C. (2007). The role of the journalist and the performance of journalism: Ethical lessons from "fake" news (seriously). *Journal of Mass Media Ethics, 22*(4), 300-314.

Bourdieu, P. (1977). *Outline of a theory of practice.* Cambridge, MA: Cambridge University Press.

Bourdieu, P., & Wacquant, L. J. D. (1992). *An invitation to reflexive sociology.* Chicago: University of Chicago Press.

Brewer, P., & Marquardt, E. (2007). Mock news and democracy: Analyzing The Daily Show. *Atlantic Journal of Communication 15*(4), 249–267.

Carter, B. (2010, March 30). CNN fails to stop fall in ratings. *The New York Times*, p. B1.

Elliott, S. (2010, April 13). CNN fights back with "objectivity" arguments. *The New York Times.* Retrieved March 30, 2011, from http://mediadecoder.blogs.nytimes.com/2010/04/13/cnn-fights-back-with-objectivity-arguments

Hackett, R. A., & Zhao, Y. (1998). *Sustaining democracy? Journalism and the politics of objectivity.* Toronto: Garamond Press.

Iggers, J. (1998). *Good news, bad news: Journalism ethics and the public interest.* Boulder: Westview Press.

Jones, J. (2010). *Entertaining politics: Satiric television and political engagement* (2nd ed.). Lanham, MD: Rowman & Littlefield.

Jones J., & Baym G. (2010). A dialogue on satire news and the crisis of truth in postmodern political television. *Journal of Communication Inquiry, 34*(3), 278–294.

McBride, S. (2010). The changing face of news in a major U.S. city; Hyper-local websites try to fill the void in Chicago. In J. Rosenberry & B. St. John (Eds.), *Public journalism 2.0: The promise and reality of a citizen-engaged press* (pp. 113–125). New York: Routledge.

McKain A. (2005). Not necessarily not the news; Gatekeeping, remediation, and The Daily Show. *The Journal of American Culture, 28*(4), 415–430.

Merritt, D. (1998). *Public journalism and public life* (2nd ed.). Mahwah, NJ: Erlbaum.

Mindich, D. T. Z. (1998). *Just the facts: How "objectivity" came to define journalism.* New York: New York University Press.

Painter, C., & Hodges, L. (2010). Mocking the news: How The Daily Show with Jon Stewart holds traditional broadcast news accountable. *Journal of Mass Media Ethics, 25*(4), 257-274.

Pew Research Center (2004, June 8). *News audiences increasingly politicized.* Washington, DC: Pew Research Center for the People and the Press.

_____. (2009, September 12). *Public evaluations of the news media: 1985–2009.* Washington, DC: Pew Research Center for the People and the Press.

_____. (2011, March 14). *The state of the news media, 2011: An annual report on American journalism.* Washington, DC: Pew Research Center for the People and the Press.

Robinson, S., DeShano, C., Kim, N., & Friedland, L. (2010). Madison commons 2.0: A platform for tomorrow's civic and citizen journalism. In J. Rosenberry & B. St. John (Eds.), *Public journalism 2.0: The promise and reality of a citizen-engaged press* (pp. 162–175). New York: Routledge.

Rosen, J. (1999). *What are journalists for?* New Haven: Yale University Press.

Ryan, M. (2001). Journalistic ethics, objectivity, existential journalism, standpoint epistemology and public journalism. *Journal of Mass Media Ethics, 16*(1), 3–22.

Sotos, R. (2007). The fake news as the fifth estate. In J. Holt (Ed.), *The Daily Show and philosophy* (pp. 28–40). Malden, MA: Blackwell.

Tenenboim-Weinblatt, K. (2009). Jester, fake journalist, or the new Walter Lippmann?: Recognition processes of Jon Stewart by the U.S. journalistic community. *International Journal of Communication, 3,* 416–439.

Tuchman, G. (1972). Objectivity as strategic ritual: An examination of newsmen's notions of objectivity. *American Journal of Sociology, 77*(4), 660–679.

_____. (1978). *Making news: A study in the construction of reality.* New York: Free Press.

Warner, J. (2007). Political culture jamming: The dissident humor of The Daily Show with Jon Stewart. *Political Communication, 5*(1), 17–37.

Wimmer, R., & Dominick, J. (2010). *Mass media research: An introduction* (9th ed.). Belmont, CA: Thompson Wadsworth.

Woo, W. (2007). *Letters from the editor: Lessons on journalism and life.* Columbia: University of Missouri Press.

Young, D. G. (2008). The Daily Show as the new journalism. In J. Baumgartner & J. S. Morris (Eds.), *Laughing matters: Humor and American politics in the media age* (pp. 241–259). New York: Routledge.

13

Gatekeeping in the Digital Age

*A New Model for
a Post-Objective World*

KIRSTEN A. JOHNSON

Over the past decade the notions of objectivity and gatekeeping have been threatened by non-journalists who create content and post it online. These non-journalists, whether they are blogging, tweeting, or commenting on stories reported by professional journalists, are challenging newsrooms to re-examine news gatekeeping practices. Studies suggest that journalists are resistant when it comes to relinquishing control of the gate, even though news operations allow users to participate in content generation (Cassidy, 2006; Domingo et al., 2008; Harrison, 2010; Hermida & Thurman, 2008; Robinson, 2011; Ryfe, 2011; Singer, 2006; Singer & Ashman, 2009). Professional journalists cite the need to keep tight control on content so as to maintain the credibility of their profession. Meanwhile, the role of the journalist is shifting from mere reporting, toward collaboration with different audiences. In fact, journalists are now called upon to help audiences sift through and interpret ever-increasing tides of information (Kovach & Rosenstiel, 2001; Singer, 2011). However, current theories of gatekeeping fail to take into account user-generated content in the news production process, as well as how newsrooms are evolving to respond to content produced by non-journalists. This chapter offers an extensive review of scholarly writings with an eye toward reconceptualizing the gatekeeping process by taking into account the roles that news consumers and journalists assume in the news production and distribution process.

Traditional Notions of Objectivity and the Role of the Press

Objectivity—perhaps no other word associated with the free press in America has drawn so much debate over its origins and meaning. Whether one believes the origins of objectivity derive from commercialism, philosophical movements, and/or technological changes (McNair, 1998), the notion of objectivity lingers as an ideological cornerstone in mainstream media outlets across the United States.

Objectivity became a well-known concept in journalism by the 1930s (Schudson, 1978, 2001) and many believe that objectivity is still relevant. According to Ryan (2001), objectivity must be present in a free society: "It is difficult to overstate the importance to a free society, and to all the groups that comprise that society, of information that has been collected and disseminated by individuals who are committed to the ideals of objectivity" (p. 3). Throughout history scholars have offered several definitions of objectivity. Some, like Tuchman (1972), asserted that objectivity in reporting is demonstrated only when journalists focus on facts, maintain an unemotional tone, and ensure that all sides to a story have been represented fairly. Others, like Ryan (2001), define objectivity as "the collection and dissemination of information that describes reality as accurately as possible" (p. 3).

Richards (2005) pointed out that many journalists realize that objectivity can severely limit reportorial practices. Still, many news workers believe that objectivity leads to truth which, above all else, must be inherent in journalistic practice (Jamieson & Waldman, 2004; Kovach & Rosenstiel, 2001; Manjoo, 2011; Schudson, 2001). According to Deuze (2009) objectivity can add legitimacy and credibility to reporters' and editors' work; when combined with autonomy, he said, objectivity can allow journalists to do their jobs effectively.

However, some observers argue that journalists often hide behind objectivity. Said Cunningham (2003), "Objectivity can help journalists make decisions fast and also protects journalists from the consequences of the stories they write" (p. 26). He maintained that journalists like to think that objective reporting leads to credibility but, he said, the reality is that the two do not correlate. Sometimes, objectivity can be dangerous, especially if it stops journalists from digging into a story and finding the truth. For example, Cunningham asserted, objectivity can lead to reporters who are afraid to argue with officials because they risk losing access to them. Another danger of objectivity is that journalists begin to rely heavily on officials to present opposing sides of a story—offering, through balancing sources, a false notion of objectivity and neutrality (Dolan, 2005). Objectivity can also become something of a shield behind which journalists hide when reporting a divisive story. Tuchman said that news workers, when attacked for their accountings of the facts, often invoked "their objectivity almost the way a Mediterranean peasant might wear a clove of garlic around his neck to ward off evil spirits" (1972, p. 660).

According to Jamieson and Waldman (2004) journalists, first and foremost, must be "custodians of fact" (p. 197). But they also acknowledged that journalists do more than just report the facts, they also craft stories and arrange information in such as way as to clearly display antagonists, heighten conflicts, and offer engaging stories. They acknowledged the many functions the press serves in a democracy — informing the public, allowing citizens to have the information they need to participate in a democracy, and serving as a watchdog. Kovach and Rosenstiel (2001) agreed that facts, truth, and the watchdog function are important, and they also added several other principles to which journalists should adhere. They suggested journalists must be loyal to citizens, display transparency, constantly verify information, remain independent from those they cover, provide a public forum for criticism, and "exercise their personal conscience" (p. 13). However, it can be difficult for journalists to remain true to all of these principles, as it appears some of them are in conflict with one another. For example, it can be difficult for journalists to depend heavily on reliable, yet agenda-driven sources and, at the same time, also allow their journalistic conscience to guide the reporting process.

Still, despite the challenges journalists face in making objectivity a reality, the concepts of objectivity and gatekeeping are inextricably linked. Long-established gatekeeping theories — conceptualizations of how journalists control the flow of information from the newsroom to the audience (Lewin, 1947; White, 1950) — partially explain a news control dynamic that persists to this day. In the 1950s, White proposed a model where sources of news send information to someone in a newsroom who then makes a decision about what gets paid attention to before it can ever be disseminated to the public. Building upon White's ideas, in 1957 Westley and MacLean further established that the multiplicity of individuals working in a newsroom operate within the confines of newsroom rules and structures that guide their decision-making processes. During the next two decades, as gatekeeping theory continued to evolve, some scholars (Bass, 1969; Chibnall, 1977; Halloran, Elliott, & Murdock, 1970) recognized the need to consider the particularized efforts of individuals in the news process (e.g., reporters, editors, news owners). They argued that gatekeeping was not just happening when the information first reached the newsroom, but it was also occurring as the information was originally gathered by reporters on the street.

Since then, news has evolved from a one-way to an interactive experience.

The audience no longer just wants to consume information, they also want to react to it, create it, and pass it along to others. Not surprisingly, the notion of objectivity and its relevance to modern-day journalism is problematic. As the notion of objectivity evolves, so too does the notion of gatekeeping. Traditional newsroom gatekeepers now encounter information that is streaming into newsrooms at a faster and faster rate, exerting increasing pressure on them to make decisions quickly. Because the information is flowing so rapidly, decisions about whether or not to include a point of view in stories may get overlooked due to the increased pace at which decisions now need to be made. Also exerting pressure on the objectivity and gatekeeping processes is increased competition from citizens who create content. The public often creates this content with a point of view since they do not feel bound by the notion of objectivity. Citizens are also not bound by organizational gatekeeping practices — they are normally only bound by their own notions of what should be disseminated. Such public-generated content may force newsrooms to release, or at least pay attention to, information they may not otherwise. There is no question that as technology continues to evolve so will the notions of gatekeeping and objectivity, but are traditional journalists ready to question these long-held tenets?

User-Generated Content Eroding Traditional Gatekeeping

To recap, increasing audience involvement in the news-gathering process puts pressure on the gate to allow more information to flow through it at a faster rate. Journalists are no longer competing with information generated by other journalists, they are also competing with news generated by users, which often contains a viewpoint. Singer (2011) argued that since journalists no longer have special access to information, and no longer control the publishing of that information, they must now try to distinguish themselves from non-journalists by emphasizing fairness and balance. At the same time, bloggers are exposing factual errors and forcing journalists to be more accountable. In this new media world "the traditional idea of gatekeeper vanishes," she said. "The journalist no longer has much if any control over what citizens will see, read or hear, nor what items they will decide are important to think about" (p. 62). Williams and Carpini (2000), in their study of the Monica Lewinsky scandal, agree with Singer, suggesting that gatekeeping is no longer relevant due to multiple news media sources. Williams and Carpini argued that if a mainstream media source chooses not to publish something, chances are someone else will.

The gatekeeping role is more important now than it has ever been due to the quantity of information available and the need for the audience to figure out whether information can be trusted (Friend & Singer, 2007). Singer (2011) argues that gatekeeping in the digital age means that journalists should filter the huge amount of information available to the public and help them figure out which information is true. Kovach & Rosenstiel (2001) offer a similar view, namely that the Internet has made the gatekeeping journalist more important because there is so much information consumers can tap into. However, these arguments appear to be somewhat counterintuitive as the audience is no longer just a consumer of information, but a "prosumer," both a producer of content and a consumer of information. The audience becomes involved in the content, adds to the story, helps shape perceptions of the story, and assists in building the permanent record of the news (Kovach & Rosenstiel, 2001).

Singer (2006) examined coverage of the 2004 presidential campaign and how it was covered on major U.S. newspaper Web sites. The study found that editors wanted to make sure that the information they provided was credible, but also realized that information they put online could be a starting point for the audience, as opposed to an ending point. The study suggested that there are evolving notions of gatekeeping due to the interactivity that can be found online:

> The Internet defies the whole notion of a "gate" and challenges the idea that journalists (or anyone else) can or should limit what passes through it. At the same time, the sheer quantity of information online, along with its wildly varying quality, reinforces the need for someone to sort it out as well as to lend it credibility and, ideally, utility [Singer, 2006, p. 265].

Studies show a grudging willingness on the part of journalists to allow traditional newsroom gatekeeping norms to evolve and change as user-created content becomes more pervasive. Harrison (2010) examined how the *BBC* handled user-generated content. He found that the traditional notion of gatekeeping has evolved in order to keep *BBC* values intact. According to *BBC* standards, all user-generated content must be moderated in some way. Sometimes this is done prior to the information being posted online (pre-moderation) and sometimes it is done after it is posted (post-moderation). However, Harrison noted that moderating content is time consuming and subjective. Hermida and Thurman (2008) surveyed how United Kingdom newspaper websites are integrating user-generated reports into its content. They found, much like Harrison (2010), that the gatekeeping process is still intact due to concerns over user-generated content eroding professional values such as trust and reputation. Hermida and Thurman (2008) also noted that newsroom personnel acknowledged that gatekeeping is expensive, but felt the associated costs were worth it. In a similar study, Singer & Ashman (2009) examined how the *Guardian* handled user-generated content. They found that journalists struggled to balance the inclusion of content produced by users with making sure the *Guardian's* credibility was maintained. Some journalists at the *Guardian* worried that user-generated content challenged their authority as journalists. Similarly, Domingo et al. (2008), in a study of 16 U.S. newspapers, found that news organizations limit opportunities for citizens to participate, reinforcing journalists' role as gatekeepers. They also found that managers always had the final say over content, never leaving this role up to citizens.

The practice of using hyperlinks as a gatekeeping mechanism was found in a study by Dimitrova, Connolly-Ahern, Williams, Kaid, and Reid (2003). The use of hyperlinks on the websites of 15 newspapers that covered the Timothy McVeigh case was examined. Results showed that only four percent of the links on the newspapers' websites directed readers to outside sources. Thus internal, as opposed to external linking, was interpreted as attempts by news organizations to keep a tight grip on the gatekeeping role (Dimitrova, et al., 2003).

In sum, while journalists show a willingness to embrace user-generated content, they still struggle with exactly how and when it should be used. This causes tensions for the traditional, gatekeeping journalist — these news workers seek to exert their control of their content while also acknowledging that user-generated material plays an increasingly valid role in the news process.

Leaving the Gate Open in an Age of Raw Information

The traditional notion of gatekeeping is being challenged and changed by those outside traditional journalism who are creating content. Journalists are no longer in charge of which information the audience is exposed to, and the credibility of information is a concern (Deuze, 2011). Singer (2011) pointed out that misinformation is often no further than a Google search away. Some journalists feel that information in the hands of users causes a devaluation of news gathering and reporting standards. Fact checking, for example, may not be pursued leading to the spread of inaccuracies (Tsui, 2009). Because journalists are no longer in charge of the information, noted Manjoo (2008), the audience not only holds different opinions from one another, but also different sets of facts. This means debates no longer take place over what should be done but, instead, center on arguments about the actual facts of a story. These debates about facts, occur, he said, because audiences do not care about objective reporting. Rather, news consumers often look for accounts that reinforce their own point of view.

One type of reporting that can reinforce the point of view of the audience is conversation-based reporting. This type of reporting is often exhibited by cable news shows. Ben-Porath (2007) found that this type of journalism causes journalists to lose control of the gatekeeping function in the short-term. Additionally, he said, the long-term consequence may be that journalism reverts to its role as a partisan medium. Competition among news outlets, and the 24-hour news cycle can lead to audience fragmentation that impacts the way journalists do their jobs (Cunningham, 2003; Deuze, 2011). In particular, media outlets monitoring each other leads to more interpretation of facts as opposed to original reporting because journalists assume that their audience already knows the basic story facts (Schudson, 2003). As a result, Cunningham (2003) called for a rethinking of objectivity, arguing that journalists must admit that subjectivity exists in reporting and avoid hiding that aspect from the public. He asserted that reporters should be encouraged to develop expertise in an area and use it to make informed judgments about what the audience needs to know. In 1979, well before the advent of online user-created content, Herbert Gans proposed a model of news gathering that relied upon getting multiple perspectives on every story, while also allowing a reporter's opinion to become part of the story. This multiperspective view of news certainly runs contrary to the way most traditional media operate. However, in a world where the audience creates its own content, journalistic immersion into the subjectivities of a story, rather than objective detachment, appears to be a valuable option for news construction.

Robinson (2011) argued that a new kind of journalism is being created by the press because raw information, hyperlinks, and other content made publicly available on the Web allows users to make the news experiential. The Internet, and particular sites such as reddit.com and Facebook, have made it very easy for readers to pass along stories. In effect, when news consumers find that an article is newsworthy, personally relevant or pertinent to someone else — and then redistribute it — they become gatekeepers (Shoemaker & Vos, 2009).

One of the ways users can choose to pass along either raw information or information reported by others is by creating a blog. Bloggers and blogging seem to pose a special concern for journalists because "objectivity is generally verboten in the blogosphere" (Smolkin, 2004, p. 39). Tensions between bloggers and traditional journalists are often notable. Bloggers occasionally demonstrate that they can break stories (some that are critical of commercial news media) that are then picked up by the mainstream press.[1] This line is becoming even fuzzier as some traditional journalists write blogs and begin to work with bloggers to report stories (Smolkin, 2004). This has prompted some scholars to examine the ethics of blogging (Cenite, Detenber, Koh, Lim, & Soon, 2009; Kuhn, 2007; Perlmutter & Schoen, 2007; Tomaszeski, Proffitt, & McClung, 2009). Many of these studies have found that bloggers are interested in the same things as traditional journalists — promoting free expression, minimizing harm, being truthful, demonstrating transparency, and promoting interactivity.

However, as Phillips (2011) pointed out, bloggers often see their work as unfinished when they publish it online and believe that the audience will correct any inaccuracies, a practice that runs contrary to traditional journalism. Not surprisingly, the advent of blogging has challenged news professionals to think about the publication process in a different way. Bloggers do not have to wait for the 6:00 P.M. news or the morning paper to publish information, and the ability to put information online means that television and newspaper reports don't have to wait that long either. Because information now moves quickly from the person who initially captures/frames the information to the audience, many news stories in the blogosphere are not finished at the time of publication, but remain open to users. Due to this shift in thinking about the publication process, Bruns (2005) advocated the idea of "gatewatching" as opposed to gatekeeping. In gatewatching, instead of generating original content and publishing it, unfinished content available on the Web is aggregated and then presented to the audience. Through this process, Bruns argued, audiences vet story content.

Such developments have revealed fractures within traditional journalism. At the first-ever World Journalism Education Congress in 2007, professional journalists and communication educators voiced concerns that bloggers are influencing the way journalists do their jobs, forcing journalists to change the way they think about journalism. In particular, said some critics, a journalistic trend toward user-generated content might represent an abandonment of journalistic core values like objectivity and fairness (Knight, 2008). Journalism has evolved from an industrial model where one journalist covers a news beat and then writes and reports stories, to a model where multiple people cover a story that is infused with individual perspectives. Such a changing news-making and news-dissemination environment has significant implication for objectivity, said Bruns:

> Objectivity is no longer a requirement here, as no one contributor "owns" the story or is responsible for it on their own; rather multiperspectivity and a willingness to engage fairly with opposing viewpoints becomes the new ideal of this more open and inclusive news production process [2005, p. 309].

Reconceptualizing Gatekeeping

Since the audience now plays a larger role in gathering and reporting information it is time to re-examine the gatekeeping process. In 1991, Shoemaker proposed a new gatekeeping model. In this model, information is brought to the attention of the media through people who act as gatekeepers. Shoemaker called them boundary role gatekeepers, and they decide whether to accept or reject the information. If the boundary role gatekeepers choose to accept the information, it may then be passed along to other news media gatekeepers who then shape the message and then transmit it to a mass audience. In this theory, both extra-media and journalistic gatekeepers play a large role in the shaping and disseminating of information. Shoemaker posited that life experiences shape the decision-making process of journalistic gatekeepers, but they must ultimately act within the rules and norms imposed upon them by their employing news organization. However, in their book *Gatekeeping Theory* (2009), Shoemaker and Vos acknowledged that the Internet has played a role in changing this model. According to the authors, each member of the audience now acts as a gatekeeper and can choose whether or not to pass along information to an online audience of friends or strangers. At times, this user-generated content has been treated by citizens as news. Therefore, journalists are now tasked with evaluating information created by citizens and making decisions about whether or not those stories should pass through the newsroom gate (Kovach & Rosenstiel, 2001; Singer, 2011).

Missing from Shoemaker's 1991 model and then Shoemaker and Vos' 2009 reassessment is the acknowledgment of audience members as creators of their own content that can be distributed to a mass audience without the help of traditional media organizations. Information created by, as Jay Rosen (2006, para. 1) called them, "the people formerly known as the audience" can be picked up by mainstream media outlets, passed along to other audience members, or not passed along.

Therefore, our understanding of gatekeeping needs to be updated so as to acknowledge how multiple content contributors distribute raw information into the world (see Figure 1). In Shoemaker's 1991 gatekeeping model, the event is the first step in the gatekeeping process — in my proposed model the first step is "raw information." It could be argued an "event" does not need to necessarily happen to begin the gatekeeping process, rather, all that needs to happen is that information exists and then someone takes an interest in that information and decides to pass it along, either in its raw or edited form, framing the material in some manner so as to appeal to various audiences. For example, in April of 2009, a citizen decided to record a city council meeting in Duncanville, Texas. Unexpectedly, during this meeting the mayor of

Duncanville ordered the arrest of a city council member who he saw as disruptive. An individual taped the meeting and then posted the unedited video on YouTube. The video was then passed on and re-posted and received nearly 30,000 views.

In the proposed model, raw information exists, then someone, either a citizen or a journalist, decides that information is worthy of being passed along. If a citizen decides something is worthy of being re-distributed, the person can choose to have an encounter with that information that can lead to one of three things happening. The information can be re-distributed (edited or un-edited) to "the world" and/or sent to the traditional media, or the information can be discarded by the citizen. The traditional media and the world can then choose to discard the information, pass the information in an unedited form further along into the world, or edit the information and then pass it along. Raw information can also enter the newsroom directly, where it can be discarded, accepted as is, or edited and re-distributed to news consumers. Additionally, once the information is received by the world, news consumers can choose to

- reject the information.
- consume the information and keep it to themselves.
- act upon the information by creating their own story based on the information and then pass that information back to newsrooms, the original content creators, or into the world again.

The cycle continues and information is filtered and refined multiple times and passed along, either changed or unchanged according to the wants, needs, and desires of the world. There are gatekeepers throughout all of these stages, making decisions about which information should be passed into the world, and which information should be discarded. In this model "citizen content creators" are defined as people who are not professional journalists, but who create content and then disseminate it, usually online. "Traditional media" is defined as trained professional journalists or information professionals who disseminate news through newspapers, television, radio, and the Internet. "The world" consists of any people who have an information need. These people may either be actively or passively seeking information. In previous models the world would have been considered the audience, but due to the confusion caused when audience members also act as content creators, the term "the world" is used.

Despite the fact that users are creating content alongside and in conjunction with traditional media, gatekeeping remains a relevant and useful approach to understanding how news is disseminated. However, it is difficult to say if objectivity will remain an important pillar in the news process, particularly as the news becomes disseminated by growing numbers of non-news professionals. Traditional media will be called upon to provide a different role in relationship to information in years to come. The traditional media, in addition to gathering and reporting news, will also be called upon to comment on the news that non-news professionals are reporting. Reporting by conservative blogger Andrew Breitbart is one example of this changing role. In 2010, Breitbart posted video excerpts of Shirley Sherrod, a United States Department of Agriculture employee, speaking at a NAACP event online. The clips intimated that Sherrod — a black woman — did not help a white farmer as much as she could have. The mainstream media credulously reported Breitbart's video. Under pressure, Sherrod resigned. Later, it was discovered that the clips had been taken out of context by Breitbart, and she was offered a new government job (she refused it). Another example of a citizen who has garnered a lot of attention is self-proclaimed undercover journalist James O'Keefe. In separate events, he secretly videorecorded an NPR official and employees of ACORN. After his videos were released, and received extensive (and unquestioning) mainstream news coverage, the NPR official was forced to resign and ACORN's federal funding was curtailed. Subsequently, O'Keefe was criticized for editing the videos in such as way as to de-contextualize the comments so that he could achieve his goal of damaging both organizations. In both the Breitbart and O'Keefe examples mainstream media were forced to respond to the raw (yet highly-edited) information promulgated by both actors. Incidents such as these reveal that journalists are struggling to figure out how to respond to reports generated outside of the traditional journalistic model. The ascent of raw information framed by non-journalists tells us that, in the wider news ecology, information no longer needs to be objective in order to appear truthful and important to an audience. In response, news workers may find that the most important tenets of journalism center on renewed commitments to ferreting out truth and displaying transparency, rather than routines that try to uphold objectivity.

Conclusion

In this new information age, journalists will be called upon to verify facts and help the audience distinguish truth from non-truth. This means that gatewatching will be increasingly important as audiences are inundated with information and need assistance trying to make sense of it. As Kovach and Rosenstiel (2001) pointed out, journalists will continue to do traditional gatekeeping, but in a different way because information is not just generated by traditional media outlets, but by citizens as well. This can lead to a wiki-style news environment where a story is reported by one citizen initially and then other citizens and journalists continue to mold and change the story after it has been released to the audience. In this scenario, emphasis is placed not necessarily on getting the story right the first time, but instead on exposing the audience to the information, and then very publicly editing and re-editing the information. This clearly raises questions about accuracy of information since the gatekeeping process now has pressure on it to move from the traditional filter-then-publish model to a publish-then-filter model.

Therefore, traditional journalists will need to learn to collaborate with citizens, which means not just being willing to listen to and act on citizens' story ideas (which some newsrooms do right now), but also partnering with citizens when telling stories and including them in the process. In this shift of thinking about news gathering and storytelling, traditional journalists still need to be vigilant about the truth and accuracy of the stories they tell in order to preserve journalistic credibility.

The new gatekeeping model offered by this chapter points to this implication: traditional journalists must realize that, in today's sped-up news environment, raw information is increasingly the stuff of news and that citizens have more opportunities to both encounter and relay this raw information. The Internet has leveled the playing field, making the information accessible to large numbers of people quickly. Once information is released to the world, it is important that traditional media recognize that the story has not necessarily ended. Those working in traditional newsrooms need to be willing to embrace audience contributions in meaningful ways. This can mean allowing comments from readers, encouraging citizens to add their knowledge and expertise to a story, and/or collaborating with a citizen to do a follow-up story.

Even though the media landscape is changing and readers are much more involved in the news-creation process, journalists are often reluctant to turn completely away from the traditional professional norm of objectivity (Ryfe, 2011). However, said Gillmor (2006), journalists do not need to relinquish traditional journalistic roles to users, but instead should think about how their roles, relative to user-generated content, are changing:

> We will learn we are part of something new, that our readers/listeners/viewers are becoming part of the process. I take it for granted, for example, that my readers know more than I do — and this is a liberating, not threatening, fact of journalistic life. Every reporter on every beat should embrace this. We will use the tools of grassroots journalism or be consigned to history. Our core values, including accuracy and fairness, will remain important, and we'll still be gatekeepers in some ways, but our ability to shape larger conversations — and to provide context — will be at least as important as our ability to gather facts and report them [p. XIV].

This is a different world for professional journalism; and truly embracing citizen contributions will absolutely have an impact on objectivity in newsrooms. Since a point of view is inherent in citizen reports, newsroom personnel will need to make a decision about how these citizen contributions fit into their current objectivity paradigm. If a newsroom would choose to publish citizen contributions with the opinions intact this could impact how the newsroom is perceived by the community at large. The community may assume that an opinion expressed in a story by a citizen contributor is also the opinion held by the newsroom. This could be problematic, particularly if an unpopular opinion is espoused. News is a business, and losing readers or viewers is not an acceptable outcome. A newsroom may wish to develop a hybrid model where only a certain amount of subjectivity is allowed, and only on certain issues. While this could help to retain an outlet's news consumers, it could also become confusing in terms of how much subjectivity in news accounts

Figure 1: Multiple Content Contributors Gatekeeping Model.

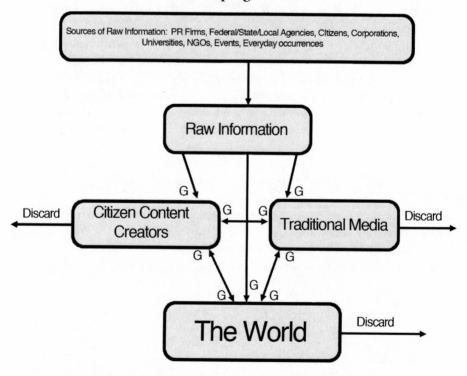

The gatekeepers in the model are represented by the letter "G." The arrows represent the direction information flows.

a newsroom would allow, and on which issues it would be appropriate to offer opinions.

As raw information continues to penetrate into the realm of news, it will be difficult for newsrooms to continue to ignore or to minimize the importance of citizen content. But, with the acknowledgement of the value of this content also comes the acceptance of material that contains opinion and does not conform to traditional journalistic models. Those who choose to embrace this content could be rewarded richly by exposing their audiences to compelling stories told through the eyes of those closest to it. However, there are also risks involved as newsroom personnel open their newsrooms to those who have not been trained in the journalistic tradition. Traditional journalism will have to make conscious decisions about what aspects of objectivity allow — or impede — its assertions that it is relevant in an age when raw information, framed and disseminated by the public, is also considered news.

Chapter Notes

1. Examples of these tensions include in 2004 when CBS news anchor Dan Rather was exposed by the blog *Free Republic* after he questioned George W. Bush's service in the military. This eventually led to Rather's resignation. Another example is in 2005 when Eason Jordan, CNN's chief news executive, said in a speech to the World Economic Forum that journalists in Iraq were being targeted by the military. His comments were released by bloggers and he resigned from CNN. Pressure by bloggers on mainstream media also forced the resignation of Senator Trent Lott. Lott made comments at Senator Strom Thurmond's birthday party about how he supported Thurmond when he was a segregationist. The story was initially ignored by mainstream media, but pressure by bloggers forced the press to cover the story (Tomaszeski, Proffitt, & McClung, 2009).

References

Bass, A. Z. (1969). Refining the "gatekeeper" concept: A UN radio case study. *Journalism Quarterly, 46,* 69–72.

Ben-Porath, E. (2007). Internal fragmentation of the news. *Journalism Studies, 8*(3), 414–431.

Bruns, A. (2005). *Gatewatching: Collaborative online news production.* New York: Peter Lang.

Cassidy, W. (2006). Gatekeeping similar for online, print journalists. *Newspaper Research Journal, 27*(2), 6–23.

Cenite, M., Detenber, B. H., Koh A. W. K, Lim, A. L. H., & Soon, N. E. (2009). Doing the right thing online: A survey of bloggers' ethical beliefs and practices. *New Media & Society, 11*(4), 575-597.

Chibnall, S. (1977). *Law-and-order news: An analysis of crime reporting in the British press.* London: Tavistock.

Cunningham, B. (2003). Re-thinking objectivity. *Columbia Journalism Review, 42*(2), 24–32.

Deuze, M. (2009). Technology and the individual journalist: Agency beyond imitation and change. In B. Zelizer (Ed.), *The changing faces of journalism: Tabloidization, technology, and truthiness* (pp. 82–98). New York: Routledge.

_____. (2011). What is journalism? Professional ideology of journalists reconsidered. In D. Burkowitz (Ed.), *Cultural meanings of news* (pp. 17–32). Los Angeles: Sage.

Dimitrova, D., Connolly-Ahern, C., Williams, A., Kaid, L., & Reid, A. (2003). Hyperlinking as gatekeeping: Online newspaper coverage of the execution of an American terrorist. *Journalism Studies, 4*(3), 401–414.

Dolan, K. (2005). Blinded by "objectivity": How news conventions caused journalists to miss the real story in the "Our Lady" controversy in Santa Fe. *Journalism, 6*(3), 379–396.

Domingo, D., Quandt, T., Heinonen, A., Paulussen, S., Singer, J., & Vujnovic, M. (2008). Participatory journalism practices in the media and beyond. *Journalism Practice, 2*(3), 326–342.

Friend, C., & Singer, J. (2007). *Online journalism ethics.* New York: M.E. Sharpe.

Gans, H. J. (1979). *Deciding what's news: A study of CBS Evening News, NBC Nightly News, Newsweek, and Time.* New York: Random House.

Gillmor, D. (2006). *We the media: Grassroots journalism by the people, for the people.* Sebastopol, CA: O'Reilly.

Halloran, J. D., Elliott, P., & Murdock, G. (1970). *Demonstrations and communication: A case study.* Baltimore: Penguin.

Harrison, J. (2010). User-generated content and gatekeeping at the BBC hub. *Journalism Studies, 11*(2), 243–256.

Hermida, A., & Thurman, N. (2008). A clash of cultures: The integration of user-generated content within professional journalistic frameworks at British newspaper websites. *Journalism Practice, 2*(3), 343–356.

Jamieson, K. H., & Waldman, P. (2004). *The press effect: Politicians, journalists, and the stories that shape the political world.* New York: Oxford University Press.

Knight, A. (2008). Journalism in the age of blogging. *Journalism Practice, 9*(1), 117–131.

Kovach, B. & Rosenstiel, T. (2001). *The elements of journalism.* New York: Crown.

Kuhn, M. (2007). Interactivity and prioritizing the human: A code of blogging ethics. *Journal of Mass Media Ethics, 22*(1), 18–36.

Lewin, K. (1947). Frontiers in group dynamics, II: Channels of group life; Social planning and action research. *Human Relations, 1,* 143–153.

Manjoo, F. (2008). *True enough: Learning to live in a post-fact society.* Hoboken, NJ: John Wiley and Sons.

McNair, B. (1998). *The sociology of journalism.* New York: Oxford University Press.

Perlmutter, D., & Schoen, M. (2007). If I break a rule, what do I do, fire myself? Ethics codes of independent blogs. *Journal of Mass Media Ethics, 22*(1), 37–48.

Phillips, A. (2011). Transparency and the new ethics of journalism. *Journalism Practice, 4*(3), 373–382.

Richards, I. (2005). *Quagmires and quandaries: Exploring journalism ethics.* Sydney, Australia: University of New South Wales Press.

Robinson, S. (2011). Someone's gotta be in control here. In D. Burkowitz (Ed.), *Cultural meanings of news,* (pp. 151–164). Los Angeles: Sage.

Rosen, J. (2006). The people formerly known as the audience. Retrieved May 19, 2010, from http://archive.pressthink.org/2006/06/27/ppl_frmr.html

Ryan, M. (2001). Journalistic ethics, objectivity, existential journalism, standpoint epistemology, and public journalism. *Journal of Mass Media Ethics, 16*(1), 3–22.

Ryfe, D. (2011). Broader and deeper: A study of newsroom culture in a time of change. In D. Burkowitz (Ed.), *Cultural meanings of news* (pp. 165–178). Los Angeles: Sage.

Schudson, M. (1978). *Discovering the news.* New York: Basic Books.

_____. (2001). The objectivity norm in American journalism. *Journalism 2*(2), 149–170.

_____. (2003). *The sociology of news.* New York: W. W. Norton.

Shoemaker, P.J. (1991). *Gatekeeping.* New York: Sage.

Shoemaker, P.J., & Vos, T. (2009). *Gatekeeping theory*. New York: Routledge.

Singer, J. (2006a). Stepping back from the gate: Online newspaper editors and the co-production of content in campaign 2004. *Journalism & Mass Communication Quarterly,* *83*(2), 265–280.

_____. (2011). The socially responsible existentialist: A normative emphasis for journalists in a new media environment. In D. Burkowitz (Ed.), *Cultural meanings of news* (pp. 53–66). Los Angeles: SAGE Publications, Inc.

Singer, J. B., & Ashman, I. (2009). Comment is free, but facts are sacred: User generated content and ethical constructs at the Guardian. *Journal of Mass Media Ethics 24*(3), 3–21.

Smolkin, R. (2004). The expanding blogosphere. *American Journalism Review*. Retrieved May 10, 2010, from http://www.ajr.org/article.asp?id=3682

Tomaszeski, M., Proffitt, J. M., & McClung, S. (2009). Exploring the political blogosphere: Perceptions of political bloggers about their sphere. *Atlantic Journal of Communication,* *17*(2), 72–87.

Tsui, L. (2009). Rethinking journalism through technology. In B. Zelizer (Ed.), *The changing faces of journalism: Tabloidization, technology, and truthiness* (pp. 53–55). New York: Routledge.

Tuchman, G. (1972). Objectivity as strategic ritual: An examination of newsmen's notions of objectivity. *The American Journal of Sociology, 77*(4), 660–670.

Westley, B. H., & MacLean, M. S., Jr. (1957). A conceptual model of communications research. *Journalism Quarterly, 34,* 31–38.

White, D. M. (1950). The "gate keeper": A case study in the selection of news. *Journalism Quarterly, 27,* 383–390.

Williams, B. A., & Carpini, M. X. (2000). Unchained reaction: The collapse of media gatekeeping and the Clinton-Lewinsky scandal. *Journalism, 1*(1), 61–85.

14

Contemporary News
Production and Consumption
Implications for Selective Exposure,
Group Polarization, and Credibility

ETHAN HARTSELL, MIRIAM J. METZGER,
and ANDREW J. FLANAGIN

Individuals currently have access to an unprecedented number of sources for news information obtained via digital media, including traditional news organizations, blogs, social networking sites, and microblogs.[1] This diverse media environment is characterized by a number of changes in news generation and coverage, media consumption, and perceptions about the credibility of news information.

The way news is produced has been fundamentally changed by the proliferation of digital networks and social media software. Rather than relying on monolithic news organizations to collect and communicate current events, individuals can now be active producers and disseminators of news content, through independent blogs, Twitter, CNN's iReport, and via many other means. In many cases, the traditional notion of authorship has become blurry. For example, rather than relying on a single, credentialed author to write a news article, groups of authors with no journalism credentials can work together using collaborative software like wikis or by re-posting and commenting on content and then linking to other sources or websites. Rather than relying on a single professional editor to fact-check and proof content, news articles can be reviewed and edited by thousands of readers empowered to give instant feedback.

Correspondingly, many independent blogs and collaborative news sites, appealing to partisan niches, have eschewed the traditional standard of objectivity in news reporting. This is exacerbated by similar changes in established news organizations. As traditional print and television news outlets have waned in popularity, there is evidence that they are, to some extent, being replaced by sources that slant their news coverage (Abrahamson, 2006; Bennett & Iyengar, 2008; Coe et al., 2008). Consequently, a great deal of the news available today appears not to adhere to the traditional standards of news objectivity that guided news reporting for more than a century. Journalism thus appears to be shifting to some extent from objective news reportage to "news with a view," as exemplified by Fox News, MSNBC, and blogs like Red State and Liberal Oasis.

A number of criticisms have been levied against the new methods of news generation and presentation. Generally, detractors deride the decreased professionalism and lack of ethical standards in social media like blogs, microblogs, and wikis. Critics perceive social media as offering little more than poorly written, unedited, and biased analyses of news events. Skeptics also attack news subjectivity for confirmation bias. That is, they fear that when opinion-confirming news sources are readily available consumers will selectively expose themselves to like-minded sources and avoid outlets that convey an opposing ideology. Finally, many scholars are concerned that audience fragmentation and selective exposure will be detrimental to a democratic society. Specifically, citizens may become less knowledgeable about the complexities that surround important issues and become more rigid in their own beliefs, resulting in a highly-polarized nation.

In this chapter we consider these issues by describing changes in the media environment and examining the apparent shift toward increasingly subjective news presentation. To do so, we briefly review a historical move away from, and then back toward, a partisan press and its implications for the credibility of news information. We also assess how user-generated news (UGN) and selective exposure link to individuals' preferences for attitude-congruent information. Next, we examine the relationship between credibility and news bias, while articulating new theoretical avenues to understand this relation. Finally, we discuss the implications of increased subjectivity in news — especially what a rise in post-objective journalism means for both news credibility and concerns about increased societal polarization.

News Objectivity, Past and Present

Beginning in the 1790s with the creation of the first organized political parties, newspapers reported along partisan lines (Robertson, 2001). Similarly, from the late-18th to mid-19th centuries, newspapers routinely covered news about the parties they supported, favorably edited the speeches of candidates they endorsed, and ignored news about members of opposing parties (Schudson, 2001). Objective reporting only gained momentum toward the end of the 19th century, and became standard within the news industry in the 20th century.

Recent changes to the technological and social landscape, however, appear to signal a return to more partisan news coverage. A striking development within many mainstream news outlets is the presence of partisan reporting. Cable news especially has seen a trend toward becoming more partisan in recent years, with Fox News (by far the most popular cable news station) taking a conservative stance on issues and MSNBC offering a liberal alternative (Abrahamson, 2006; Bennett & Iyengar, 2008; Coe et al., 2008). These cable news providers have seen an increase in their viewership as well, while CNN, which values neutrality in reporting, has experienced a decrease in viewers since 2009 (Carter, 2010).[2] The trend toward partisan news is even more evident on the Internet, where the most popular blogs are often overtly liberal or conservative (Meraz, 2008).

The re-emergence of partisan news, coupled with greater opportunity for amateur news content production and dissemination via digital and social media forms, has several implications for the credibility of news information, and for how news consumers themselves determine credibility. For a long time, news credibility was equated to objectivity in news analysis and reporting. Absence of bias, professional fact-checking, and journalist credentials have traditionally comprised the benchmarks for credibility. However, the marked rise of both partisanship and UGN, coupled with recent changes in the news and media industries, are complicating and, in some cases, overturning traditional objectivity approaches as credibility markers. In this chapter, we examine whether people are adapting to these changes in news by altering their criteria for judging a news outlet's credibility.

User-Generated News: Characteristics and Credibility

The return of the partisan press represents only one of several recent changes in the ways news is generated and presented. In particular, consumers have more power in producing information than ever before (Pew Project for Excellence in Journalism, 2009). User-generated news, for example, includes sources like blogs (e.g., Drudge Report), microblogs (e.g., Twitter), and CNN's iReport, that are frequently associated with the shift from top-down to bottom-up information generation. UGN news sources also include news aggregators like Yahoo! News and Google News, both of which use algorithms to rank stories according to their popularity. Wikipedia, the online collaborative encyclopedia, might also be characterized as a news source, as it is frequently updated to include current events. These sources belie objectivity in several ways.

The most salient example of UGN subjectivity is in *how* information about issues is presented. Many of the most popular blogs take positions at extreme ends of the political spectrum (Meraz, 2008), and bloggers tend to link to websites that share their personal biases, resulting in "echo chambers" that amplify their political ideologies (Garrett, 2009). Blogs are also subjective in *which* issues they choose to report. Institutional biases notwithstanding, traditional news sources endeavor to cover issues that are important and relevant to a great number of people, and to cover them "objectively" (e.g., presenting opposing sides of controversial issues) so as to capture the largest possible audience share while not alienating news consumers whose views fall on either side of an issue (Mindich, 1998). By contrast, many bloggers and microbloggers primarily discuss personally-important issues through a unique, idiosyncratic lens (McKenna, 2007).

Not surprisingly, UGN sources have been met with criticism and are considered by some to lack credibility. Critics contrast UGN sources with traditional journalism, which operates under established codes of ethics. For example, the Society of Professional Journalists Code of Ethics (1996) states that journalists should not plagiarize, and should avoid conflicts of interest, identify sources whenever possible, and distinguish between reporting and commentary. Newspapers and magazines are seen as better written than blogs and other social media sources because of the extensive training reporters go through before entering the workforce. Moreover, traditional journalism articles are perceived as generally more trustworthy because of codes of ethics and accountability for misreporting, and more complete if there is a balance between fact-based accounts and cause-effect interpretive reporting (Cenite, Detenber, Koh, Lim, & Soon, 2009; Keen, 2007; Usher, 2010).

Accordingly, many researchers, professional journalists, and news consumers dismiss the news value of blogs (Sweetser, 2007). Some argue that blogs offer a great deal of analysis without any actual reporting, relying instead on traditional news sources to break stories (Bardach, 2008). Others have been critical about the lack of professionalism of many blogs, arguing that bloggers-as-journalists are inferior writers and tend more toward the distortion of events in comparison to traditional journalists (Keen, 2007). Much of this fear is fueled by a sense that the transition to online reporting has resulted in a loosening of standards and an increase in carelessness in newsgathering (Pew Project for Excellence in Journalism, 2009).

Potential Advantages of User-Generated News

In spite of these concerns, there are a number of potential benefits to be derived from increasingly user-generated, and often subjective, news accounts. For instance, in the case of international coverage, traditional news reporters from foreign outlets often lack relevant local expertise and are subject to official and institutional constraints (Committee to Protect Journalists, 2011). In the case of local coverage, traditional media tend to be more conservative in their treatment of controversial issues, often leaving out relevant information and showing deference to the government (Song, 2007). In contrast, UGN allows individuals to report openly about crises and controversial topics from multiple perspectives, relatively unfettered from government or institutional interference or influence. For example, Egyptians used Facebook, YouTube and Twitter to distribute reports of the 2011 uprising that occurred within that country (Preston, 2011).

Social media also benefits from the expertise of users, which comes from individuals who are "cognitive authorities in the sphere of their own experience, on matters they have been in a position to observe or undergo" (Wilson, 1983, p. 15). CNN's iReport.com, for instance, allows users to upload video, audio, pictures, and personal accounts of news events, as well as to provide links to other websites that contain relevant information. Stories are organized based on number of views, how often they have been shared among users, and how many comments have been made on them. Although individual contributions to sites like iReport are most certainly subjective, an aggregate of many user reports could potentially present a more complete account of an event than a single journalist could ever create.

Indeed, perhaps the most compelling benefit of UGN is its ability to harness the so-called "wisdom of the crowd" in creating information. Such crowd wisdom can be a superior form of news generation and distribution when it allows individuals to fill gaps in each others' knowledge and create more complete information (Chi, Pirolli, & Lam, 2007). Mistakes are also more likely to be caught in a timely manner through collective information generation techniques than through traditional news creation. Wikipedia and blog articles essentially have hundreds, if not thousands, of "editors" searching for errors, in contrast to traditional news sources, which rely on a few editors to check stories before they are published (Sunstein, 2007).

Of course, there are limits to the power of the wisdom of the crowd. Sunstein (2007) argued that collaboration works best when a group is comprised primarily of experts or those possessing requisite knowledge in some area, because then each member of the group has a better chance of being right than wrong. Surowiecki (2004) argued that collective knowledge generation is best when crowds are diverse, when group members are independent and not influenced by other group members, when the group is decentralized, and when an apparatus exists to aggregate their contributions. Some UGN sources, but certainly not all, fit these criteria.

Independence also allows bloggers to play a valuable role as a sort of Fifth Estate, policing both the government and traditional news institutions. In a survey of 140 blogs, McKenna and Pole (2008) found that 80 percent of bloggers reported on bias or omissions in the traditional media. Independent news producers are also not beholden to government sources of information. Blogs offer journalists and users alike the time and autonomy to cover in depth issues they passionately care about (Carpenter, 2010; Perlmutter & Schoen, 2007). Although this can lead to biased reporting, it also may expose scandals like Trent Lott's 2002 announcement of support for Strom Thurmond's decades-old, segregation-based presidential campaign, and "Rathergate" in 2004-2005.[3]

Perceptions of UGN Credibility

Determining a news source's "actual" credibility is quite difficult, if not impossible. Not only is credibility a subjective concept, but news from a traditional source such as *The New York Times* can be inaccurate, despite all of the safeguards in place to ensure its accuracy. On the other hand, information from a personal blog can be completely accurate despite the author's lack of professional training. As a result of the inherent complexity in determining credibility, little research exists that empirically examines whether UGN sources are actually more or less credible than traditional sources. However, scholars have tried to answer this question by looking at public *perceptions* of UGN credibility, and some interesting patterns have emerged from the data.

Generally speaking, news consumers perceive that blogs and other non-traditional online news sources are low-to-moderately credible (Metzger et al., 2011; Thorson, Vraga, & Ekdale, 2010). In a survey of Internet users, for example, only about 30 percent of news consumers thought *Salon*, the *Huffington Post*, *Slate*, and the *Drudge Report* were believable news sources (Pew Project for Excellence in Journalism, 2009). Credibility ratings for traditional media outlets have been steadily declining easily since the 2000s, although mainstream media are still generally rated as higher in credibility than UGN sources (Pew Research Center, 2010). In surveys that ask respondents to compare the credibility of online and offline information directly, results have been more mixed, revealing wide variations in perceived credibility of online news sources

(Flanagin & Metzger, 2000, in press; Johnson & Kaye, 2010; Kiousis, 2001; Kohut, 1999; Mehrabi, Hassan, & Ali, 2009; Melican & Dixon, 2008; Online News Association, 2001; Schweiger, 2000).

The inconsistent results found in these studies suggest that news consumers' credibility perceptions may depend on several factors beyond simply whether information appears on the Internet or not. One factor is experience using online and UGN news sources. In a series of surveys of politically-interested Internet users, Johnson and Kaye (2004, 2009) found that people who heavily rely on blogs for news information find them more credible than mainstream sources, and that the more a person relies on blogs for news information, the more that person perceives that blogs are credible (Mehrabi, Hassan, & Ali, 2009; Sweetser, Porter, Chung, & Kim, 2008).

Another factor is experience generating online news. Cassidy (2007) found that online journalists rated UGN as significantly more accurate, comprehensive, fair, and believable than print journalists, who rated online news as low in accuracy, comprehensiveness, fairness, and believability. Moreover, in a 2009 survey by the Pew Project for Excellence in Journalism, professional (but offline) journalists indicated that the proliferation of online news sources has led to a loosening of journalistic standards, less diligence in reporting, and more superficial reporting. There is some evidence, however, that perceptions of blog credibility are changing. Messner and Distaso (2008) found a greater acceptance by traditional news media of blogs as legitimate sources for news stories. Recently, scholars have suggested that blogs may alter the way that people judge news credibility, supplanting traditional credibility markers including expertise, accuracy, and lack of bias with alternative credibility criteria such as interactivity, transparency, and source identification (Carroll & Richardson, 2011; Kang, 2010; Yang & Lim, 2009).

In sum, many of the typical criticisms of UGN appear to overstate flaws in UGN sources while ignoring their ability to provide credible news information. These criticisms also make assumptions about the objectivity of traditional sources that do not always withstand scrutiny. Nonetheless, it is still true that most UGN sources, especially blogs, tend to report from a partisan perspective, which raises legitimate concerns about information credibility and news consumption behavior. If credibility is equated with objectivity, for example, there is cause for concern about the future production of credible (i.e., objective) news information. Moreover, the question remains whether individuals avail themselves of the diverse sources at their fingertips to receive balanced accounts of events, or whether they only rely on news outlets that report from consonant political attitudes and opinions. Thus, news ecology forces may be pushing toward reduced objectivity and increased partisanship not only on the supply side of the news industry, but on the demand side as well.

Selective Exposure to Attitude-Congruent Information

Selective exposure to attitude-congruent information (i.e., partisan selective exposure) predates the Internet. In the 1940s, Lazarsfeld, Berelson, and Gaudet (1944) found evidence that during presidential campaigns voters selectively attended to messages that supported their preferred candidate. Later in that decade, researchers found evidence of selective exposure to information on United States foreign policy (Hyman & Sheatsley, 1947) and blood donation (Cartwright, 1949). However, research on partisan selective exposure in subsequent decades was less conclusive. For instance, Sears and Freedman (1967) reviewed two decades' worth of research on selective exposure and concluded that some studies supported the selective exposure hypothesis, while others showed that people had no preference for attitude-consistent or inconsistent information. They also found research that indicated some people preferred information that *disconfirmed* their beliefs (see also reviews by Cotton, 1985; Frey, 1986). These mix of findings caused some scholars to conclude that people do not actively seek out sources that confirm their beliefs (Kinder, 2003).

It is not surprising that scholars in the pre-digital age found little support for selective exposure, given that partisan sources were not nearly as prolific or as easily obtained as they are today. Today's media consumption environment, however, shows more consistent evidence of selective exposure. Two factors help make this so: (1) changes in the presentation of news toward more partisan coverage, and (2) increases in individuals' ability to use digitally-networked technologies to control their exposure to news sources and issues.

Selective Exposure in the Contemporary Media Environment

Indeed, selective exposure has been re-examined in the contemporary media context and, so far, support for it is robust. For example, Stroud (2008) found that 64 percent of Republicans consistently relied on at least one conservative news source, while only 26 percent of Democrats consistently used a conservative news source. Moreover, 76 percent of liberals relied on at least one liberal source, compared to 43 percent of conservatives. Iyengar and Hahn (2009) similarly found that when given a choice among five news sources (Fox News, CNN, BBC, NPR, and an unattributed source), conservatives significantly preferred Fox News over any other, while liberal participants avoided Fox News (although they did not converge on any source more than the others). While these studies generally focused on traditional media, the authors suggested that changes in the media environment since the 1990s may be driving the recent positive findings for selective exposure to attitudinally-congruent information. Indeed, the selective exposure phenomenon may be even more pronounced online, where maintaining readership may be contingent on taking a side. The online news landscape is populated by a diverse array of bloggers, the most popular of whom take an aggressive stance at either the liberal or conservative end of the ideological spectrum (Meraz, 2008). Accordingly, there has been recent empirical support for the existence of selective exposure within the blog context. Johnson, Bichard, and Zhang (2009), for instance, found that blog readers have a tendency to visit blogs that share their political predispositions and avoid blogs that challenge them.

Both source bias and story bias appear to impact people's decisions when selecting a source of news information online, as well as how long they will consume the information. Garrett (2009) found that individuals were more likely to view online stories, and stick with them longer, if they think the accounts confirm their opinions, and experience a slight aversion to information that appears to disconfirm their opinions. Similarly, Knobloch-Westerwick and Meng (2009) found that people chose attitude-congruent sources of online news information significantly more often than counter-attitudinal sources when cued to story bias by article headlines, and spent more time reading attitude-congruent stories after choosing them.

Fischer, Schulz-Hardt, and Frey (2008) also found evidence for selective exposure to attitude-consistent information under conditions of abundant content choice. Under high-choice conditions (10 available sources compared to only a few), individuals preferred attitude-congruent information. Fischer, Jonas, Frey, and Schultz-Hardt (2005) also found that placing limits on the amount of information for which an individual can search heightens selective exposure. This study also reflects actual Internet search behavior, in that individuals typically have a limited amount of time and energy that they are willing to spend on information searches online.

Most strikingly, fears about the effect of partisan news on information consumption behaviors appear to be justified. While research on selective exposure to attitude-congruent sources found limited support for the phenomenon before the proliferation of ideologically-biased sources, research on selective exposure in the current media environment consistently supports the phenomenon. It appears that individuals have a strong preference for news sources that share their ideology and confirm their beliefs. Although this is understandable in some ways, it is puzzling given that news consumers have traditionally determined credibility largely in terms of objectivity. We next consider the role that source credibility plays in selective exposure, as a means to extend the theoretical understanding of these phenomena.

The Selective Exposure Paradox: The Role of Source Credibility

To recap, we see that recent findings concerning selective exposure appear to contradict decades of research on source credibility. Once, news credibility was seen as based upon a source's expertise and trustworthiness — both indicated by the degree to which a news outlet, acting as an objective source, provided information in "balanced" or unbiased ways (Berlo, Lemert, & Mertz, 1969; Bowers & Phillips, 1967; Hovland, Janis, & Kelly, 1953; Whitehead, 1968). Yet, as discussed before, while individuals may believe that unbiased sources are more credible than unbalanced ones, they still seem to seek out attitude-consistent information over less biased sources. Several possible explanations exist for these apparently contradictory findings.

The first explanation is that selective exposure decisions are a simple matter of dissonance avoidance. Cognitive dissonance theory (CDT), for example, suggests that people are motivated to avoid information that is incongruent with their beliefs, attitudes, or behavior because it makes them feel uncomfortable (Festinger, 1957). Selective exposure to attitude-congruent information is one way to reduce or prevent dissonance (Cotton, 1985; Taber & Lodge, 2006), and so people may choose to attend to attitude-congruent news sources and information to avoid the discomfort brought about by dissonant information. In this case, the credibility of the source has little to do with exposure, as this explanation centers on dissonance prevention as the primary driver of news selection decisions. However, cognitive dissonance theory by itself cannot adequately explain selective exposure behavior observed in several studies. For example, CDT fails to account for a body of studies that find people do not necessarily avoid attitude-discrepant information (Iyengar, Hahn, Krosnick, & Walker, 2008; Kobayashi & Ikeda, 2009). The theory predicts that if people were concerned with dissonance, they would actively avoid information that challenged their beliefs, and yet that is often not what is observed.

Instead, studies of bias perception in media coverage find that people notice and devote greater attention to information that is antagonistic to their point of view, as opposed to attitudinally-congruent information, and to feel that attitude-congruent information is more fair and valid (Gunther &

Schmitt, 2006; Vallone, Ross, & Lepper, 1985). Moreover, news consumers tend to attribute antagonistic biases even to *neutral* sources, especially when these news consumers are highly involved in the issue being covered (Christen, Kannaovakun, & Gunther, 2002; Giner-Sorolla & Chaiken, 1994; Perloff, 1989). So, while selective exposure could result from a drive to reduce dissonance, it is more likely also due to people perceiving information that agrees with them as more impartial, and thus more credible. Put another way, this suggests that *people process biased information in biased ways*: They are quite keen to notice bias when the source or message contradicts their attitudes and they then use this as a strong *negative* credibility cue. At the same time, they are rather blind to bias when the source or message is congruent with their attitudes and, in this case, use attitude congruity as a *positive* credibility cue.

The idea that people may attribute higher levels of quality and fairness to biased, but like-minded sources was first suggested by Fischer et al. (2005), and support for this as an explanation of selective exposure comes from Kahan and colleagues' *cultural cognition thesis*. This perspective combines elements of Wildavsky's Cultural Theory of Preference Formation (1987) with research in psychology on cognitive heuristics (Kahan et al., 2009, 2010). Wildavsky's Cultural Theory of Preference Formation suggests that people filter information through their personal, cultural identities, and subsequently form opinions about that information. For example, when considering a proposed piece of legislation, people gauge the legislation's ramifications against their own values, consider the opinions of others who have similar values, and evaluate the values of the legislation's source. Kahan et al. (2010) argued that they do this because people tend to perceive like-minded sources as more honest, knowledgeable, and impartial than differently-minded sources.

Thus, individuals appear to find biased, yet attitude-congruent information more credible than neutral or opinion-challenging information because they perceive attitude-congruent information as (ironically) more impartial, and they are more likely to seek out and rely on like-minded sources as a result. As such, credibility offers a new theoretical explanation that is superior to those offered in the past to account for the somewhat paradoxical patterns of selective exposure observed in the literature. It also plays a more complex role in the selective exposure process than previously thought. As new media, including UGN, continue to bring news consumers greater choice and control over news content selection, some scholars fear that repeated exposure to attitude-congruent information over time will hamper knowledge of important issues, increase opinion rigidity, decrease willingness to compromise, and breed intolerance toward attitude-challenging ideas.

Selective Exposure to News, Cyberbalkinzation, and News Credibility

Sunstein (2007) argued that the multiplicity of sources combined with increased control over issue exposure will lead to the "Daily Me": a personalized collection of news stories that filters out unwanted information. Potential negative consequences of the Daily Me include declines in political knowledge as individuals avoid reading about issues they perceive as uninteresting or unimportant, and more extreme political views as individuals expose themselves to only likeminded information. Some evidence for the Daily Me can be found in a recent survey by the Pew Internet & American Life Project (2010), which found 67 percent of Americans report paying attention to only those subjects that interest them, while 31 percent of online news users prefer sources that share their own point of view.

Sunstein's fear that the public will be less aware of, or misinformed about, political issues appears warranted to some degree. Evidence suggests that democracy functions best when citizens are well-informed about multiple aspects of issues, as this helps them make educated voting decisions and strengthens the democratic dialogue (Mutz & Martin, 2001). Over the last several decades, research has revealed knowledge gaps among individuals who selectively expose. For example, Sweeney and Gruber (1984) found that Richard Nixon supporters were far less knowledgeable about the Watergate scandal than neutral parties and Nixon detractors. More recently, Nir (2011) found that individuals who sought out information that supported a preferred conclusion were more likely to hold misconceptions about their opinion's popularity, both on a national level and in small-scale discussion groups. This phenomenon has been described as the "false consensus effect," which is the tendency for individuals to overestimate the popularity of their own opinions, especially when presented with attitude-confirming information (Bosveld, Koomed, & van der Pligt, 1994).

Effects at the individual level are almost certainly reflected at the societal level. Putnam (2000) broadly described social fragmentation resulting from the fractured media environment as "cyberbalkanization." The Web allows people to only expose themselves to others who share their interests, whether political, spiritual, or physical. This fragmentation results in a decrease in social capital and shared cultural experience, which may in turn lead to social divisions based on political and cultural values. Recent research suggests that cyberbalkanization may be escalating. For instance, voters have become gradually less likely to vote for a member of the opposing party over the last 60 years (Abramowitz & Saunders, 2006). And Stroud (2008) found that cable news viewers became more polarized over the course of the 2004 election.

News consumers' propensity toward selective exposure also has interesting implications for news producers, in terms of traditional news corporations as well as journalists. News organizations, especially those like the Tribune, the Hearst Corporation, the Washington Post Company, and the New York Times Company (whose revenue is generated mainly by newspapers), must look for ways to remain profitable in a changing news landscape. One option is to follow the lead of News Corporation (owner of Fox News, *The Wall Street Journal*, and the *New York Post*, among others) in targeting niche audiences through slanted news coverage. Another is to adapt their product to a digital world. However, this adaptation often enables selective exposure just as much as presenting slanted news does. For example, subscribers to the digital version of *The New York Times* can customize their homepage to only show certain areas of interest (i.e., national news, sports news, entertainment, etc.). Other news sites (cnn.com, msnbc.com) have features that rank news stories according to popularity, directing users' attention to stories that are entertaining but not necessarily essential. Additionally, by enabling news organizations to track which stories provide the biggest audiences, these features could jeopardize the coverage of issues that are boring but important or that are only followed by a small, fervent group of people.

Professional journalists are placed in an unenviable position by these developments. They cling to the ideals and ethical standards promoted in journalism school, arguing that a free and independent press should provide a voice to the voiceless, a check on the government, and tie communities together, while also deriding their corporate employers that dilute the ethical foundation of news (Usher, 2010). Thus, they face an uncomfortable choice: either work for "big media" and compromise their ideals, or maintain their ideals but venture into the less profitable, tumultuous world of online news. Either decision undermines the very notion of "professional" journalism. If journalists working for traditional media no longer follow codes of ethics, then what separates them from independent news bloggers other than the institutional backing behind their articles? And if a journalist must start an independent blog to uphold their ethical standards and cover issues they are passionate about, then why go to journalism school at all?

These trends present significant implications for the credibility of news. As discussed earlier, the resurgence of the partisan in news production and consumption is negatively affecting the credibility of news. However, people are also likely to *perceive* partisan news as quite credible if it conforms to their personal political views. To some degree, this apparent contradiction is a function of which dimensions of credibility are emphasized. Furthermore, if credibility is understood to mean unbiased, professionally-vetted information, then clearly the migration toward news information that is produced by individuals who are largely untrained in news production signals the erosion of news information credibility.

However, if news credibility is not viewed as stringently yoked to objective accounts by trained professionals, other possibilities emerge. For example, if dimensions other than objectivity and institutionally-approved authority are privileged — such as independence from corporate news organizations, timeliness, authentic firsthand accounts, opportunities for cross-validation across numerous independent sources, and interactivity — then contemporary UGN accounts may in fact be viewed as more credible than traditional news reports (Carroll & Richardson, 2011). In this model, credible news information could legitimately emerge from people with high experiential credibility, though they lack traditional credentials, or from a diversity of sources who in the aggregate are likely to produce a trustworthy account of news events.

Moreover, when looking across the enormous amount of news information currently available from a vast array of personal and political perspectives about any particular issue or event — including traditional news organization accounts — the addition of UGN accounts provides a significantly more complete and credible analysis of current affairs. Compared to the handful of media conglomerates that have dominated traditional news production for the past century or so, the addition of a significant number of user-generated news reports can be seen as a tremendous boon to people's understanding of the world. Viewed this way, the complete "body" of news information now available eclipses that formerly known, which likely can enhance the overall credibility of news information today.

Finally, professional journalism (vetted, trained) and UGN accounts (experiential, biased) need not stand in contrast to one another. Not only do many news venues actively feature both perspectives (CNN's iReport is a prominent example), but users themselves have the option to seek out both types of reportage. The extent to which they do so, however, is an open research question. Selective exposure complicates the picture. Not only does it affect what content people pay attention to but also their selection of perceived credible sources from among the wide range of professional and UGN outlets.

Conclusion

The notion of an objective press dominated the U.S. mass media for over a century, but recent trends in news consumption and markets point toward new iterations of more subjective news. One instance of this trend discussed here is user-generated news, where news reports are produced by independent individuals or groups of interested people, rather than by professional journalists affiliated with large media organizations. Although the user-generation of news presents problems with source credibility, there are some possible credibility advantages, including the benefits of the news purveyor's personal experience with issues and events, the aggregation of diverse voices and views, and independence from a news owner apparatus that can sometimes constrain mainstream reporters' ability to provide pertinent and relevant news accounts.

Accompanying these potential advantages of a more post-objective journalism, however, are serious concerns about news consumers' selective exposure to attitudinally-congruent information. In the digital media environment, where news consumers are faced with a plethora of options, individuals are more likely to selectively expose themselves to like-minded others and views consistent with their own opinions. They do so because they appear to find attitude-congruent information to be credible, which is surprising in light of its inherent bias. Source credibility research provides a new and superior theoretical explanation to account for the somewhat paradoxical patterns observed, suggesting that perceptions of source credibility assume a more complex role in the selective exposure process than previously thought. Such an explanation is important since exposure to information that largely fails to contradict individuals' pre-existing beliefs has the potential to lead to group polarization and the diminution of informed debate, which is the cornerstone of the Jeffersonian ideal of an informed populace and vibrant democracy. Thus, in the end, the recent evolution toward "news with a view" is accompanied both by tremendous opportunities and potentially significant costs, the ultimate balance of which remains to be determined.

Chapter Notes

1. A "microblog" is a truncated form of a blog; the format is commonly visible in online vehicles such as Twitter and Facebook.

2. The most popular cable news shows still trail behind traditional news programs like *NBC Nightly News* in terms of viewership (Bauder, 2011; Shea, 2010). People are not abandoning traditional news sources entirely. There is merely a downward trend in reliance on sources that use traditional, unbiased methods of reporting, and an uptick in use of biased sources.

3. Thurmond ran for president in 1948 on a segregation platform, carrying the states of Mississippi, Louisiana, Alabama, and South Carolina. At a celebration of Thurmond's 100th birthday, Lott, a Senator from Mississippi, said, "I want to say this about my state: When Strom Thurmond ran for president, we voted for him. We're proud of it. And if the rest of the country had followed our lead, we wouldn't have had all these problems over all these years, either" (Edsall, 2002, para. 2). Bloggers helped propel this event into the mainstream news. Additionally, during the 2004 presidential election, a report by Dan Rather on *60 Minutes* claimed that President George W. Bush received special treatment while in the National Guard in 1968. The report used documents showing that President

Bush had his flight status revoked for missing a physical as evidence. Bloggers questioned the authenticity of these documents, which were later found to be fake (Folkenflik, 2005). Months later, Rather resigned.

References

Abrahamson, D. (2006). The rise of the new partisan press: Forward into the past. *Journal of Magazine and New Media Research, 8*(1). Retrieved August 15, 2011, from http://aejmcmagazine.arizona.edu/Journal/Spring2006/Abrahamson_notes.pdf.

Abramowitz, A. I., & Saunders, K. L. (2006). Exploring the bases of partisanship in the American electorate: Social identity vs. ideology. *Political Research Quarterly, 59*(2), 175–187.

Bardach, A. L. (2008). A crisis in the newsroom. In R. Rice (Ed.), *Media ownership: Research & regulation* (pp. 221–242). Cresskill, NJ: Hampton Press.

Bauder, D. (2011). Network evening news ratings up across the board. *The Huffington Post.* Retrieved August 15, 2011, from http://www.huffingtonpost.com/2011/07/13/network-evening-news-rati_n_896883.html

Bennett, W. L., & Iyengar, S. (2008) A new era of minimal effects? The changing foundations of political communication. *Journal of Communication, 58*(4), 707–731.

Berlo, D. K., Lemert, J. B., & Mertz, R. J. (1969). Dimensions for evaluating the acceptability of message sources. *Public Opinion Quarterly, 33*(1), 563–576.

Bosveld, W., Koomen, W., & van der Pligt, J. (1994). Selective exposure and the false consensus effect: The availability of similar and dissimilar others. *British Journal of Social Psychology, 33*(4), 457–466.

Bowers, J. W., & Phillips, W. A. (1967). A note on the generality of source credibility scales. *Speech Monographs, 34*(3), 185–186.

Carpenter, S. (2010). A study of diversity in online citizen journalism and online newspaper articles. *New Media & Society, 20*(10), 1–21.

Carroll, B., & Richardson, R. R. (2011). Identification, transparency, interactivity: Towards a new paradigm for credibility for single-voice blogs. *International Journal of Interactive Communication Systems and Technologies, 1*(1), 19–35.

Carter, B. (2010). CNN fails to stop fall in ratings. *New York Times.* Retrieved August 15, 2011, from http://www.nytimes.com/2010/03/30/business/media/30cnn.html

Cartwright, D. (1949). Some principles of mass persuasion. *Human Relations, 2*(4), 253–267.

Cassidy, W. P. (2007). Online news credibility: An examination of the perceptions of newspaper journalists. *Journal of Computer-Mediated Communication, 12*(2), 478–498.

Cenite, M., Detenber, B. H., Koh, A. W., Lim, A., & Soon, N. E. (2009). Doing the right thing online: A survey of blogger's ethical beliefs and practices. *New Media & Society, 11*(4), 575–597.

Chi, E. H., Pirolli, P., & Lam, S. K. (2007). Aspects of augmented social cognition: Social information foraging and social search. *Online Communities and Social Computing, 4564,* 60–69.

Christen, C. T., Kannaovakun, P., & Gunther, A. C. (2002). Hostile media perceptions: Partisan assessments of press and public during the 1997 United Parcel Service strike. *Political Communication, 19*(4), 423–436.

Coe, K., Tewksbury, D., Bond, B. J., Drogos, K. L., Porter, R. W., Yahn, A., & Zhang, Y. (2008). Hostile news: Partisan use and perceptions of cable news programming. *Journal of Communication, 58*(2), 201–219.

Committee to Protect Journalists. (2011). *Mubarak intensifies press attacks with assaults, detentions.* Retrieved April 12, 2011, from http://cpj.org/2011/02/mubarak-intensifies-press-attacks-with-assaults-de.php.

Cotton, J. L. (1985). Cognitive dissonance in selective exposure. In D. Zillmann & J. Bryany (Eds.), *Selective exposure to communication* (pp. 11–33). Hillsdale, NJ: Lawrence Erlbaum.

Edsall, T. B. (2002). Lott decried for part of salute to Thurmond. *The Washington Post.* Retrieved August 20, 2011, from http://www.washingtonpost.com/ac2/wp-dyn?pagename=article&contentId=A20730–2002Dec6

Festinger, L. (1957). *A theory of cognitive dissonance.* Evanston, IL: Row, Peterson.

Fischer, P., Jonas, E., Frey, D., & Schultz-Hardt, S. (2005). Selective exposure to information: The impact of information limits. *European Journal of Social Psychology, 35*(4), 469–492.

Fischer, P., Schultz-Hardt, S., & Frey, D. (2008). Selective exposure and information quantity: How different information quantities moderate decision makers' preference for consistent and inconsistent information. *Journal of Personality and Social Psychology, 94*(2), 231–244.

Flanagin, A. J., & Metzger, M. J. (2000). Perceptions of Internet information credibility. *Journalism and Mass Communication Quarterly, 77*(3), 515–540.

_____. (in press). Digital media and perceptions of source credibility in political communication. *Oxford Handbook of Political Communication.* New York: Oxford University Press.

Folkenflik, D. (2005). Q&A: The CBS "Memogate" mess. *National Public Radio.* Retrieved August 20, 2011, from http://www.npr.org/templates/story/story.php?storyId=4279605

Frey, D. (1986). Recent research on selective exposure to information. In L. Berkowitz (Ed.), *Advances in experimental social psychology* (Vol. 19, pp. 41–80). San Diego: Academic Press.

Garrett, R. K. (2009). Echo chambers online? Politically motivated selective exposure among Internet news users. *Journal of Computer-Mediated Communication, 14*(2), 265–285.

Giner-Sorolla, R., & Chaiken, S. (1994). The causes of hostile media judgments. *Journal of Experimental Social Psychology, 30*(2), 165–180.

Gunther, A. C., & Schmitt, K. (2006). Mapping boundaries of the hostile media effect. *Journal of Communication, 54*(1), 55–70.

Hovland, C. I., Janis, I. L., & Kelley, H. H. (1953). *Communication and persuasion.* New Haven: Yale University Press.

Hyman, H. H., & Sheatsley, P. B. (1947). Some reasons why information campaigns fail. *Public Opinion Quarterly, 11*, 412–423.

Iyengar, S., & Hahn, K. S. (2009). Red media, blue media: Evidence of ideological selectivity in media use. *Journal of Communication, 59*(1), 19–39.

Iyengar, S., Hahn, K. S., Krosnick, J. A., & Walker, J. (2008). Selective exposure to campaign communication: The role of anticipated agreement and issue public membership. *The Journal of Politics, 70*(1), 186–200.

Johnson, T. J., Bichard, S. L., & Zhang, W. (2009). Communication communities or "cyberghettos"? A path analysis model examining factors that explain selective exposure to blogs. *Journal of Computer-Mediated Communication, 15*(1), 60–82.

Johnson, T. J., & Kaye, B. K. (2004). Wag the blog: How reliance on traditional media and the Internet influence credibility perceptions of weblogs among blog users. *Journalism and Mass Communication Quarterly, 81*(3), 622–642.

_____, (2009). In blog we trust? Deciphering credibility components of the Internet among politically interested Internet users. *Computers in Human Behavior, 25*(1), 175–182.

_____, (2010). Still cruising and believing? An analysis of online credibility across three presidential campaigns. *American Behavioral Scientist, 54*(1), 57–77.

Kahan, D. M., Braman, D., Cohen, G. L., Gastil, J., & Slovic, P. (2010). Who fears the HPV vaccine, who doesn't, and why? An experimental study of the mechanisms of cultural cognition. *Law & Human Behavior 34*. Retrieved November 12, 2010, from http://www.culturalcognition.net/papers-topical/

Kahan, D. M., Braman, D., Slovic, P., Gastil, J., & Cohen, G. L. (2009). Cultural cognition of the risks and benefits of nanotechnology. *Nature Nanotechnology, 4*, 87–91.

Kang, M. (2010). Measuring social media credibility: A study on a measure of blog credibility. Institute for Public Relations. Retrieved June 21, 2011, from http://www.instituteforpr.org/topics/measuring-blog-credibility/

Keen, A. (2007). *The cult of the amateur: How today's Internet is killing our culture*. London: Nicholas Brealey.

Kinder, D. R. (2003). Communication and politics in the age of information. In D. O. Sears, L. Huddy, & R. Jervis (Eds.), *Oxford handbook of political psychology* (pp. 357–393). Oxford: Oxford University Press.

Kiousis, S. (2001). Public trust or mistrust? Perceptions of media credibility in the information age. *Mass Communication and Society, 4*(4), 381–403.

Knobloch-Westerwick, S., & Meng, J. (2009). Looking the other way: Selective exposure to attitude-consistent and counterattitudinal political information. *Communication Research, 36*(3), 426–448.

Kobayashi, T., & Ikeda, K. (2009). Selective exposure in political Web browsing: Empirical verification of "cyber-balkanization" in Japan and the USA. *Information, Communication, & Society, 12*(6), 929–953.

Kohut, A. (1999). *The Internet news audience goes ordinary*. Washington, DC: Pew Research Center.

Lazarsfeld, P. F., Berelson, B., & Gaudet, H. (1944). *The people's choice*. New York: Columbia University Press.

McKenna, L. (2007). "Getting the word out": Policy bloggers use their soap box to make change. *Review of Policy Research, 24*(3), 209–229.

McKenna, L., & Pole, A. (2008). What do bloggers do: An average day on an average political blog. *Public Choice, 134*(1), 97–108.

Mehrabi, D., Hassan, M. A., & Ali, M. S. S. (2009). News media credibility of the Internet and television. *European Journal of Social Sciences, 11*(1), 136–148.

Melican, D. B., & Dixon, T. L. (2008). News on the net: Credibility, selective exposure, and racial prejudice. *Communication Research, 35*(2), 151–168.

Meraz, S. (2008). Is there an elite hold? Traditional media to social media agenda setting influence in blog networks. *Journal of Computer-Mediated Communication, 14*(3), 682–707.

Messner, M., & Distaso, M. W. (2008). The source cycle: How traditional media and weblogs use each other as sources. *Journalism Studies, 9*(3), 447–463.

Metzger, M. J., Flanagin, A. J., Pure, R., Medders, R. B., Markov, A. R., & Hartsell, E. H. (2011). *Adults and credibility: An empirical examination of digital media use and information credibility*. Research report for the John D. and Catherine T. MacArthur Foundation.

Mindich, D. T. Z. (1998). *Just the facts: How "objectivity" came to define American journalism*. New York: New York University Press.

Mutz, D. C., & Martin, P. S. (2001). Facilitating communication across lines of political differences: The role of mass media. *American Political Science Review, 95*(1), 97–114.

Nir, L. (2011). Motivated reasoning and public opinion perception. *Public Opinion Quarterly, 75*(3), 1–29.

Online News Association (2001). *Digital journalism credibility survey*. Retrieved May 24, 2011, from www.journalists.org/Programs/ResearchText.htm

Perlmutter, D. D., & Schoen, M. (2007). "If I break a rule, what do I do, fire myself?" Ethics codes of independent blogs. *Journal of Mass Media Ethics, 22*(1), 37–48.

Perloff, R. M. (1989). Ego-involvement and the third person effect of televised news coverage. *Communication Research, 16*(2), 236–262.

Pew Project for Excellence in Journalism: State of the News Media. (2009). *Citizen-based media*. Retrieved February 15, 2009, from http://www.stateofthemedia.org/2009/index.htm

Pew Research Center for People and the Press. (2010). *Americans spending more time following the news*. Retrieved August 16, 2011, from http://people-press.org/2010/09/12/americans-spending-more-time-following-the-news/

Preston, J. (2011). Movement began with outrage and a Facebook page that gave it an outlet. *The New York Times*. Retrieved February 11, 2011, from http://www.nytimes.com/2011/02/06/world/middleeast/06face.html?_r=1&partner=rss&emc=rss

Putnam, R. D. (2000). *Bowling alone*. New York: Simon & Schuster.

Rhine, R. J. (1967). Some problems in dissonance theory research on information selectivity. *Psychological Bulletin, 68*(1), 21–28.

Robertson, A.W. (2001). "Look on this picture ... and on this!" Nationalism, localism, and partisan images of otherness in the United States, 1787–1820. *The American Historical Review, 106*(4), 1263–1280.

Schudson, M. (2001). The objectivity norm in American journalism. *Journalism, 2*(2), 149–170.

Schweiger, W. (2000). Media credibility — Experience or image? A survey on the credibility of the World Wide Web in Germany in comparison to other media. *European Journal of Communication, 15*(1), 37–59.

Sears, D. O., & Freedman, J. L. (1967). Selective exposure to information: A critical review. *Public Opinion Quarterly, 31*(2), 194–213.

Shea, D. (2010). Cable news ratings: Top 30 programs. *The Huffington Post*. Retrieved August 29, 2011, from http://www.huffingtonpost.com/2010/03/31/cable-news-ratings-top-30_n_519737.html#s77244&title=1_The_OReilly

Song, Y. (2007). Internet news and issue development: A case study on the roles of independent online news services as agenda-builders for anti-U.S. protests in South Korea. *New Media & Society, 9*(1), 71–92.

Stroud, N. J. (2008). Media use and political predispositions: Revisiting the concept of selective exposure. *Political Behavior, 30*(3), 341–366.

Sunstein, C. R. (2007). *Republic.com 2.0*. Princeton, NJ: Princeton University Press.

Surowiecki, J. (2004). *The wisdom of crowds*. New York: Anchor Books.

Sweeney, P. D., & Gruber, K. L. (1984). Selective exposure: Voter preferences and the Watergate affair. *Journal of Personality and Social Psychology, 46*(6), 1208–1221.

Sweetser, K. D. (2007). Blog bias: Reports, inferences, and judgments of credentialed bloggers at the 2004 nominating conventions. *Public Relations Review, 33*(4), 426–428.

Sweetser, K. D., Porter, L. V., Chung, D. S., & Kim, E. (2008). Credibility and the use of blogs among professionals in the communication industry. *Journalism & Mass Communication Quarterly, 85*(1), 169–185.

Taber, C. S., & Lodge, M. (2006). Motivated skepticism in the evaluation of political beliefs. *American Journal of Political Science, 50*(3), 755–769.

Thorson, E. (2010). The journalist behind the news: Credibility of straight, collaborative, opinionated, and blogged "news." *American Behavioral Scientist, 55*(5), 100–119.

Thorson, K., Vraga, E., & Ekdale, B. (2010). Credibility in context: How uncivil online commentary affects news credibility. *Mass Communication & Society, 13*(3), 289–313.

Usher, N. (2010). Goodbye to the news: How out-of-work journalists assess enduring news values and the new media landscape. *New Media and Society, 12*(6), 911–928.

Vallone, R. P., Ross, L., & Lepper, M. R. (1985). The hostile media phenomenon: Biased perception and perceptions of media bias in coverage of the Beirut massacre. *Journal of Personality and Social Psychology, 49*(3), 577–585.

Whitehead, J. L. (1968). Factors of source credibility. *Quarterly Journal of Speech, 54*(1), 59–63.

Wildavsky, A. (1987). Choosing preferences by constructing institutions: A cultural theory of preference formation. *American Political Science Review, 81*(1), 3–22.

Wilson, P. (1983). *Second-hand knowledge: An inquiry into cognitive authority.* Westport, CT: Greenwood.

Yang, S. U., & Lim, J. (2009). The effects of blog-mediated public relations on relation trust. *Journal of Public Relations Research, 21*(3), 341–359.

About the Contributors

Aaron **Barlow**, an associate professor of English at New York City College of Technology of the City University of New York, is the coauthor, with Robert Leston, of *Beyond the Blogosphere: Information and Her Children*, the last volume of a trilogy relating to new media. His other books include *Quentin Tarantino: Life at the Extremes*. He edited *One Hand Does Not Catch a Buffalo*, an anthology of essays by Peace Corps Volunteers who served in Africa.

Robin **Blom** is a doctoral student in the Media and Information Studies program and a graduate assistant for the School of Journalism at Michigan State University. He earned his journalism degree at the Hogeschool van Utrecht, Netherlands, and a master's degree in journalism and mass communication at Point Park University, Pittsburgh. He has worked as a reporter for national and local newspapers. His interests include media bias perceptions, agenda setting, and the influence of news media on political involvement and the marketplace of ideas.

Serena **Carpenter** joined the Arizona State University faculty in 2007 specializing in the research and teaching of newer media after finishing her doctorate in Media and Information Studies at Michigan State University. She teaches courses in the areas of online/multimedia journalism, social media, and mass communication theory in the Walter Cronkite School of Journalism and Mass Communication. Her research focuses on media sociology, news characteristics, and alternative journalists.

Deborah S. **Chung** is an associate professor in the School of Journalism and Telecommunications at the University of Kentucky. She earned her Ph.D. from Indiana University–Bloomington in 2004. She is interested in opportunities afforded to information consumers through the adoption of new technological tools (e.g., blogs, social bookmarking, interactive features) and the framing and perceptions of various types of interactive and social media.

Elina **Erzikova** is an assistant professor of public relations in the Department of Journalism at Central Michigan University. Her research interest includes the role of power in state-media relations and cultural aspects of public relations practice. Her studies have been published in *Political Communication, Journalism Studies, Public Relations Review, Public Relations Journal,* and *Russian Journal of Communication.*

Andrew J. **Flanagin** is a professor in the Department of Communication at the University of California–Santa Barbara, where he also serves as the director of the Center for Information Technology and Society. His research focuses on the ways in which information and communication technologies structure and extend human interaction.

Ethan **Hartsell** is a doctoral student in the University of California–Santa Barbara Department of Communication. He studies media effects, social media and credibility, and has coauthored several works on online information credibility, social media and media effects.

John A. **Hatcher** is an assistant professor of journalism in the Department of Writing Studies at the University of Minnesota–Duluth. He is the coeditor with Bill Reader of *Foundations of Community Journalism*. His research focuses on community journalism and the sociology of news, and a comparative analysis of community journalism in Norway, South Africa, and the United States. He worked for years as editor and columnist at the *Daily Messenger* in upstate New York.

John **Jirik** is an assistant professor in Journalism and Communication at Lehigh University. Before pursuing graduate study at the University of Texas–Austin, he was a television news producer at Reuters, based in Moscow, Hong Kong and Singapore. His research focuses on the way power works in and through media.

Kirsten A. **Johnson** is an associate professor and chair of the Department of Communications at Elizabethtown College. She earned her Ph.D. from Drexel University and teaches in the areas of broadcast news writing and television production. Her research interests include citizen journalism and online credibility. Johnson worked in local radio and television for nearly a decade at KRNT and WOI-TV in Des Moines, and WGAL-TV in Lancaster, Pennsylvania.

Gerry **Lanosga** is an assistant professor of journalism at Ball State University. He earned his Ph.D. in mass communications from Indiana University after a 20-year career as a print and broadcast journalist. He has won such awards as an IRE Medal, a Silver Baton in the duPont–Columbia Awards, and a George Foster Peabody award. His teaching and research interests include investigative reporting, media law, and journalism history.

Wilson **Lowrey** is an associate professor of journalism in the College of Communication and Information Sciences at the University of Alabama. He earned a Ph.D. from the University of Georgia after seven years in the newspaper industry. His research focuses on the sociology of news work and emerging media forms. He is the coeditor of *Changing the News: The Forces Shaping Journalism in Uncertain Times* and he has published in *Journalism & Mass Communication Quarterly*, *Political Communication*, and *Mass Communication and Society*.

Doreen **Marchionni** earned her Ph.D. from the Missouri School of Journalism. She specializes in online news research/credibility and journalism-as-a-conversation. A 17-year veteran of newspapers, most recently as an assistant metro editor at *The Seattle Times*, she teaches news reporting and writing, social media, and editing at Pacific Lutheran University in Tacoma, Washington, and runs a Tumblr blog (blog.sasquatchmedia.com).

Sharon **Meraz** is an assistant professor in the Department of Communication at the University of Illinois–Chicago. Her interdisciplinary research centers on the political impact of new media such as blogs, social networking sites, and mobile media. She also studies the impact of these technologies on the evolution of the traditional mass media industry, and mass media effect theories.

Miriam J. **Metzger** is an associate professor in the Department of Communication at the University of California–Santa Barbara. Her interests lie at the intersection of media, information technology, and trust, especially how information technology alters our understandings of credibility, privacy, and the processes of media effects.

Seungahn **Nah** is an assistant professor of community communications in the Department of Community and Leadership Development, University of Kentucky, and the director of the Kentucky Citizen Media Project: The Lexington Commons. He earned his Ph.D. from the University of Wisconsin–Madison. He researches the interrelationships among communication, community, and democracy. His work has appeared in *Javnost—The Public*, *Mass Communication & Society*, and *Journalism: Theory, Practice & Criticism*.

David Michael **Ryfe** is a senior scholar and associate professor in the Reynolds School of Journalism, University of Nevada–Reno. He writes in the areas of presidential communication, public deliberation, and the history and sociology of journalism. His most recent book is *Will Journalism Survive? An Inside Look into American Newsrooms*.

Burton **St. John** III is an associate professor of communication at Old Dominion University. He is the author of *Press Professionalization and Propaganda: The Rise of Journalistic Double-Mindedness, 1917–1941* and coeditor of *Public Journalism 2.0: The Promise and Reality of a Citizen-Engaged Press*. His work has appeared in the *Journal of Communication Management*, *Journal of Mass Media Ethics*, *Journalism Studies*, *Public Relations Review*, and *Journalism Practice*.

Daxton R. "Chip" **Stewart** is an assistant professor at the Schieffer School of Journalism, Texas Christian University, where he teaches courses in media law and ethics. His research has focused on the First Amendment, freedom of information and open government laws, and intellectual property. He earned a J.D. at the University of Texas School of Law. He later worked as a newspaper editor and columnist and earned a Ph.D. in journalism and an LL.M. in dispute resolution from the University of Missouri.

Index

ABC in Australia 171
Africa 173
agenda setting 80–81, 90, 157, 178
aggregators, news 79–85, 87–92, 179, 201, 241
Ahearn, Chris 177
Ailes, Roger 30
Al Jazeera 171
Allan, Stuart 171, 174
Al-Qaeda 171
Altschull, J. Herbert 63, 153, 155
American Society of Newspaper Editors
    (ASNE) 172
Ancel, Judy 38
Andrews, Stephen Pearl 20
Asbury Park Press 66
Asia 173
Associated Press (AP) 170–180, 183–185
Association of Community Organizations for
    Reform Now (ACORN) 29, 35, 232
attitude-congruent information 245–248, 252
Audit Bureau of Circulations (ABC) 122
Austin, Texas 62, 202

Bagdikian, Ben 154
balance, journalistic 7, 27, 29–30, 44, 49, 53,
    69, 112, 136, 145, 170, 173, 181, 190, 205–220,
    225, 227, 241, 244, 247
Barney, Ralph D. 155, 165
Bayart, J.-F 173
Baym, Geoffrey 207–208
Benkler, Yochai 194, 198
Bennett, James Gordon 17, 19, 191
Ben-Porath, Eran N. 228
bias, journalistic 6, 15, 27–29, 32, 44, 53–54,
    62, 74, 78, 98, 101, 112, 135, 165, 170, 172,
    239–252
Blitzer, Wolf 209–211, 214
blog (blogs, bloggers, blogging) 4, 26, 28, 32,
    61, 66–67, 75–76, 78, 81–82, 85, 90, 102,
    104, 150, 182, 205, 212–213, 215, 222, 225,
    228–229, 232, 235, 238–244, 246, 250,
    252–253
Boston 202, 209
Boston Globe 37
Boston Post 52

Boudana, Sandrine 1–2
Bourdieu, Pierre 141, 150–151, 190, 200, 203,
    206–207, 217, 220
Bowles, Tom 199
Boyd-Barrett, Oliver 173–175
Breitbart, Andrew 29, 37–38, 232
Britain 171–172, 184
British Broadcasting Corporation (BBC) 171,
    174, 178, 226, 245
British press 172, 175
Bruns, Axel 4, 229
Bush Radio 161–162, 164

Cable News Network (CNN) 171, 174, 205–
    220, 235, 238, 240, 242, 245
Canadian Broadcasting Corporation (CBC)
    171
Cape Town 161–162, 163
Carey, James 65, 177
Carpenter, Serena 100
Castells, Manuel 165
CBS radio 30
Chicago 122
Chicago Daily News 51
Christians, Clifford 155, 159
citizen journalists 6, 75, 97–113, 164
Civil War 11–12, 23–24
cognitive dissonance theory (CDT) 247
collaborative filtering 80, 82–84, 89
community newspaper 101, 112, 120, 156–157
contextual objectivity 173–175, 184
Cooper, Anderson 214, 219–220
co-orientation 66–67, 69–71, 73, 75; *see also*
    homophily
Costello, Carol 217
Coughlin, William 156–157
credibility, journalistic 2, 4, 7, 38, 61–62, 66–
    67, 69–75, 91, 98, 100, 126–127, 143, 145,
    155, 158, 160, 166, 199, 206, 222–223, 226–
    227, 233, 238–241, 244, 247–252
crowdsourcing 80–82, 84, 87–88
cultural theory of preference formation 248
Cunningham, Brent 191, 223, 228
cyberbalkanization 249

263

Daily Kos 32
Daily Show (TDS) 205–220
Day, Benjamin 14, 17
Des Moines Register 123, 125
detachment, journalistic 46, 50, 54–55, 65, 98, 155, 159, 190, 199, 205–220, 228
Detroit Free Press 124
Dewey, John 64, 183–184
Dobbs, Lou 217, 219
Downie, Leonard 27–28, 34
doxa 205–207, 209, 214–219
Drudge Report 5, 240, 243

Eberle, Robert 32
Egyptian uprising 242
Elements of Journalism 22
El Paso Herald 47
Erickson, Erick 216–217
Erie Gazette 14
ethics, journalistic 11–12, 23, 26, 45, 136, 149, 154, 241, 250
Ettema, James 46, 48–49, 52

Facebook 3, 5, 75, 79, 88, 92, 121, 179, 182, 213, 215, 228, 242, 252
facts, and journalism 1, 3, 5–6, 11, 17–18, 34, 43–44, 47, 52, 54–55, 61, 63, 67, 75, 98–99, 113, 127, 136, 139, 144, 146–147, 154, 166–167, 170–172, 174–175, 179, 182–183, 190–192, 206, 209–211, 220, 222–235
Fallows, James 32
Fenton, Thomas 28, 30–32
field theory 137, 140, 144, 146–147, 190
filter-then-publish model 233
First Amendment 13, 16, 37, 39, 63
Fowler, Mayhill 201
Fox.net 38
Fox News 2, 27, 30, 61, 66, 78, 89, 205, 216, 218, 239, 240, 245–246, 250
Fuller, Margaret 20

Gannon, Jeff 31–33, 37
Gans, Herbert 228
Gardner, Susan 32
gatekeeping (gatekeepers) 2, 37, 82, 90, 222–235
gatewatching 4, 81, 229, 232
Gillmor, Dan 3, 191, 233
Glass, Stephen 36
Glasser, Theodore 46, 48–49, 52
Globalpost 202
Google 103, 201, 227, 241
Gorbachev, Mikhail 135, 151
Government 141, 144–146
Great Debate 181
Greeley, Horace 11–24
guard dog theory 156
Guardian 227
Guckert, James *see* Gannon, James

Habermas, Jurgen 181
Haidt, Jonathan 119
Halberstam, David 28, 39
Hale, William Harlan 19
Hannity, Sean 2
Hartsville Today 6
Hearst Corporation 250
homophily 67, 69–73, 87; *see also* co-orientation,
hubs 189, 195, 197–199
Huffington Post 5, 201, 243

impartiality, journalistic 12, 43–44, 170–172, 182–183; *see also* neutrality, journalistic
Industrial Revolution 62
informational cascades 82, 91–92
Ingersoll, Lurton 13
Internet 3, 5, 26, 30, 31, 33, 78, 81–82, 91, 93, 97, 100, 102, 104, 127, 171, 175–179, 182–184, 189, 194–195, 197–198, 201, 212–213, 217, 226, 228, 230–231, 233, 240, 243–246, 249
Investigative Reporter's Handbook 53
Iran 213
iReport(s) 213, 215, 238, 240, 242, 251

Jamieson, Kathleen Hall 224
Jeffersonian 15–16
Jenkins, Henry 31
Journal of Commerce 14, 17, 21
Jurkowitz, Mark 1

Kaiser, Robert 27–28, 34
Kamwangamalu, Nkonko M. 158–159
Kansas City Star 50
Kitty, Alexandra 27
Knight Citizen News Network 100, 103
Kovach, Bill 22, 190, 223–224, 226, 232
Kremlin 142, 145, 148
Kurtz, Howard 216

Latin America 173
LeBon, Gustave 120–121
Lemon, Don 213
Limpopo Mirror 160
Lippmann, Walter 53, 64, 172, 183–185, 191
Log-Cabin 15–16
London 172, 181
Long, Gerald 173
Los Angeles 122
Los Angeles Times 37, 50, 157
Lott, Trent 235, 243, 252

Maddow, Rachel 2
Makoya 160–161, 166
Mandela, Nelson 159
McVeigh, Timothy 227
media choice model 61, 66, 69
Medvedev 139, 145, 152
Mencken, H.L. 191
Merritt, Davis "Buzz" 26–27, 39, 206, 212

Mexican War 172
Meyer, Phil 53, 69
microblogs 238–240
Mindich, David 3, 44, 127, 189–190, 206
Minneapolis Star-Tribune 124
Minnesota Public Radio 68, 74
Miraldi, Robert 44–46
Mirror 161
morality 116–128
Morning Courier and New-York Enquirer 14
Moscow 142, 145, 149, 151
MSNBC 2, 78, 87, 205, 216, 218, 239–240, 250
My Space 213

Nass, Clifford 73
National Association for the Advancement of Colored People (NAACP) 35–36, 50, 232
National Public Radio (NPR) 36, 201, 232, 245
Nerone, John 18, 22
neutrality, journalistic 11–24, 42–46, 49, 52–55, 139, 208, 223, 240; *see also* impartiality, journalistic
New Republic 36
New World Information and Communication Order (NWICO) 173, 186
New York 13–15, 17, 22, 122, 172, 209
New York Evening Post 14, 52
New York Herald 15, 17, 19, 21
New York Morning Post 14
New York Post 250
New York Sun 14–15, 17–19, 21–22, 47
New York Times 17–18, 20, 37, 75, 178, 193, 243, 250
New York Times Company 250
New York Tribune 11–12, 15–18, 20–24
New York University 65
New-Yorker 11–12, 15–19, 22–23
Newhagen, John 73
News Corporation 201, 250
Northern Spectator 14
Norwegian Massacre 180
Nyhan, Brendan 29–30, 33

objectivism 29, 40
O'Keefe, James 31, 34–40, 232

Pareto principle 82, 197
Parton, James 12, 24
Penny Press 11–15, 17, 19, 21–23
Pereosmyslenie 139
Perestroika 135, 136–138, 143, 151
Peter the Great 137
Pew Research Center, 1–2, 40, 97, 218–219, 244, 249
Phillips, Kyra 210–211, 213
power law 82, 84–86, 196–198, 202
pragmatism 64
Private 142–146, 148–149
produser 81, 90; *see also* prosumer

Project Veritas 34
Propublica 202
prosumer 112, 226; *see also* produser
Public and Its Problems 64
public journalism 3, 65, 99
public opinion 64, 90–91, 116, 127
publish-then-filter model 233
Publitsistika 138
Pulitzer Prizes 45–47, 50–52, 54, 156–157
Putin, Vladimir 94, 96, 139, 151–152
Putnam, Robert D. 155, 249

Rathergate 243
raw information 227–228, 230–233, 235
Raymond, Henry J. 17–18
Regional Branch 142, 144, 147
Reifler, Jason 29–30, 33
Reuters 170–185, 201
Righteous Indignation 29
Riverdale Press (the Press) 157, 166–167
Robinson, Sue 228
Rochester Democrat and Chronicle 123
Roegsen, Susan 216
role conceptions, journalistic 3–4, 11–13, 18–20, 23, 28, 34, 38, 43, 46, 64–65, 80–81, 86, 97–113, 135–150
Rosen, Jay 65, 201, 205–206, 230
Rosenberry, Jack 120
Rosenstiel, Tom 22, 190, 224, 226, 232, Rousseau, Jean-Jacques 63–64
Russia 135, 137–138, 142–146
Ryan, Michael 223

St. Louis 50
St. Louis Post-Dispatch 51
Salon.com. 5, 243
San Francisco 202, 209
Satanic Verses 157
Schudson, Michael 11, 14, 43–44, 46, 54–55, 127, 190, 192
Seattle 202
Seattle Post-Intelligencer 201
Seattle Times 74
selective exposure hypothesis 245
Serrin, Judith 42–43, 50
Serrin, William 42–43, 50
Sherrod, Shirley 35–36, 38, 232
Shoemaker, Pamela 80–81, 230
Silver, Nate 75
Singer, Jane 4, 120, 225–226
Slate.com 201, 243
Smith, Anna Nicole 215
social capital 249
social media 66, 75, 78–92, 179, 182–183, 201, 238–239, 241–242
social presence 66–67, 69–73
sociality 78–92
Society of Professional Journalists (SPJ) 154, 241
South Africa 154, 158–159, 162–164, 166–167
spiral of science theory 118

Sports Illustrated 199
Steiger, Paul 65
Stein, Bernard 157, 158, 167
Stewart, Jon 30, 205–220
Sunstein, Cass R. 242, 249

Talon News 31–33
Tatton, Abbi 212
Thurmond, Strom 235, 243, 252
Tocqueville 153
Today Show 219
Traditional 141, 143–145, 147
Tribune organization 250
Tuchman, Gaye 44, 47, 192, 209, 223–224
Twitter 3–5, 38, 69–73, 75, 79, 90, 92, 121,
    179–180, 182, 199, 201, 213–215, 238, 240,
    242, 252

Ubuntu 158–159, 164
University of Texas-Austin 12
user-generated content 4, 6, 97, 120, 222,
    225–230, 233
user-generated news (UGN) 239–244, 248,
    251

Vallejo Times Herald 123
Vedomosti 137

Velshi, Ali 217
Venda 160–161, 163
Vos, Timothy 81, 230

Wall Street Journal 65, 250
Wallace, Chris 30
Washington Daily News 156
Washington Post 27, 47–48, 87, 154, 201, 250
Washington Post Company 250
watchdog journalism 34, 63, 99, 101, 138, 143,
    146, 224
Web 2.0 78–83, 90–93, 99
White, David Manning 224
Wichita Eagle 26
wiki 232, 238–239
Williams, Robert C. 24
World War I 1–2, 44, 171–172
World War II 30, 175
World Wide Web (the Web) 4, 31, 61, 65–67,
    73–74, 78–86, 88–93, 97, 99, 102, 104,
    153, 178, 198, 226, 228–229, 249

YouTube 79, 97, 231, 242

Zoutnet newspaper group 160–164
Zoutpansberger 160